The list of policing's contemporary woes is long and has led many to question whether the organization and practice of policing can endure in their present form. Yet few alternatives have been put forward, because to do so requires returning to, questioning, and re-imagining the fundamentals. Morrell and Bradford do exactly that, in a remarkable work that draws on high theory, inter-disciplinary insights, and a wide-ranging empirical grounding to deliver a new and compelling understanding of the meaning of good policing and how to bring that public good into being.

Professor Nigel Fielding, Emeritus Professor, Department of Sociology, University of Surrey

This engaging book provides a new and valuable analysis of what we mean by police legitimacy, public good and how this impacts on the ethics of the police. By offering new insights into this complex and changing topic the authors provide a thought provoking examination into how governance is managed through these complexities.

Emma Williams, Deputy Director Canterbury Centre for Policing Research, Canterbury Christ Church University

Policing and Public Management fills a much needed gap in understanding policing from a governance and organisation viewpoint. It is theoretically sophisticated but also engaging and accessible. Frontline police will recognise the account of their work, at the same time academics will draw upon its theoretical insights.

Professor Graeme Currie Professor of Public Management, Warwick Business School

POLICING AND PUBLIC MANAGEMENT

Policing and Public Management takes a new perspective on the challenges and problems facing the governance of police forces across the UK and the developed world. Complementing existing texts in criminology and police studies, Morrell and Bradford draw on ideas from the neighbouring fields of public management and virtue ethics to open the field up to a broader audience. This forms the basis for an imaginative reframing of policing as something that either enhances or diminishes "*the public good*" in society.

The text focuses on two cross-cutting aspects of the relationship between the police and the public: public confidence and public order. Extending award-winning work in public management, and drawing on extensive and varied data sources, *Policing and Public Management* offers new ways of seeing the police and of understanding police governance.

This text will be valuable supplementary reading for students of public management, policing and criminology, as well as others who want to be better informed about contemporary policing.

Kevin Morrell, Professor of Strategy, PhD Programme Director, Business School, Durham University, UK.

Ben Bradford, Professor of Global City Policing, University College London Jill Dando Institute of Security and Crime Science, UK.

POLICING AND PUBLIC MANAGEMENT

Governance, Vices and Virtues

Kevin Morrell and Ben Bradford

LONDON AND NEW YORK

First published 2019
by Routledge
2 Park Square, Milton Park, Abingdon, Oxon OX14 4RN

and by Routledge
711 Third Avenue, New York, NY 10017

Routledge is an imprint of the Taylor & Francis Group, an informa business

© 2019 Kevin Morrell and Ben Bradford

The right of Kevin Morrell and Ben Bradford to be identified as authors of this work has been asserted by them in accordance with sections 77 and 78 of the Copyright, Designs and Patents Act 1988.

All rights reserved. No part of this book may be reprinted or reproduced or utilised in any form or by any electronic, mechanical, or other means, now known or hereafter invented, including photocopying and recording, or in any information storage or retrieval system, without permission in writing from the publishers.

Trademark notice: Product or corporate names may be trademarks or registered trademarks, and are used only for identification and explanation without intent to infringe.

British Library Cataloguing in Publication Data
A catalogue record for this book is available from the British Library

Library of Congress Cataloging in Publication Data
Names: Morrell, Kevin, author. | Bradford, Ben, author.
Title: Policing and public management governance : vices and virtues / Kevin Morrell and Ben Bradford.
Description: 1 Edition. | New York : Routledge, 2018. | Includes bibliographical references and index.
Identifiers: LCCN 2018007514 (print) | LCCN 2018011357 (ebook) | ISBN 9781315172569 | ISBN 9781138044173 (alk. paper) | ISBN 9781138044180 (alk. paper) | ISBN 9781315172569 (ebk)
Subjects: LCSH: Police–Great Britain. | Police-community relations–Great Britain. | Public administration–Great Britain.
Classification: LCC HV8195.A3 (ebook) | LCC HV8195.A3 M67 2018 (print) | DDC 172/.2–dc23
LC record available at https://lccn.loc.gov/2018007514

ISBN: 978-1-138-04417-3 (hbk)
ISBN: 978-1-138-04418-0 (pbk)
ISBN: 978-1-315-17256-9 (ebk)

Typeset in Bembo
by Taylor & Francis Books

Fear and confidence and appetite and anger and pity and in general pleasure and pain, may be felt both too much and too little ... to feel them at the right times, with reference to the right objects, towards the right people, with the right aim, and in the right way ... is characteristic of virtue. *Aristotle*

If I can't do something for the public good, what the hell am I doing? *Anita Roddick*

I was in command in Parliament Square, state opening of Parliament, and two American women came up to me. This was when there was a stop the war camp and they'd dug in toilets and vegetables and everything onto the green in Parliament Square, and tents and all sorts of things, and so it was all being covered by the media and all sorts. And I can remember these American women coming up to me and saying "why do you, you know, why do you guys allow this?" and all this sort of stuff ... and funnily enough there was a statue of Winston Churchill only a few metres from me and I pointed, related the story of – I can't remember the chap that Winston took out of his cabinet – and said, you know "Winston Churchill took a chap out of the cabinet because he was very unpopular and asked a lot of difficult questions but he actually ended up bringing him back and said you've got to protect people who ask difficult questions because they make you, you know, think about your decisions and they challenge you, you've got to protect those people." But, and it kind of, in a simple way, was effectively that actually there are probably people inside Parliament, probably not everybody, but people inside Parliament they're the people like Winston Churchill. Although we might not necessarily agree with some of that protest, it is actually a really important part of our democracy that people can do this. *"Paul"*

CONTENTS

List of illustrations   *x*
Acknowledgements   *xi*
Preface   *xii*

1   Governance   1

2   The public good   22

3   Legitimacy   35

4   Identity   53

5   Work   67

6   Training   86

7   Disorder   105

8   Evidence   128

References   *145*
Index   *177*

ILLUSTRATIONS

Figures

1.1	Governance and Policing	20
2.1	Policing for Public Good	34
3.1	A Model of Trust and Legitimacy	40

Tables

1.1	Changes to Hierarchical Governance Modes in Policing	9
4.1	Organizational Identification and Membership	63
5.1	Cop-managers, Civilian-managers and Stakeholders	76
6.1	Data Sources Relating to Public Order	96
7.1	"Impossible Jobs" Policing and the Public Good	107
8.1	The Value of Stories in Understanding Threats to Life	141

Box

8.1	The College of Policing Definition of Evidence-Based Policing	129

ACKNOWLEDGEMENTS

Nothing would be possible without the support of our families: Sarah, Emily, Ruby, Jake – thank you! And the same to Amra and Emil.

Kevin would like to thank the British Academy for their award of a Mid-Career Fellowship which made co-authoring this book possible. For their comments and support over time, we also thank Gareth Stubbs, Les Graham, Layla Branicki, Ross Ritchie, Claire Davis, Keith Floyd, Kelvin Jackson-Robbins, Emma Williams, Mark Learmonth, Loizos Heracleous, Dave Hollies, Bas Javid, Paul Robinson, Mark Cooper, Dawn Hands, Jenna Allen, Natalie Tomlinson, Ian Morton and Steve Peckwood. To this list Ben would like to add Jonathan Jackson, Betsy Stanko, Sarah MacQueen, Jenna Milani, Chris Giacomantonio and Mike Hough. Thanks also to Judith Lorton, at Routledge for her support and encouragement and also to Lucy McClune, Peter Stafford and Dominic Corti.

Particular thanks are due to people who helped with work supporting data collection or analysis: to Graeme Currie and Andrew Lockett for generously allowing us to draw on data from interviews with police managers and other stakeholders (in Chapter 5); to Stephen Brammer in reviewing contemporary literature in applied ethics (in Chapter 6). Thanks to those participating in interviews and survey work without whom no analysis would be possible. The usual disclaimers apply.

PREFACE

This book develops a new way to think about policing. It takes a normative perspective, meaning we are interested in building up a picture of what good policing "should" be like. Books on highly specialized areas of practice like policing often start by describing current practice and then offer analysis and critique or recommendations. What we want to do here, although it is still informed by current practice, is different. We want to re-imagine the role and purpose of policing in contemporary democratic societies. We base this on the concept of "the public good" because this gives us an alternative and novel starting point.

Outline

Chapter 1 discusses policing and "governance" from the perspectives of public management and a branch of applied ethics: virtue ethics. We define governance as "the production of order", partly because order has particular resonance in policing, and introduce a list of contemporary challenges in the governance of policing. This definition and our list raise both "how" and "why" questions to do with governance. Focusing on the "why" questions, we build up a theoretical framework to assess "good governance".

Chapter 2 considers challenges that come when we try to apply this broad idea of serving "the public good" to policing, where activities are often about limiting harm in crisis situations and involve force, and there is conflict between different stakeholders. We use a case study that highlights these features to refine "the public good". This helps to apply this concept to policing.

Chapter 3 considers legitimacy, describing it as an *institutional virtue*. We identify two dimensions that frame the space within which institutional virtues take shape: legitimacy in the relationship between police and public (Chapter 3) and social identity within the police organization (Chapter 4). In doing so, we move from the broader ranging literatures on applied ethics and public management to focus more specifically on the relevant literature in sociology, criminology and police studies.

Chapter 4 considers the topic of "police" identities. This allows us to focus in particular on ways normatively appropriate policing might be encouraged, and on the challenges posed by the social and operational context of policing. The discussion in this chapter forms an important link between our opening chapters on governance and the public good, and the chapters in the following sections which look at particular aspects of police practice.

Chapters 5 and 6 consider *individual virtues* by focusing on police work and character. The concept of character connects "the public good" to the development of virtue (or vice). It is also a way of understanding how to scale from the individual to the level of the service as a whole. Chapter 5 identifies and discusses a rarely mentioned aspect to police work, namely that some "policing" involves managerial work. This has implications for identity and character because managerial work can bring people into tension with their identity as front-line "cops". Chapter 6 looks more closely and in depth at virtues in context and on the role that training can play in developing individual virtues. To do so we consider the importance of habit in developing character.

Chapter 7 focuses on public disorder, using a framework that has been applied to a number of jobs in public management . This is the idea of an "impossible job". This is a phrase coined by Hargrove and Glidewell (1990), and has a particular meaning which we discuss. Drawing on extensive multi-site, multi-method data we analyse public disorder and conclude by outlining three extensions to the "impossible jobs" framework which help us understand "street-level" policing.

Chapter 8 applies insights from virtue ethics to criticize "evidence-based policing". We identify tensions between virtues and this account of evidence, and develop some useful directions for future research using stories. Our goal is to move the conversation about policing and evidence forward, so it is not suffocated by an overly simplistic and reductionist picture of how we learn about the world, or how this learning can inform practice. In doing so we underline the central role of ethics and situated judgement in policing.

Why this book, why now?

The scale and scope of contemporary change in policing make many existing perspectives and practices look at risk of being outdated, or even obsolete. These include reforms to institutions and the leadership of policing, the changing nature of crime, cuts, complex demands and new technologies. Simply because of such change there is a need for new work in this area. But more than just providing an updated account of the context for policing, we are trying to offer something different. This book is different because it seeks to understand policing not just from the specialist perspectives of criminology or police studies, but also from the broad, interdisciplinary topic of "governance" and looking through the lens of virtue ethics. This complements many existing insights from criminology in particular and allows us to bring in ideas from public management, applied ethics and management studies, combining these with a richer sensitivity to understanding the nature of public sector work. There is a gap in existing understanding here because few, if any, books on policing are purposefully as interdisciplinary as this. The different literatures we draw on do not really "talk" to one another, and we want to change that because it is often in the gaps between disciplines that new insights emerge. Also, policing is such a complex and contested activity that no one discipline has "the answers", and neither can any one discipline even frame all the relevant questions.

Why "the public good"?

Policing is not always portrayed or understood as a public service that contributes to the public good. This is partly because it is often about limiting harm and partly because the police have the unique power to use force against the public. They represent state power, and this power is not necessarily always turned toward the good, sometimes in the UK and very often in other parts of the world. Policing is also sometimes seen as the province of specialist disciplines: criminology and police studies. Taken together these features mean that "the police" are often seen as separate from other public services. This is despite the fact that policing as an activity (for instance in relation to missing persons and mental health) may be primarily about the provision of care rather than the use of force, and despite the fact that the police are often the last resort when provision fails in other public services. Drawing on "the public good" helps to connect policing more closely to other public services. It also helps us to connect more closely to the choices of government.

This connection to the public good means our analysis is informed not just by policing studies and criminology, but also by a wider understanding of public sector work. This builds on our contributions to understanding policing, and also on work that considers the nature of relations between the state and the public in a number of different settings: in analysis of reforms to public services such as the NHS (Morrell, 2006a,b; Morrell and Hewison, 2013), in UK national government (Morrell, 2009), in local government (Morrell and Hartley, 2006a,b) the Inland Revenue / HMRC (Currie, Morrell and Tuck, 2015; Morrell and Tuck, 2014); and in a post-conflict setting (Morrell and Harrington-Buhay, 2012).

This book draws not just on fresh theory but brings together a great deal of empirical work from surveys, observations and interviews with the police and the public. Using a new normative perspective and drawing on rich and diverse data sources gives us a strong theoretical and empirical basis to think about policing in a new way. For simplicity, "we" is often used to describe data collection and analysis, but many people have helped at different stages with different projects, some of whom we thank in the acknowledgements.

For, against or about the police?

Critical management scholars sometimes use a distinction between scholarly work that is "for" management, work that is "about" management, and work that is "against" management (Parker, 2002). A great many popular texts on management are unthinkingly and one-sidedly "for" management, never considering the impact on other stakeholders. But there are few such nakedly "for" books in policing because policing is a much more contested activity. Even the most pro-police texts typically acknowledge problems or failings in terms of, for examples, relations with the public or failures of process or structure. At the same time, there are few texts resolutely "against" policing in the way some critical management scholars are "against" management. Critics of policing identify failings, abuses and inequalities, but they are rarely against the role in entirety.

An additionally useful distinction is between "insider" and "outsider" perspectives, reflecting that policing and its associated disciplines and practices are highly specialized. Insider texts tend to be written by figures within policing, or by retired officers, or are in some ways institutionally sponsored or endorsed (e.g. Allen et al., 2005, 2006; Brain, 2010, 2013; Great Britain, 2012; Centrex, 2006; DCLG, 2006, 2007; HMIC, 2009; Home Office, 2013; Ministry of Justice, 2011, 2012; Villiers, 1997; Villiers, 2009). This picture is somewhat complicated because many officers become academics. Outsider texts, such as textbooks (Drew and Prenzler, 2015; Roberg et al., 2014), and critical reviews (Savage, 2007), tend to be more "about" the police and often developed from within specific disciplinary perspectives, mainly sociology, law and criminology (Bowling and Foster, 2002; Skolnick, 1966), although some – particularly edited texts – combine insider and outsider perspectives (Fleming, 2015).

Joining these categories together, this book is "about" the police, from an "outsider" perspective.

Whom is the book "for"?

If policing is a highly specialized and distinctive area of practice, then texts on policing tend to be similarly specialized. In considering "the public good", our aim is to give a broader account of policing as a public service and as a form of work. Our ultimate goal is to improve understanding of policing in order to benefit the public. To try to achieve this, our book is written to interest anyone with an intellectual or practical stake in how policing is governed. It is of broader relevance to public policy too. It could appeal to those working in the police or contributing to policing policy and education, as well as students and researchers in public policy, policing studies, criminology, criminal justice, sociology and law. We hope this volume can be used as a guide to other relevant literature as well, since we connect to a lot of other work across different disciplines. For readers unfamiliar with this style of referencing, or to reading text cluttered by a flurry of names and dates (as the previous paragraph is), please do not let this convention distract or deter you. Citations (Name, Date) signpost other work and give credit to other people for their words or ideas. These are listed in the references, but you can read this book without following the signposts.

1
GOVERNANCE

This chapter examines governance, which we define as the "production of order". This definition makes it clear "governance" is not just about practical, "how questions" (control and coordination) or the outcomes associated with a social system. It is more fundamentally about ethical "why questions" (fairness and openness to alternatives). This helps us to connect the governance of policing to "the public good".

Governance and order

Order in social systems (like society, organizations, institutions, corporations, political administrations and public services) has many benefits: reduction of uncertainty, predictability, ease of exchange, control and coordination, the ability to plan ahead. Order also has disadvantages: it means that an unfair or inefficient system will be maintained, that inequalities will be reproduced, that harmful routines or patterns are entrenched, and it can close down alternative, better ways of organizing.

To use a simple, but also rich metaphor, governance is not just about playing a game within the rules. It involves setting up or changing the rules which make the game work in the way it does. If we extend this a little to consider "good governance", this does not just mean securing winning outcomes, it also involves defining what "good" means and for whom. It is not just about making good choices, it is about the basic architecture of choice. For example, often, a government, or Home Secretary, or the people responsible for leading a police force, will tell the public they have an efficient and effective police force that provides excellent value. This claim will communicate that they have been making optimal choices about how to govern the police. They will use measures and statistics to support these claims, and in criminal justice there are plenty of measures to choose from. But "good governance" is not simply about measures of efficiency or effectiveness or value. It is more fundamentally about the very meaning given to terms like "efficiency" or "effectiveness" or "value". When we consider governance as the "production of order" and when we consider the benefits and costs of order this prompts underlying questions: efficient and effective at doing what, in whose interests, and, who determines value?

These questions are important partly because they connect the governance of policing much more closely with the actions of government. This matters because governments regularly make claims about the effective management of public services and this forms the justification for their ownership of power. As they try to balance political with economic costs they face an imperative to persuade the electorate tax revenue is being spent effectively (Ezzamel, 2001) and that they deserve to be in power. One task the academic community has is to ask the most basic "why" questions and therefore subject the claims those in power make to scrutiny (e.g. Bache, 2003; Jann, 2003; Starkey, 1995). This task is helped if we start with a broader definition of governance as the production of order, rather than simply considering existing measures and outcomes.

Debates using "governance" are most prominent in "corporate governance" (Daily, Dalton and Cannella, 2003; Sundaramurthy and Lewis, 2003). This tends to focus on the need to keep some corporate vices (corruption, fraud, mis-selling, misreporting) in check by improving control and measurement. Corporate scandals – including the Global Financial Crisis (Tomasic, 2011) – are often described as failures in "corporate governance". But "corporate governance failure" does not tell us much. It is like saying that two different patients, one with pneumonia and one suffering from dementia, are "seriously ill" – or that paper burns because it has flammable properties. Unless we take care to define it, then to use "governance" to label something can mislead us into thinking we also have an explanation. Unfortunately, just as labelling a corporate scandal a "corporate governance" failure tells us very little about private sector organizations, there is a danger that talking about governance in policing tells us little. "The public" want "good governance" in their public services, and we recognize that when things go wrong this is a governance failure, but what do we know beyond this?

Currently, in policing in England and Wales questions of governance can be thought of quite narrowly in terms of the Police and Crime Commissioner (PCC) model. But there have been many other changes with implications for policing governance (Jones, 2009; Loader, 2000; Walsh and Conway, 2011). Although by no means immune from New Labour's reforms associated with the New Public Management, policing budgets in England and Wales were protected and officer numbers grew throughout the early 2000s. More recently, policing has been the latest public sector service to go through the seismic reductions in funding that are a consequence of the Global Financial Crisis, and the chosen policy response of austerity. Policing has come under the same pressures of reform and cuts as other parts of the public sector. Moreover, deep cuts in local government, adult social care and public health also impact on policing because it can be a service of last resort (Toynbee, 2015). A slightly more complex consequence of cuts is that the police may end up taking the role of lead agency in situations where they are not the most appropriate agency to do (owing to lack of investment elsewhere). New forms of collaborative working have arisen to cope with cuts as well as to address demand complexity.

New institutions – the College of Policing (CoP) and the National Crime Agency (NCA) – offer (as one potential benefit) the prospect of integration and efficiencies, but they also impinge on the identities and traditions of over 40 separate police forces, promoting a service-wide agenda of professionalization and "evidence-based policing" and more controversial schemes such as Direct Entry. At the same time, CoP and the NCA replaced institutions with arguably clearer mandates, namely the Serious Organised Crime Agency, the Child Exploitation and Online Protection Centre, the National Cyber Crime Unit, and the National Policing Improvement Agency. At the same time, Brexit has placed into doubt many of the transnational institutions and arrangements that are increasingly important as crime continues to "globalize".

The institutional arrangements for overseeing policing have changed, comparatively recently, not just with the introduction of Police and Crime Commissioners (PCCs) in England and Wales but with new systems of inspections and audit. PCC powers, responsibilities and their accountability framework, and more fundamentally their role, are all still not fully understood by the public. There remains a substantial democratic deficit since the turnout for these elections is so low. Mergers between forces, or even takeovers are a potential outcome of the twin effects of cuts and this emerging model for overseeing policing.

There are new technologies and threats such as the rise in cyber-crime, terrorism and the fear of terrorism, and increasing awareness of the problems posed by child sexual abuse, people trafficking and modern slavery. These challenge received practices and taken-for-granted understandings of police territory, powers and jurisdiction. Legislation continually changes, and meanwhile "traditional" problems remain as problematic as ever, with up to half of all crime being drug-induced, and each force incurring massive regular costs relating to alcohol use (Bacon, 2013; Barton, 2011; Plant and Plant, 2006), while mental health issues account for around a third of police time. To summarize this as a list, contemporary policing in England and Wales faces many things that could be described as governance challenges:

- cuts in budgets (loss of personnel and station closures)
- cuts to neighbouring public services
- new institutions
- new legislation
- PCC model
- new technologies
- the changing nature of crime

- growing awareness of "hidden" crimes
- rising levels of demand
- demand complexity
- drug and alcohol-related crime
- mental health and missing persons
- inspection regimes
- direct entry
- "evidence-based" policing
- potential mergers or takeovers
- Brexit and other challenges to international frameworks

These are complex and difficult issues, and they pose many questions of those in charge of the police. But this list gives only a very restricted and even sanitized perspective on the governance of policing. The picture becomes a lot more complicated once we sign up to a definition of governance as the "production of order" and recognize that order has disadvantages as well as benefits. This definition helps us to see that, beyond the province and even perhaps influence of the police, there are many things excluded from this list which produce order in relation to policing and criminal justice. There is no acknowledgement here of the broader responsibilities the state has in setting the context for society and policing, or the relationship between the public and their police. There is also no acknowledgement, expressing it simply, that society is not fair.

We have said above that "good governance" in a social system is about the architecture of choice. But people's individual choices are often "governed" and their own power, opportunities or "life chances" limited by the cards dealt to them at birth (Dahrendorf, 1979). Often this takes the form of different kinds of membership: poverty, ethnicity, religion, class, gender and race, age, sexuality, geography or social capital. Many of these memberships are allocated rather than chosen. These can intersect (Crenshaw, 1991) in ways that accentuate disadvantage (Emejulu, 2008). This aspect to social order also gives some (affluent, white, males) life-long advantages. In crucial senses, there is not one public whom the police serve but many "publics".

Decades of research in criminology show that people can have different experiences of the criminal justice system and of the police because of these memberships (Alexander, 2008; Anderson, 1990; Brogden, 1991; Brown and Heidensohn, 2000; Coleman, 2004; Millie, 2013; Crawford, 2009; Keith, 1993; McAra and McVie, 2005; Skogan, 2006; Westmarland, 2001, 2002; Whitfield, 2004). These memberships may affect the likelihood of people wanting to join the police, affecting its prospects of being seen as an institution representative of multiple publics. Even after joining, police officers' own memberships (e.g. in terms of gender and ethnicity) influence their work experiences and identity (Dick and Cassell 2002; Holdaway, 2010; Silvestri, Tong and Brown, 2013).

Also excluded from, or at least downplayed in, lists of the type above are some of the fundamental challenges for the governance of police that exist in all times and places. These include, first, the lived reality of being subject to the power of the police: arrest, the cell, at times the state-sanctioned violence, but also at times the protection and care. Second, the nature of policing as a job of work: the mundane daily routine punctuated by fear and panic; the life-changing moments that define people or institutions; the camaraderie with colleagues but also the isolation of the police from the public, the temptations accompanying unique powers, the distance of police "forces" from other public "services". And third, the loss, terror or violence that victims experience, their gratitude or deep despair to the response of the police.

To start this book with a definition of governance as the "production of order" is to build a broader and multi-layered picture of the relationship between the police and the public. The definition we choose has particular resonance in policing, where the maintenance and reproduction of order are a central role of the police and essential for the state (Waddington, 1999). If we aim to build this more complex picture of governance, there is a need to lay deeper theoretical foundations. This chapter and the following chapter do so by developing an account of governance and "the public good" that is specifically relevant for policing. We begin by reviewing existing attempts to define "governance" across different fields before discussing governance modes. We use this to introduce a distinction between the "how questions" relating to governance and the "why questions", which are key to our definition of governance as the production of order. To conclude the chapter we begin to connect governance to the idea of the public good – the focus of Chapter 2. The "public good" is our way of addressing these "why" questions.

How do we define "governance"?

There is a lot of rhetorical flexibility in the word "governance", partly because it is used across different disciplines. It is commonplace in commenting on policing (Crawford, 2006; Den Boer, 2002; Goldsmith and Lewis, 2000; Loader, 2000) but also in: organization studies (Jones, Hesterly and Borgatti, 1997; Starkey, 1995); international relations (Kooiman, 1993; Senarclens, 1998); development studies (Hyden and Bratton, 1992; Leftwich, 1994); socioeconomics (Campbell, Hollingsworth and Lindberg, 1991; Crouch, 2006; Hollingsworth and Boyer, 1997; Hollingsworth, Schmitter and Streeck, 1994); political science (Pierre and Peters, 2000); public management (Bache, 2003; Bevir, Rhodes and Weller, 2003; Morrell, 2009; Rhodes, 2000); social policy and policy implementation (Daly, 2003; Rhodes, 1997).

Across these disciplines, "governance" has no agreed definition. It has been described as a "vague", "pre-theoretical", "buzzword" (Jessop, 1998), having a "breadth and ambiguity of definitions" (Lynn, Heinrich and Hill, 2001: 5). Bache (2003: 301) says, "its use often lacks definitional clarity", and Rhodes, (1997: 15) that it has, "too many meanings to be useful". This means its "usage has been both loose and universalising" (Daly, 2003). Others describe governance more cynically, as "fashionable" "neologism" (Pollitt and Bouckaert, 2004: 10), or a "political catchword" (Pierre and Peters, 2000: 50). Jann (2003: 113) suggests it is, "an all-purpose political concept", resonating with Bevir, Rhodes and Weller's (2003: 14) description of an "elastic" term.

What we call rhetorical flexibility can be helpful. "Governance" can be a banner term that allows us to connect quickly to important ideas, problems and relationships at interlocking levels of analysis (Karllson, 2000). However, when trying to apply "governance" to a particular problem or domain, like policing, this rhetorical flexibility is also limiting. Part of the motivation for writing about the governance of policing is a frustration with how "governance" is often taken as comparable across different sectors. "Governance" is typically understood as a system for regulating individual agents and using different kinds of contracts (with penalties and incentives) to oversee different kinds of transaction (Kocher, Kumar and Subramanian, 1998; Lister and Herzog, 2000; Mayers, Shivdasani and Smith, 1997; Saleh, Vaughn, Rohrer and Linden, 2002). This reflects a number of assumptions about the nature of people; for instance that they choose freely and out of self-interest, and about organizations or institutions; for instance that they are closed systems, sealed off from the effects and influences of wider society, and also self-interested.

When considering the governance of policing we want to emphasize basic differences between sectors. We argue policing is something that should be "public sector" and we also see the public sector as fundamentally different from the private sector. Across the public sector, terms like "public sector ethos", "public service", "publicness", "public duty" and "civic duty" capture different aspects of these basic differences (Kelman, 2005; Marquand, 2004; Morrell, 2006a, 2009; Pettigrew, 2005). This is important in policing because of the nature of police work and the legal and political context for this work. Another factor is that when it is done well, policing involves carrying out certain duties and services discharged to "the public". In contrast to private sector corporations and their "customers", there are, and should be, marked differences with the relationship between a public servant and their client (Loader and Walker, 2007). In policing, there are additionally distinctive aspects to this relationship owing to the nature of police work and its connections to the state. The police officer is a "mediator of relations in power in a society" Reiner (2010: 118), with authority to use force against the public (Jones, 2008; Waddington, 1999). Even if "the public" were to be described as an ultimate or end customer, many of the direct recipients of police services (or force) are unwilling "customers". The police as an institution play a broader role in maintaining order. There are also distinctive historical, cultural and social factors in play, in England and Wales and in many mature democracies, where there is a model of policing by consent, and a Peelian ideal that the public are the police and the police are the public (which we return to later in the book). These public/private differences have implications in terms of policing and one vector for governance – "governance modes".

Governance modes

Conventionally there are three governance modes: hierarchies, markets and networks (Rhodes, 1997; Sbragia, 2000). These produce order – using our definition of governance – because they shape how resources are allocated in a social system (Starkey, 1995). To revisit our simple but powerful metaphor, they set the rules of the game. Each mode has merits and limitations. Hierarchies may be inefficient but they may also preserve equity and principles; markets may reproduce or exaggerate inequalities, but competition can encourage efficiency; networks may be difficult to scrutinize and regulate, but establishing partnerships and trust may offset some of the risks associated with markets – the benefits of "relational" governance (Akbar and Venkatraman, 1995; Poppo and Zenger, 2002).

There are many different variations on "hierarchy", "market" and "network" depending on the type of social system, the economic and political context, the type of good or resource being allocated, institutional histories and identity, professional jurisdiction and so on. For example, Hollingsworth and Boyer (1997) differentiate between clans, clubs and communities, which would all fall under the broad category of network. The three basic modes also combine and coexist: markets rely on a legislative framework (a hierarchical mode) and are rarely perfect, so trade often depends on some prior connection (a network mode). Hierarchies can be undermined by different kinds of relationships or "ties" (a network mode) or some forms of bargaining (a market mode). Nonetheless there is a stable appeal to these modes – even at this high level of abstraction.

Governance modes feature in both private and public sectors of course, but one reason they are helpful in relation to policing is there is more conflict about choice of mode in the public sector. Often, changes in governance are most controversial when they are attempts at privatization or marketization – shifting from hierarchical modes to markets, or sometimes as an intermediate step, networks or partnerships (Davies, 2007; Sheaff and West, 1997). Examples of marketization include outsourcing; public–private partnerships; personalization of services such as "patient choice", insurance schemes, voucher schemes, capitation (payment per client); selling off companies (e.g. British Steel, British Petroleum, Rolls Royce, British Airways) and utilities (water, electricity); "right to buy"; creation of internal markets, the "purchaser / provider split", private finance initiatives, commodification of – say – "science" or "knowledge", tuition fees (Cooper and Taylor, 2005; Gibbons et al., 1994; Hyde and Davies, 2004; Harrison and Wood, 1999; Kazancigil, 1998; Morrell, 2006b; Mrotek, 2001; Seymour, 2012).

More broadly, phrases like "New Public Management", or a culture of "managerialism", often mean an attempt to dismantle hierarchical modes of governance, and swap "administration" with "management" (Learmonth, 2003, 2005, 2017), or "leadership" (Ballas and Tsoukas, 2004; Diefenbach, 2009; Hewison and Morrell, 2013; Learmonth and Morrell, 2016; Morrell and Hartley, 2006a). These shifts produce conflicts and tension, and lead to unanticipated consequences. The effects are far-reaching, though often justified by a narrow consideration of costs. For example, analysis of the Scottish Executive's programme of prison privatization found it was insensitive to contextual factors and notions of the wider public, "a failure to capture social costs or benefits" or even acknowledge basic assumptions about cost over time (Cooper and Taylor, 2005: 500). Examples of some contemporary changes in policing are shown below in terms of governance modes. Each shows a move away from hierarchy (see Table 1.1):

Changes to governance modes in the public sector are often a pragmatic or short-term response to challenges of how to do more with less. This leads to a focus on "how" questions that concern processes and outcomes – management, control and measurement (Chaudhuri, Graziano and Maitra, 2006; Crawford, 2006; Jones and Goldberg, 1982).

The how of governance

Policing and criminal justice are certainly not short of data or measures (Loveday, 2006) that can be used to track the how of governance. But as we discuss in Chapter 2, measuring the ultimate purpose of good governance – the public good – is difficult. A more fundamental and far-reaching definition of governance – as the production of order – creates space for accounts that look beyond metrics, indicators and auditing to take in a much broader context (Jackson and Carter, 1995; Starkey, 1995). It also opens up more possibilities in terms of methods – for example, in depth qualitative study that can allow more scope to study interaction, process and structures (Pettigrew and McNulty, 1995; Roberts, 2001).

The challenge of defining governance is not just an academic exercise. It translates into real world problems to do with implementation and analysis and also the allocation of responsibility or blame. For example, although governance is occasionally portrayed as a systemic or cultural phenomenon (Starbuck, 2003), a lot of research looks at the "how" of governance and understands it in much more narrow terms of control, drawing on a private sector "corporate governance" paradigm:

> Corporate governance regulates the ownership and control of organizations ... It sets the legal terms and conditions for the allocation of property rights among stakeholders, structuring their relationships and influencing their incentives, and hence, willingness to work together.
> *(Konzelmann, Conway, Trenberth and Wilkinson, 2006: 542)*

Studying governance in this "ownership and control" sense is vital, but – like our opening list of bullet points – it is also limited. Often control is the only focus of discussion, particularly in settings like criminal justice where measures dominate discussion. This is problematic because a narrow focus on particular actors or a specific set of outcomes can eclipse broader, underlying questions. These broader questions are not just about governance as control, but governance as the "production of order".

TABLE 1.1 Changes to Hierarchical Governance Modes in Policing

Example	How is this a move away from hierarchy	Implications
Cuts in budgets to policing and their consequent effects on police numbers. Office of National Statistics data show police numbers were cut by more than 10% in the five years since 2010 (Nardelli, 2015).	Police budgets have three main components: personnel (by far the largest), estates (such as police stations) and equipment. The softest target in the largest, personnel category (in terms of police officers) is police and community support officers (PCSOs) because they have fewer employment protections (the legal protections in employment contracts are a different example of a hierarchical mode). However cuts can also affect staff in finance, HR, support services training and development etc. Although imposed centrally, their effects are not evenly distributed in terms of the hierarchical mode of governance that is the chain of command. Instead their consequences can be very difficult to anticipate and fall differentially, undermining established hierarchical orderings of practice.	Taking one example, cuts to PCSOs has meant many forces losing what former Commissioner Lord Blair described as "the eyes and the ears inside the community" (May, 2015). As one consequence, loss of visibility can compromise the effort to combat terrorism (Morrell, 2015). While the work of PCSOs can be seen as mundane (located at the bottom of a hierarchical ordering of practice) it can be vital. PCSOs build and sustain public confidence, hate crime, take on specialist liaison roles, carry out routine patrols, analyse crime associated with preparing for terrorism, develop connections with local businesses and communities, undertake outreach activities, use local knowledge to evaluate and sense-check remotely gathered intelligence, contribute local expertise during covert operations, cultivate – over time – local contacts and information sources. Losing support services also has many hidden consequences and costs.
Introduction of PCCs, locally elected and accountable responsible for overseeing the policing budget and related commissioning of police services.	Devolution can be understood as a shift towards greater democratic accountability but it is also about divesting responsibility. A comparatively small portion of police budgets comes from local tax so this shift away from hierarchy is a way of distancing central government from the consequences of cuts.	Low turnout, and foot-printing of PCC candidates and outcomes on the results of national elections each undermine the idea these elections are reflections of any candidate's individual competence. Direct elections may also increase police politicization. Policing is a national capability and problems and challenges to policing will often come from factors outside PCC control (such as levels of poverty).

Example	How is this a move away from hierarchy	Implications
New forms of collaborative working to address demand complexity for instance Multi-Agency Safeguarding Hubs (MASH) which combine police, adult social care and children's services.	Collaborative or partnership working is a shift from hierarchies to network modes. This potentially offers advantages for dealing with complex social problems and may also result in efficiencies and learning across different jurisdictions. However it can also blur lines of accountability and increase rather than reduce duplication across agencies. Reorganization may also mask the extent of cuts because changes and new institutions can make it harder to measure agency performance year on year.	One issue can be that problems that "should" be the province of one service are now distributed across a network. This can compromise what is sometimes called "domain consensus" – clear understanding of who owns a problem. Working across boundaries brings different expertise together but by the same token can also erode professional boundaries and duties. In relation to mental health for example, one could argue this should be a "health" issue rather than a "policing" issue. Combining services does not necessarily lead to improved governance across different functions – to use a cliché problems shared may be doubled.
Direct entry, allowing recruits from outside policing to enter the police at Superintendent and Inspector levels, without carrying out the same level of formal, front-line training.	Traditional career paths within the police are based on progression in terms of an internal labour market where all have had training as a front-line police officer. Direct entry is marketization because it is opening up this internal labour market.	It lowers morale – breaking a psychological contract in terms of expectations about career progression, and potentially increases risks because people in senior management roles may make decisions that are not informed by practical experience and therefore put the public or officers at risk.
Fast Track Schemes or Cohorts, designed to identify and more quickly progress high potential officers.	These represent investment in improving standards and practices which is welcome, but these can also be seen as attempts to break up the internal labour market and whilst they encourage people to form networks for good reasons, this can have undesirable consequences.	This can have unforeseen consequences because unethical police practices are often a function of networked power – for instance word-of-mouth that can affect chances of promotion (Hales, May, Belur and Hough, 2015).

Example	How is this a move away from hierarchy	Implications
The professionalization agenda, for instance pushing for police officers to have a degree-level qualification (Police Education Qualifications Framework).	A project of professionalization is not so much moving away from hierarchy, but remaking a new kind of hierarchy that is institution-wide rather than force-wide. A key aspect of professionalization is that it supports jurisdictional claims – professionals own certain activities. This is why professionals can be difficult to manage, because they have field-wide rather than organization-specific status. Accreditation offers a way for force-specific controls to be introduced. These can reshape the labour market and offer additional managerial "levers" so that (using Mintzberg's term) the Professional Bureaucracy becomes easier to "manage". This imposes greater, standardized control of learning.	The ideal of equivalent recognition to other public servants is helpful in many ways. However differences will remain because policing as an activity involves use of force and is often understood (by police and other groups) as a kind of "dirty work" (Dick, 2005). Foregrounding "professional" qualifications without acknowledgement of prior experiential learning would devalue craft skills (a similar threat to morale as Direct Entry). Allowing recognition of craft (accreditation for prior expertise) ideally gives some kind of equivalence to experience, but typically in any professional project abstract, codified knowledge becomes more prized over time so status differences are likely to remain. Over time, entry criteria are likely to change so this also potentially moves away from the ideal of the police being able to represent all sections of the public. This touches on a general concern for policing – representativeness of some minority communities is very poor (though of course a powerful argument for a common qualification is it could improve representativeness if it encourages people from different backgrounds to apply).

Example	How is this a move away from hierarchy	Implications
Evidence-based policing, foot-printed on evidence-based medicine this is the pursuit of the best available evidence to solve problems.	The ideal of best evidence redirects the gaze beyond traditions, force boundaries and local, received practices to an aggregated understanding of relevant work "out there" where the best available evidence is, which will indicate "what works". One consequence is that it creates a new marketplace made up of those skilled in the language and techniques of evidence. Implicitly it is a "work smarter" discourse that can be reworked to suggest that cost cutting can be managed by using best evidence.	Ideals of being informed by best evidence are helpful in many ways, but one unfortunate consequence can be a revaluing of situated expertise so professional experience and "craft" are devalued. The claim to be value free is problematic given the irresolvable ethical dilemmas policing often involves. EBP can be seen as part of a programme of culture change associated (above) with professionalization. A target of this culture change is the middle ranks who are often positioned as relying on outmoded ideas or patterns of thinking and a barrier to be removed or needing to be challenged.
Private police schemes as in Frinton-on-sea and Kensington. Frinton is a low-crime area but cuts meant the nearest police station will close. Local residents each agreed to pay £100 a year so a private security firm can patrol at night.	Privately funded officers breaks a very important link between policing and the public. Privatization would mean instead of one national institution comprising 43 richly connected local forces (plus one or two more) with a common history, potentially hundreds of new borders and boundaries will be established, which could cause havoc as firms jostle for business and territory.	If a wealthy suburb can subsidize regular patrols and its poorer neighbour cannot, private security may displace not stop crime. Security guards are employees of businesses. They are not expected to focus on serving the public good over the interests of their paymasters. It is not clear privatizing policing will even save money. As shown by the debacle over security at the London 2012 Olympics, police will still be left holding the responsibility for mistakes and the public purse is being left significantly exposed to the threat of miscarriages of justice.

Example	How is this a move away from hierarchy	Implications
Performance management through key performance indicators and cross-force comparisons through rankings in the Police Effectiveness, Efficiency and Legitimacy programme (the PEEL reviews).	Although ostensibly about sharing best practice, and maintaining standards, one effect of these reports is to introduce an element of competition between forces. Rather than simply being a new form of hierarchical mode of control from the centre, identifying and publicizing differences across forces makes this more like a market because it introduces contestability.	The problem with any system of comparative measurement is that these can become vehicles for carrying blame. In turn this reinforces a view of power and governance as the province of individuals. As well as introducing aspects of competition and potentially misleading stakeholders about the reasons for differences in KPIs, focus on outcomes can disguise underlying problems caused by resource constraints. Some performance measures cannot accurately reflect demand scope, or differentiate well enough between response and proactive prevention. These schemes are hugely vulnerable to how measures are conducted and it can be a mistake to confuse proximate goals with the ultimate goal.

A definition of governance as the production of order takes us beyond "how" questions by getting us to consider deeper "why" questions. This distinction offers a new way to think about the links between political administrations or public services and the public(s) they serve. Understandably, given their unique powers, the governance of the police is often seen in terms of controls that apply at the level of an individual officer: laws, sanctions, procedures, records, various surveillance mechanisms (see Chapter 4). Less frequently, and more recently, forces as a whole are evaluated on a range of metrics through a system of inspections. But when it comes to complex, large-scale problems like combating terrorism (Pockrass, 1986; Sentas, 2014; Walsh, 1983), discrimination and racism (Pryce, 1979; Whitfield, 2004), child abuse (Morgan and Zedner, 1992), organized crime (Hobbs, 1995), the horrors of Hillsborough (Scraton, 2016), or simply understanding crime itself, this focus on individuals is too thin and simplistic. If instead we look at the broader concept of order and how this is produced, we can build a richer picture that takes in the tradition, history and context for policing, interrelations with other stakeholders, the political and economic climate and so on. As we argue in Chapters 2 and 6, virtue ethics can help with this attention to context.

Focusing on individuals and on individual forces may not help if the sources of problems are more deeply ingrained. It can even be harmful by distracting from underlying problems which we describe in terms of the why of governance and the public good.

The why of governance – the public good

We discuss how to apply "the public good" to policing in more specific detail in Chapter 2. Here, in relation to the "why" of governance, we will begin by outlining the concept in much broader terms and connect it to our main theoretical framework on ethics: virtue ethics.

Rawls (1999: 217) usefully defines the common good as, "certain general conditions that are in an appropriate sense equally to everyone's advantage". Pickhardt (2005) suggests this is served by adherence to principles of justice, a system of government that combines efficiency with fairness, *Gemeinsinn* or a sense of togetherness and community, and the altruistic behaviour of the public both individually and as a collective. The policy of a government or agency such as the police, or the actions of a transnational body such as the United Nations or European Union could all harm or benefit the "public". So too could the actions of an individual public servant.

At a national level, assessment of the public good could involve considering a portfolio of different measures, for instance employment levels, skills, productivity, income differentials, access to core services, educational attainment, health indices, levels of crime and violence, electoral turnout, home ownership, rates of blood and organ donation, charitable giving, emigration and inward migration, levels of homelessness, malnutrition, debt and so on. In policing there is also a wide range of indicators that could be used: victim satisfaction, public confidence, reported levels of trust or legitimacy, representativeness, efficiency measures, different types of costing, sickness and absenteeism, ill-health retirement, staff turnover and, of course, a whole host of measures relating to crime(s).

A problem we will discuss in the next chapter in more detail is that these things are impossible to trade off against one another or to measure using a single index. This makes contributing to the public good very different from maximizing "shareholder value" (Kincaid 1997; Morrell, 2009; and Rhodes and Wanna, 2009).[1] Policing is also a last-resort service and recipients of police services are often unwilling, whether being arrested or subject to force, or having to rely on the police in distress. Maximizing "value" can be a clumsy way to describe these dynamics. In addition, when, for instance, the police face severe cuts, the challenge seems more sensibly understood as coping, or maintaining service provision, not "maximizing value".

A more fundamental point is that any approach that tries to understand the public good exclusively in terms of performance indicators faces difficulties (Stoker, 2006). This is because (recalling our list of "governance challenges" facing the police) consideration of the public good is never simply about "how" questions to do with measurement and control. Instead it raises "why" questions about what is right and what is good. In the case of policing, as mentioned, a host of measures could provide indicators for the public good. But we would argue that it is impossible to trade these indicators off against each other. Is one violent crime against a person, or a child, in any sense ever equivalent to a crime against property? The law and sentencing guidelines provide bases for comparison, and a harm index is also one way to approach this, but then these only cover crime. Much of policing is not about crime, and whereas crime affects victims directly there is always the question of the wider public to consider. What are the appropriate levels of spending to improve public confidence or feelings of safety? Would money be better spent trying to secure more convictions, or pursuing tactics that are proven to be effective at catching criminals, or deterring them, even if these damage public confidence, feelings of safety, or the ability of certain groups (or indeed everyone) to use public spaces?

The ideal of "the public good" moves us beyond thinking about individual indicators to a more general assessment of what is good for society. However, people are likely to arrive at different accounts of the public good if they begin from different starting assumptions (Ross, 1980). For instance, if we wanted to re-imagine our society from the roots up, we could begin with a basic principle of individual liberty. But then even this means different things – is liberty principally about kinds of ownership, and the freedom of choice? Or is liberty about things like identity, association and belief? Should liberty be understood as freedom from any form of tyranny or as the ability to realize one's full potential? All have different implications for how we might try to realize "the public good". For example, Nozick (1974) argues if we make individual liberty the foundation of a society there is a compelling case for market modes of governance. Alternatively, we could begin with a different basic principle that we used to understand "the public good": that we should have social justice. This leads to a quite different vision of the ideal society. If our primary concerns are at a societal level and concern justice, there is likely to be a case for overriding individual liberty (Rawls, 1999), and introducing more hierarchical modes of governance.

These differences between accounts of "the public good" for society underline the need for a firm foundation when considering the relationship between governance and the public good. To define this more precisely we base our account of the public good on virtue ethics. We use "virtue" throughout the book, but in closing this chapter it is helpful to introduce this perspective in a little more detail and in relation to the "public good". In Chapter 2 we consider more carefully the need to contextualize public good before applying this to policing.

Governance – a virtue ethics perspective

A virtue ethics perspective on "the public good" has advantages over vaguer appeals to "good governance" and we also think it has many advantages over using a suite of performance indicators. It connects to a well-established ethical tradition which is not just focused on individual agents or decisions, nor on outcomes or processes, but instead considers how people and institutions act in a given context over time (MacIntyre, 1984a; Nussbaum, 2001; Sen, 2005). This greater sensitivity to context and to actions over time helps us continue to develop an account of governance as the production of order. This can be illustrated by considering the two main rival systems of ethics: Utilitarianism and Kantian ethics.

Utilitarianism and Kantian ethics are rule-centred approaches that are designed to help derive solutions to ethical problems (Mellahi, Morrell and Wood, 2010; Morrell, 2004a). If the question is, "what should I/we do in this situation?", a Utilitarian answer would be – whatever leads to the most benefit all round (or greatest utility); a Kantian answer would be – whatever is in line with established duties (also considering what the world would be like if everyone acted in that same way). Utilitarianism emphasizes the consequences of a decision, so it is an example of a consequentialist approach to ethics. Duty in Greek is "*deon*" so Kantianism is called a deontological approach (the "golden rule" of "do unto others …" is a deon and it is the essence of Kant's ethical system).

These are brief summaries, but to apply them in policing, if the operational focus is on minimizing potential harm, that is a consequentialist approach. The basic duty of having to "enforce the law" is deontological. One can imagine the kinds of difficulties that come about when trying to apply these very abstract principles in policing and that also signals well-known problems with these two systems. In policing it is very difficult to compare different outcomes, it is very difficult to measure harm, and one cannot always predict what the consequences will be (so Utilitarianism / consequentialism is problematic). Kantian or deontological approaches can be hard to follow because different duties might conflict and also because resources are constrained.

Virtue ethics can be compatible with both traditions (Morrell, 2004a), but it is also different because it draws attention to the individual (or institution) as a moral agent, and to their context in the widest sense. Utilitarianism and Kantianism are based on ideals of abstractness and impartiality because they rely on the idea that these principles apply in every situation. Virtue ethics takes a different approach by considering questions such as what does it mean to be a good person? What would a good person do in these circumstances? What is meant by being "good" or living the good life? Virtue ethics is not about abstract rules. A point that we will return to in our concluding chapter is that virtue ethics can be thought of as an ethic of stories – since it considers the implications of actions in terms of an agent's environment and personal history, as well as the future implications of that action on the agent's moral worth, or character. Virtue ethics prioritizes the cultivation of virtue, or moral excellence; through following good habits and acting in accordance with the pursuit of the good. It is a constant struggle to meet standards of excellence so evaluation of someone's character and moral excellence can only really be done at the end of their life (Morrell, 2004a).

Virtue ethics strives for "the good" by trying to move beyond consideration of a list of things that we take to be "good" and towards a more general understanding of the overall form that is "the good" (Kraut, 2002). In other words, as well as aiming to do a variety of good things, we also try to consider what is our ultimate aim – in relation to policing this involves considering what is "the public good".

"The public good" has an ancient heritage. There are limitations with these origins but this does not mean we have to adopt any ancient vision of the ideal society and it does not mean we cannot adapt them if we find they offer potential to generate new insights (Morrell, 2007, 2012a). For instance, you could simply see if you agree with the argument set out in the following two paragraphs.

One of the earliest advocates of virtue ethics, Aristotle, acknowledges that many things are held to be good. He goes on to argue that although these things are diverse, they are also connected in some way. To develop a systematic account of "the good", he suggests we need to understand how these good things are related. He suggests different activities "aim" at different good things, "the end of the medical art is health, that of shipbuilding a vessel, that of strategy victory, that of economics wealth" (Aristotle, 1094a7–10). These are proximate goals, which is to say each goal is in itself subordinate to other activities and goals. So in terms of his examples, health is not an end in itself, it enables us to do other things; a ship once built is used for other activities; victory may be necessary for peace, which is necessary for political administrations to pursue other ends; wealth is not an end in itself but creates potential for more choices and so on. Analogously, the various indicators used in policing that we mention above (frequency of different crimes, complaints, levels of convictions, feelings of safety, public confidence) are proximate goals – because people who feel safe and do not suffer crime are more likely to be able to live their lives as they want.

To connect these different things together, he suggests there is an ultimate goal at which all activity aims. He calls this *eudaimonia*. This is often translated as happiness, which is unhelpful because it is not a state of mind or mood, instead it is an ongoing activity. When rejecting the idea happiness is a temporary state he gave us the famous metaphor: "one swallow does not make a summer". He also said, "a short time does not make a man blessed and happy" (1098a17–19). A better translation for *eudaimonia* – which we will use – is "flourishing": activity that helps us to realize our potential and where we pursue those things that make us distinctively human. Evaluation of whether one has successfully aimed at flourishing is finally realized at death. (Virtue ethics is also sometimes called a *teleological* account of ethics because *telos* means goal or end.) Evaluation of ethical behaviour – of whether one has aimed at the good – applies not only to individuals, but to institutions, "though it is worthwhile to attain the end merely for one man, it is finer ... to attain it for a nation or for city states" (1094b10–11).

In terms of what this means for the public good, the implications of a virtue ethics perspective are that:

1. Political administrations govern the provision of public services and try to maximize beneficial outcomes across various indicators, but these things (like ship-building and wealth creation) are only proximate goals.
2. The role of politics is to achieve excellent administration by pursuit of proximate goals, and an ultimate goal of a society where the public can flourish.
3. In addition, it is not enough for the state and its servants to achieve these goals; the actions of the state and of its servants and any public service – such as policing – should themselves exhibit virtue.

Two broad illustrations of this perspective, at the level of national government, may be helpful since we will come on to talk more specifically about policing.

Illustrations

First: the UK Conservative Governments 1957–64. Prime Minister MacMillan and his successor Douglas-Home formed cabinets of remarkable cliques. MacMillan showed astonishing nepotism, giving government posts to 35 family members, employing 7 in his cabinet (Marr, 2007). Both were fond of including Old Etonians in their cabinets. These crude versions of network governance: by old school tie and nepotism, clashed with the liberalization of the early 1960s. This elitism heightened the impact of the Profumo affair and the legacy of this era is hypocrisy and scandal: vices antithetical to the public good. Using the virtue ethics framework above, these governments failed to contribute to the public good in each regard. The way they controlled power over time was through reliance on nepotism and cliques (crude distortions of network governance). This meant they were out of touch with their citizenry at a time of liberalization. The gulf between the ruled and the ruling elite was prejudicial to pursuit of the good life. In undermining confidence in the institutions of the state, and being so demonstrably unrepresentative, they damaged the link between government and civil society.

Second: the Blair era. There are parallels between "sofa government" and the cosy networks of MacMillan and Douglas-Home. More distinctive to New Labour were the arrogation of powers to Number 10 and influence of unelected advisers. Blair's government eroded civil liberties: curtailing freedom of speech and right to protest; establishing DNA databases and affording police the power to swab people by force; persisting with an ID card agenda; curtailing rights to trial by jury; extending the rights of the state to detain without trial (Porter, 2006). They pursued war in the face of unparalleled opposition. These describe a particular way in which order was produced over time: a presidential style inconsistent with the UK's model of democracy. Measures to curb liberty, and the Iraq war, were justified with reference to terrorism. Guarding against terrorist threat should be something governments "aim" at in several ways (including enlightened foreign policy). This is so the public can pursue the good life. If this is compromised by curtailing liberty and creating a climate of fear, and by increasing the power and reach of the state, an administration is not aiming at *eudaimonia*, but totalitarianism.

Unlike political administrations, policing never ends, but there can be transition periods or eras marked by boundaries. These might come when governments are elected, when new legislation or practices are implemented, after watershed events, or when leaders of forces change. Another complication is that police forces have various constraints, most obviously the legal framework within which they operate, but also pressures from society and of course the level of resources given to them by government.

To apply the framework above to look at the governance of policing, virtue ethics suggests we should study:

1. Proximate goals relating to policing and criminal justice, in their political and social context.
2. An ultimate goal – the extent to which the police create conditions which enable the public to flourish.
3. How the police (individually and collectively) exhibit virtue (or vice), where virtue is understood in a wider context, over a given time period.

Good governance in policing then, ideally, is not simply about limiting harm, but about providing conditions that allow people to flourish. Existing criminal justice measures are part of this picture. Whether individual officers or forces themselves exhibit virtue is also a critical consideration.

Figure 1.1, below, summarizes our perspective on governance in policing.

Illustration

We will look at many examples of attempts to apply virtue ethics in the course of the book, but to complement the analyses of different governments above it is useful to provide a comparable analysis of governance in policing informed by this framework.

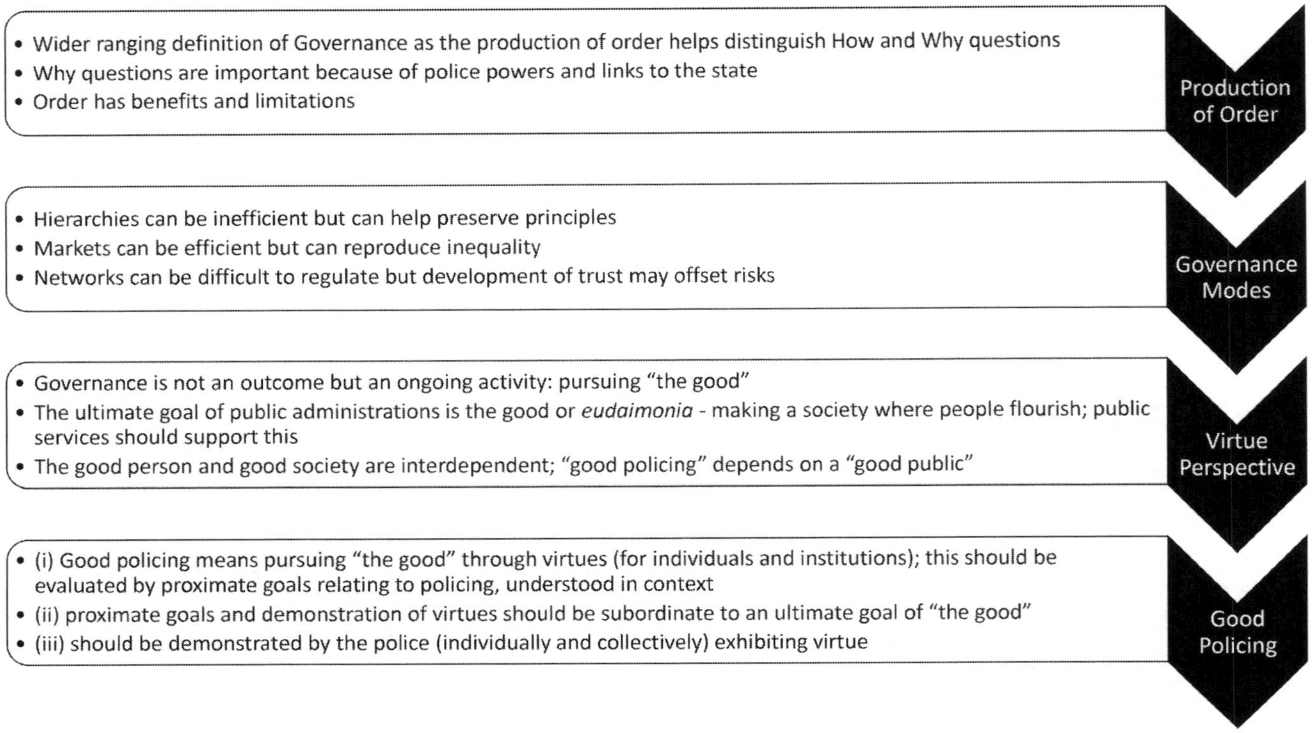

Production of Order
- Wider ranging definition of Governance as the production of order helps distinguish How and Why questions
- Why questions are important because of police powers and links to the state
- Order has benefits and limitations

Governance Modes
- Hierarchies can be inefficient but can help preserve principles
- Markets can be efficient but can reproduce inequality
- Networks can be difficult to regulate but development of trust may offset risks

Virtue Perspective
- Governance is not an outcome but an ongoing activity: pursuing "the good"
- The ultimate goal of public administrations is the good or *eudaimonia* – making a society where people flourish; public services should support this
- The good person and good society are interdependent; "good policing" depends on a "good public"

Good Policing
- (i) Good policing means pursuing "the good" through virtues (for individuals and institutions); this should be evaluated by proximate goals relating to policing, understood in context
- (ii) proximate goals and demonstration of virtues should be subordinate to an ultimate goal of "the good"
- (iii) should be demonstrated by the police (individually and collectively) exhibiting virtue

FIGURE 1.1 *Governance and Policing*

The miners' strike (1984–5) (or "dispute" as the state and police at the time referred to it) was a vicious watershed in British policing. This is often seen as a pivotal point because it is the signal period during which the police became politicized as part of the state's attempt to break Trade Union power. From a very low base, police pay and conditions increased significantly throughout the Thatcher government and during the strike officers were sent across the country ostensibly to police an industrial dispute, but in reality to provide protection to those who wanted to break strikes (lawfully) by crossing picket lines.

There was a tension between proximate goals: protecting lawful crossing of a picket line; and other less proximate goals: community cohesion, perpetuating injustice. As a whole, the dispute created deep divisions in society that also compromised the Peelian ideal that the public are the police and the police the public. Over the course of the strike, impoverished miners were brought face to face with those breaking the strike and at the same time confronted by a well-fed and extremely well-paid arm of the state. This was often made up of people with little or no lived appreciation of the life of mining communities. Many thousands of police were involved and so speaking of their individual virtues or vices is impossible, but in terms of policing as a whole and how order was produced, often officers were drawn from urban areas and asked to police more remote, rural communities (given their location by pits). During this period the police recruited from among the (predominantly) white working class so there was a fracturing of class and of class identity. Action lasted over a year and was nationwide during which an astonishing 14,000,000 police overtime hours were approved (Wallington, 1985). This indicates an expression of hierarchical, state power rather than a choice based on market considerations and this figure does not, as far as we can see, seem factored into any economic case for changing the coal industry in this way. One of many incoherences here is that one of the grievances of the miners was they were facing restrictions on earnings because of a ban on overtime.

Conclusion

This chapter offers an account of governance as the production of order. Claims to effectiveness in the delivery of public services inescapably relate to power and politics. One role of the academic community is to scrutinize the case that those in power make. The framework presented here serves as a means to scrutinize the production of order, and its relationship to the public good which we discuss more specifically in relation to policing in the next chapter.

2
THE PUBLIC GOOD

This chapter discusses the concept of the public good in more depth and considers how to apply this term to policing. It describes two problems: first, that "the public good" is a goal that can never be reached (the "utopia problem"); second, that it is difficult to quantify (the "measurement problem"). After proposing three solutions to the utopia problem, we introduce a fivefold framework to help explain how it is we can use "the public good" with as unique an institution as policing.

The public good

The public good is at the heart of contemporary writing on religious, social and applied ethics (Carcello, 2009; Dorrien, 2008; Hollenbach, 2002; O'Brien, 2009) as well as in the contemporary literature on public management (Barabashev and Straussman, 2007; Bozeman, 2007; Dillman, 2008; Lewis, 2006; Morrell, 2009; Rhodes and Wanna, 2009). As Lewis (2006) has suggested, the terms "public good", "public interest" and "common good" can have different nuances but they are also often used interchangeably. For instance, Grandy (2009: 1119) aligns the public good with collaboration and citizenship, "the values of collaboration, the public interest, and citizenship". Simo and Bies (2007: 125) discuss cross-sector collaboration in terms of "orientation toward the public good". Vigoda-Gadot and Meisler (2010: 73) use the public good to discuss outcomes associated with public work, as do Moynihan and Pandey (2007: 40). Barabashev and Straussman (2007: 380–381) describe corrosion of the public good in an absence of neutrality among public workers, where, "personal interests dominate the public interest". Tullock (1984: 89) defines public interest as "abstract devotion to the public good". At their core, these accounts all resonate with Rawls' (1999) definition of common good that we mentioned in Chapter 1, "certain general conditions that are in an appropriate sense equally to everyone's advantage" (also cited in Carcello, 2009 and Morrell and Clark, 2010).

At the same time as consensus about the core meaning of "the public good", there are problems with using this as an analytic concept (Schubert, 1962). Critical feminist scholars reject the notion because, "the insistence that there is such a thing as a generalized common interest has typically served the advantage of male elites who define the content of 'public' and 'private' (2004: 11–12)." O'Brien (2009: 25) echoes this as he suggests we should be, "suspicious of the idea that a good can be anything more than a perspective on reality that reflects the best interests of a certain elite group, often hiding behind the veil of the common good". Working out what the public good means in any particular setting should always require critical reflection and care. In this chapter we try to do this by building on our discussion of governance in Chapter 1. This helps us to set out what we mean specifically when we talk about "policing and the public good".

Policing and the public good

Since policing is often central to the administration of the state, it is often directly implicated in many of the state's failings. Many crimes (with the notable exception of "white-collar" crimes) are often foot-printed on deprivation and the "production of order" favours those who are already in positions of power and privilege. The police are also sworn to uphold the law and we know from social history that laws can be oppressive and unfair or can disenfranchise particular groups. Policing is often seen in a negative light because of these things and, relatedly, it comes under scrutiny from different stakeholders who have concerns about the use and legitimacy of police powers. In their day to day work, since they are an emergency service and a "last resort" provider, where the police respond and act it is often in crisis situations. On these occasions something has already gone badly wrong and in that immediate sense there can be no "good" outcome. All these factors would seem to suggest that doing policing well is less a matter of enhancing the public good and more a question of limiting various kinds of harm, or managing risk. The list of challenges we set out in the previous chapter – for instance relating to cuts and the changing nature of crime, together with rising, more complex demands – create additional pressures. This all suggests there is a need to think through the meaning of "public good" carefully if we want to use it in relation to policing.

To do so, we will begin by discussing two problems with applying "the public good" that are important considerations in any setting. The first is that it is impossible ever to attain the public good, the second is that it is difficult to turn something the public good into something that can be quantified. The first of these problems we will call the "utopia problem", the second we will call the "measurement problem". These two problems make it a challenge because "the public good" is unlike any conventional performance measure.

The utopia problem

There will never be a time when "the public good" has been reached or fulfilled. If we consider society as a whole, governing is a perpetual process, where different interest groups have goals and values that may be destined to be in conflict. Indeed, democratic societies are by nature made up of groups who express different interests. People's hopes and aspirations are potentially limitless, but resources are not. If we consider policing more particularly, to reach "the public good" would require utopia where (among other things) there were no causes of risk or harm – like poverty, drug and alcohol dependencies, mental illness; and no sources of conflict – like racism, misogyny or unequal life chances. Since we can never arrive at a point where the public good has been fulfilled, it could seem unsatisfactory to use the idea of an end goal that is unrealizable. Three different perspectives from virtue ethics can serve as solutions to this "Utopia" problem.

Perspective one: institutional virtues

Using virtue ethics, solving the "utopia problem" requires a shift in perspective. To acknowledge that we cannot ever reach an ultimate goal is not a recipe for despair, it is really just opening up a different way of thinking about performance, although this will jar with existing ways that we measure performance in criminal justice. From a virtue ethics perspective, we are in a sense "allowed" to have a goal that is bold and noble, but that we cannot reach. As we mentioned in the previous chapter, "the good", or *eudaimonia*, cannot be a target that we could reach, because it is an activity not an end state. However, this does not mean that we have no attainable goals. The pursuit of "virtue" can involve all kinds of proximate goals. However, proximate goals – doing good things – are subordinate to an ultimate goal – pursuing the good. Far from being utopian, virtue ethics is a very pragmatic approach, in ways that utilitarian and Kantian principles are not. For example, if we fall short of ideals, or fail in some decisions, that does not compromise a goal of living well over time. Additionally, built into the language of virtue and vice is an acknowledgement that people and institutions can be more or less virtuous without having to be perfect. Also, because context is important in attributions of virtue, we can acknowledge that sometimes circumstances, or "bad luck", prevents otherwise good people from acting virtuously. (Other traditions of virtue ethics can lead to different perspectives on some of these issues.)

"Good policing" then, is not so much an outcome as it is an ongoing activity. One aspect of this is the cultivation of (what we call) "institutional virtues". Institutional virtues are shared normative criteria that administrations aspire to when governing institutions well and which also speak to the rights and duties of the public. In policing these could be things like competence, fairness, representativeness and – most importantly – legitimacy (which we discuss in Chapter 3). These could in turn be tracked using different indicators. Cultivating institutional virtues does not involve commitment to a utopian destination. Continually striving for an ultimate end goal through the pursuit of a series of more proximate goals is a fairly simple idea to communicate, but in practice it involves a radical reimagining of policing. We suggest there would be huge cultural barriers to fully accepting this because policing is so often about hard metrics and categories and reviewing past performance. In police practice, even where there is ambiguity, very often the role of the police is to resolve dilemmas, remove this ambiguity and definitively classify something or someone. Indeed this is a key function of a broader category of public servants, "street-level bureaucrats" (Lipsky, 2010) (which we discuss in Chapter 7). Police officers are often pragmatists and solution oriented, but "virtue ethics" does not necessarily offer a category, classification or solution.

Perspective two: individual virtues

The language of institutional virtues opens up a different way of talking between relations between policing and the public, and about the role of police in society. From an individual perspective, and thinking about the jobs of individual officers or others working in police forces, it can also be beneficial to focus on the work that the police do as public servants. For individual public servants, the public good can be thought of as an ongoing, individual obligation rather than a destination. This is often how public servants describe and understand their work – as a continuing duty that is discharged to the public (Lewis, 2006). One of the things we do in this book is emphasize that policing is a kind of work. This seems important because "the police" are often seen in monolithic terms – as a collective force in society. This can make it harder to build up an idea of policing as contributing to the public good, or to provide more context-sensitive accounts of virtuous or vicious behaviour.

Understanding police work (Chapter 5), and the role of training in police work (Chapter 6) helps shed light on the nature of this obligation and on how it is learned and discharged. This gives insights into the importance of individual virtues and character, which is an important idea in the virtue framework. The idea of the police officer as a developing character or indeed as a kind of character is useful because it helps us to think about relationships between the individual and the service as a whole. At the level of the service as a whole this concept of ongoing obligation is consistent with the idea that good governance involves pursuing equity and justice, in the progress discharging an obligation to future generations (Frederickson, 1994). This is another way to answer the utopia problem by again reframing the public good as a process rather than a destination (see also Goodsell, 1985, 1990).

Perspective three: the police are the public, the public are the police

We can also work to relate individual and societal perspectives on the "public good" to one another. Doing so means building on a central idea at the origins of virtue ethics: that the good person and good society are defined relationally (Morrell, 2009). On this view, policing that contributes to the public good is understood as something that makes it possible for the public to flourish or to live the good life. In addition, part of this good life as a member of the public is consent and co-operation, solidarity with other members of the public and supporting policing and the criminal justice system (where this system is just). The public are also responsible for governance – producing order (or disorder). If we have "good policing" then this is only made possible because there are "good members of the public", good members of the public can only flourish because they have faith in public institutions, such as good policing and belief in governance – the production of order. This account of a recursive relationship between policing and the public is already very familiar because it is the most often quoted Peelian principle:

> To maintain at all times a relationship with the public that gives reality to the historic tradition that the police are the public and that the public are the police, the police being only members of the public who are paid to give full time attention to duties which are incumbent on every citizen in the interests of community welfare and existence.

Again this leads to a process perspective on the utopia problem. Rather than seeing the public good as an end point, it is a continual process, and one which relates the person to the state or to their public services. "Good policing" is an activity ideally carried out by the police and the public in concert.

These three perspectives on the utopia problem can complement one another. They can support an account of "public good" as something understood in terms of: (i) a number of subsidiary institutional virtues (competence, responsiveness, representativeness and so on); (ii) an ongoing obligation realized through cultivating individual virtues and the development of character; and (iii) a mutually constituted relationship between the public and the state. Each of these refinements moves us further away from a "utopia" picture of "the public good", and closer to an account that is more flexibly applied to a particular context and that takes shape in the pursuit of proximate goals. They are refinements to the definitional framework we built in the first chapter, building on the idea that public services can be evaluated over time in terms of how they "produce order", how well they demonstrative virtue themselves, and how well they allow the public to live the good life.

The measurement problem

As well as the utopia problem, there is a second and related problem with using the notion of the public good. This is that it is difficult to quantify; summed up most dramatically by Schubert's (1962) suggestion that the public good, "makes no operational sense" (in Denhardt and Denhardt, 2007: 67). This makes it an open question as to whether using such a general term like public good has any additional analytic benefit. Is it an empty re-description? Are we in the same territory as chatter about "corporate governance failure" – buzzwords masquerading as analysis. Is this saying as little as we would if we "explained" paper burns because it has flammable properties?

We would argue that the picture we are building up of the public good is already much more robust than vague appeals to "good governance". The public good has an established, core, sense which ties it to well understood questions and problems in practical ethics. One answer to the measurement problem could be to say that the very process of seeking a definition in a given setting is what is important. A dialogue about the public good could be an important part of deliberative democracy – this is potentially the role that a new Royal Commission on Policing could play (Morgan and Newburn, 1997; Newburn, 2017). "The public good" can – at the same time – be a term which is hard to measure because its meaning changes in different settings, and be indispensable because it is part of a common language with a rich heritage. Indeed, the idea is already understood quite flexibly, if not on a case-by-case basis, in the courts. "Public interest" is used when ruling on new, disruptive technologies whose effects could not have been foreseen (Gurses and Ozcan, 2015). It plays a useful role there because, in a sense, "the public good" stretches forward in time. Laws lag behind societal changes, but the idea of the public good is flexible and robust enough to evaluate new and unforeseen innovations.

There is potential for using "the public good" in policing, and we would argue that this has not been given sufficient attention in the literature to date. This is perhaps because understanding of the public good is predominantly based on the study of Western, developed democracies and on an assumption that "the public good" is something that is somehow added to. So, "good" public services enhance or contribute to the "public good". Less attention has been given to the idea that people or institutions might still serve the public good when the circumstances are far from ideal, when what they do is remove a source of harm, or act in ways that use force.

Policing is often about crisis-response, focused on limiting harm and involving the use of control and force (Holdaway, 1977). Also, different stakeholders can have extremely contrasting views about the police and the purpose of the police. These factors mark differences between the police and other public services such as health or education, which can perhaps be linked more easily to *eudaimonia* and ideas of flourishing (this is not to deny these settings can involve different kinds of state-sanctioned discipline or, for instance, symbolic violence). We need to think more radically about what "the public good" actually involves when applying it to a public service as distinctive as policing.

Comparative governance studies tell us that the meaning of "the public good" is very complex and differentiated when we evaluate governments as a whole (Morrell and Harrington-Buhay, 2012). This challenges assumptions we might make in the West. Taking one example, "democracy" is sometimes held out as necessary for the public good (Kim et al., 2005; Lewis, 2006). But many societies (through history or across the world) are not democracies (also societies described as democracies are undemocratic in many ways). This need not necessarily mean their public services have no possibility of ever contributing to the public good, or that individual public servants cannot be virtuous. Comparative work on governance is helpful to acknowledge in passing when considering policing because our language about the public good is often tied to assumptions about democracy and the ideal society, referencing back to the idea that the public good is often considered as something administrations and public services enhance, whereas much of policing is about limiting harm. As our definition of governance also suggests, policing often involves the use or threat of force and curtailing some people's liberties in order to "produce order". This makes the issue of "rights" and policing in some other jurisdictions complex (Cordone, 1999).

Policing is a highly contested activity and there are multiple publics with conflicting, even irreconcilable, perspectives. Analogously, if we stop to consider governance in developing contexts, many elements in the Western recipe for "good governance" are deficient or absent. As a result, governments are often preoccupied with preventing harm and in making complex trade-offs that try to balance conflicting outcomes and constituencies – for instance in dealing with the legacy of civil war. Comparing across countries reveals there is no one model of "good governance" and also that the Western model of the public good can be based on limiting assumptions. In the following section we adapt and apply a framework that has been developed for thinking about public good in comparative governance (discussed in much more detail in Morrell and Harrington-Buhay, 2012). We suggest that several elements of this model are useful for thinking through distinctive aspects to policing and for evaluating how policing can contribute to the public good.

1. The need for a "shock absorber"

One thing Morrell and Harrington-Buhay (2012) discovered when looking at the public good in a post-conflict society was the need for a trusted interlocutor between state actors and wider society. This was because constituencies were so polarized. We describe this role as providing oxygen and breathing space as well as a shock absorber. Models of "the public good" do not recognize the need for this shock absorber role because there is no acknowledgement that different parties may not be listened to because they are associated with force, nor is there acknowledgement that stakeholders can be polarized. These elements also apply in policing, and much more so than in other public services. Moreover, implicit in some models of criminology is the idea that policing only exists because of market and state failures – because poverty can explain crime or at least predict the response of the criminal justice system, "the rich get richer, the poor get prison" (Reiman, 1998).

This puts policing in tension with other public services (social work, housing, education, health) that might see themselves as trying to improve the lives of those in poverty. Combined with the exercise of force and sworn duties to protect property and uphold the status quo, or order, this leads to quite radical tensions. It also means the basic morality of policing is open to question, and that it is perennially important to ask what the police are for. Discussion and debate about policing is often polarized, so understanding "policing and the public good" may well require a trusted interlocutor because some constituencies feel so disenfranchised or distrustful. Potentially this is an important role for the academic community to play and one which is very different from the kind of service-provider role envisioned in evidence-based policing (cf. Loader and Sparks, 2013).

For instance, one commonly expressed grievance for families of those who have died in custody has been that the Independent Police Complaints Commission (IPCC) have not been independent:

> We believed it [the investigation] would be independent, but it was never independent," said one person. "Our case was played out in the media ... It took three to four days for the IPCC to contact his mother.
>
> *(in Allison and Hattenstone, 2017)*

Neither the IPCC nor the media play this shock absorber role, so one implication for policing is to think about the potential institutional "home" for examining highly contentious issues. In a different sense, the role of Her Majesty's Inspectorate of Constabulary and Fire and Rescue Service (for brevity we will abbreviate this to HMIC) – now could be seen as interlocutor between the police and the government, however it also is not trusted sufficiently to warrant the "shock absorber" description. HMIC are often seen as pursuing an agenda on behalf of the government of the day rather than merely evaluating the service – even though recent reports, at the time of writing, have been critical about the consequences of cuts (e.g. HMIC, 2017). Picking up the "insider/outsider" distinction with which we opened the book, perhaps this interlocutor needs to be a genuine outsider to absorb the shock of force. If we are not going to have a Royal Commission style, wide-ranging discussion of what the police are for, then for academia to play this role would require greater separation and distance than is envisioned in "evidence-based policing", or encouraged in the governance of academia itself where there can be an overly narrow focus on "impact".

2. Avoid "bads"

Policing is often not about the choice of the optimal solution to a problem. Rather, as Bittner (1974: 18) says, the role of the police is to "impose or ... coerce a provisional solution" (Newburn, 2017). Whilst this solution may be seen as a bad outcome for all parties, an important aspect to this is trying to take into account what other – far worse outcomes might result. Both at the level of individual scenarios and in mass disorder, choices can be more easily thought of as about avoiding "bads" rather than enhancing "the good". This extract from a police officer we interviewed (data collection is described in more detail in Chapter 6) described responding to a fight between a far-right group (the English Defence League or EDL) and an anti-fascist movement (Unite against Fascism or UAF):

> There's UAF to one side and then obviously the EDL at the other side of Peterborough and they'd broke out, EDL had broke out their lines and run round over the bridge and actually managed to get to the UAF and we went over the bridge, there was only myself, another officer from Peterborough, another Leicestershire officer and we got there and all we saw was this massive basically like a fight in the park. It looked like medieval times where people were running up to each other and they were fighting with sticks, punching each other and all we did – we had to – obviously we run across the park to them and we basically went to like primal instincts basically trying to tear people apart from fighting, detaining people. But then you'd detain one person and you'd see some more fighting, people with sticks so you think that's more dangerous, that's more important so you'd go there.

This is helpful in showing the limits with our assumed way of talking about whether a service "enhances" the public good. When things get "medieval", the good might take shape in following basic imperatives – to save life, or to save one's own or one's colleagues' lives.

3. Account for alternatives

Part of calculating the public good means considering the effect of what would happen if we did not have a basic or taken-for-granted ingredient of the public good – such as order. What we might call the Western "shopping list" of good governance – democracy, rule of law, property rights, effective civil society and institutions, etc. – does not really apply in all instances when the police have to confront bads, such as avoiding the kind of conflict described in the extract above. In some circumstances we might sacrifice almost anything to preserve some basics. Any critic of what seems to be an inappropriate use of force (either excessive or inadequate) could reasonably identify failures. But at the same time, they might need to account for the alternatives and to see policing in the context of the actions of the state as a whole, and the actions of the public.

To try to give an example, one might consider the police response to the 2011 disorder (that we discuss in Chapter 7). The police were criticized as being slow to act and different politicians suggested they should have used much greater force: plastic baton rounds (rubber bullets), water cannon or that the government should have involved the army. Whilst there may have been potential failures to act quickly enough, critics would need to reflect on what a more militarized and swifter response by the state would have meant for ongoing relations between the police and public. A quote we also use in Chapter 7 from Hugh Orde is relevant here since he cautioned that: "excessive force will destroy our model of policing in the long term" (Hoggett and Stott, 2012: 174).

4. Lowest common denominator of values

There are many components to "the public good", some of which we have discussed in this chapter and in Chapter 1. These include: shared objectives and established "rules of the game"; methods to bring about consensus and institutionalized consensus; mechanisms for dialogue and goal setting across sectors; recognition of inequity and the need to reduce it; the capacity to reconcile differences without resorting to violence; the ability to overcome vested interests who benefit from order (Snyder and Mahoney, 1999); governmental legitimacy and coherence between its avowed and actual intent (Brinkerhoff and Brinkerhoff, 2002); capacities for governing, and capacities for public service delivery; a sense of nationhood, and national ownership of solutions. Underlying these are peace, security, political and economic stability and basic infrastructure.

One other ingredient we would want to apply to our model of public good in policing comes from a particularly powerful phrase in our case study (Morrell and Harrington-Buhay, 2012), namely, "a lowest common denominator of values". Indeed perhaps this is an essential social good. In policing, the imperative to save life might be the very heart of this, as this extract from someone policing the first night of the 2011 disorder shows:

> I thought "Right, it's quite clear, the fire brigade are here, the ambulances are here, buildings are being set alight, it's clear both those emergency services have got to be protected to save life, so unless anyone tells me any different that's what I'm doing, and I'm keeping this crowd back so that London Ambulance Service and London Fire Brigade can do their job. Save life, that's got to be more important than anything else that's going on at the moment, and the issue here is to just keep that crowd back, because if they filter round the side of us or break us down and come through the LAS and the LFB have got no other option, they'll just have to abandon their vehicles and run, and people who are trapped inside burning buildings will die." (Again, data collection is described in more detail in Chapter 6).

5. Multiple publics

Frederickson (1991) notes that responses to the question of "who is the public?" depend directly on the purpose for which the question is asked. This suggests the need to explore and explicitly define the public when working with the public good. This is an important consideration because (as we discuss in more depth in Chapter 6) often different publics are in conflict. The importance of multiple publics is also crucial to understanding policing because very different measures such as "public confidence" and "satisfaction" can be taken as assessing "the public". Actually the public is fractured, not just because of divisions in wider society and different kinds of memberships, inclusion and exclusion – but because people's impressions of policing are likely to be very different depending on whether they come into contact with the police or not. They will almost certainly differ according to whether they are subject to some form of punishment carried out by the police, or whether they are victims of crime. People's experiences and likelihood of coming into contact with the criminal justice system also varies according to different kinds of membership: ethnicity, gender, age, lifestyle choices, geographical location – and in terms of intersections between these memberships. Again, these are different publics.

The public good needs to be understood in the light of social and institutional arrangements – of actors, institutions, the role of the state, multiple publics, government (Kohn, 2000). In policing there is a clear need to consider this because in many situations the police respond as an emergency service and a "last resort" provider. This can make it hard to connect "policing and the public good" because we inevitably consider limitation of harm, or responses to failure where there may be no good outcomes, rather than something that would enhance flourishing and "the good life". We suggest these different features outlined above (the need for a shock absorber, avoidance of bads, accounting for alternatives, lowest common denominator of values, multiple publics) offer a way of reconciling the practices and institutions of policing with the ultimate goal of "the public good".

Conclusion

Part of the value of such broad terms as the public good is that they invite scrutiny, making us ask what they mean in any given context. For instance, the very term "public" can be misleading. There is a plurality of publics, and different institutional arrangements can be understood as being more or less beneficial to particular publics. Policies can even bring new publics into being – perhaps where they recognize and legitimate the interests of a disenfranchised minority. Small institutions can even be thought of as having their own publics. Berkman and Plutzer (2005) capture the essence of this in the title of their study of US public school districts: *Ten Thousand Democracies*. Challenging the monolith "the public good" can be valuable if it means we pay more attention to groups whose influence and power chances differ. This is important because across all kinds of state it is those in power who construct what "public" is.

Terms like public can imply a coherence and stability which may be an illusion in some settings. They can also wrongly imply a collective capacity or sense of shared identity. Comparative governance studies highlights how such assumptions are questionable. In the developing world, there are some very obvious and very pertinent "bads", such as war, famine and disease, which do not feature in developed countries. Rather than suggest these are lower down a notional hierarchy of interests, or directly comparable, we would argue these are qualitatively different and require a rethinking of "the public good". Rather than transcendent or universal, "the public good" is situated, contextual and culturally freighted. In transferring lessons to policing, the importance of interlocutors, acknowledgement of the value of avoiding "bads", accounting for alternatives, and recognizing multiple publics are all important.

Figure 2.1, below, is a conceptual model that summarizes our framework for policing and the public good as set out in this Chapter.

At the base we have listed the three core challenges we identified in relation to working with the public good in this setting:

1. The utopia problem (the public good can't be attained).
2. The measurement Problem (the public good is hard to quantify and also context-specific).
3. Policing is a unique institution (making it harder to apply established models of the public good).

We argue the utopia problem can be addressed by taking a virtue ethics perspective because this is an approach that understands good governance in terms of activities that aim at proximate goals and an ultimate goal (which is importantly different from the kinds of targets associated with performance management). Virtue ethics help us to consider different ways in which public good can be implemented in policing:

1. *Institutional virtues* – "good policing" is not an outcome but an activity in accordance with institutional virtues, the foundation for which is legitimacy (Chapters 3 and 4).
2. *Individual virtues* like competence and fairness are expressed through ongoing individual obligation to serve the public and learned through becoming a police officer (Chapters 5 and 6).

In relation to challenge 3 (existing models of the public good are harder to apply to a unique institution like policing), the top of the model sets out additional considerations when it comes to implementation:

1. *A shock absorber*: Force and conflict can mean the need for a trusted interlocutor.
2. *Avoid bads*: Policing involves stark trade-offs – it may be a choice to avoid horrific "bads" rather than enhance the public good.
3. *Account for alternatives*: Critics need to provide an alternative and consider the effects over time of actions on policing as an institution.
4. *Lowest common denominator of values*: Discussing what the public good means is a useful way of finding basic common ground.
5. *Recognize multiple publics*: With conflicting stakeholders it is useful to think of many publics rather than necessarily "the public good".

In the next two chapters we discuss institutional virtues.

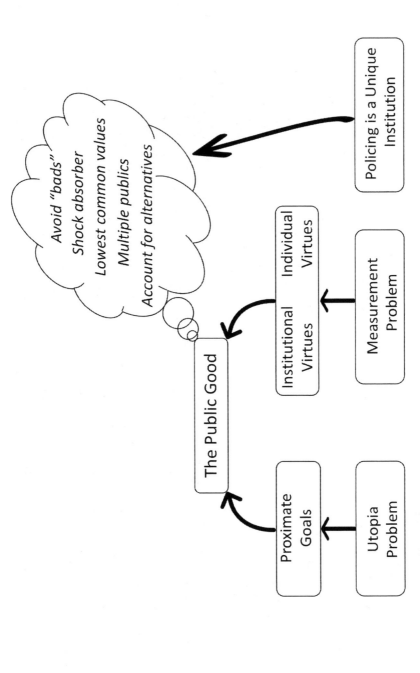

FIGURE 2.1 *Policing for Public Good*

3
LEGITIMACY

This chapter argues that for policing to enhance the public good, it needs to be associated with certain institutional virtues. Where it is associated with vices, it diminishes the public good. Foremost among these institutional virtues is legitimacy. We begin by setting out why legitimacy is such an important aspect of the relationship between police and public. We do this by considering legitimacy as an empirical component of the relationship between police and public, with a particular emphasis on how legitimacy is formed and reproduced, and the extent to which legitimate – or illegitimate – policing can influence the behaviours and indeed subjectivities of the policed.

Police legitimacy

The question of legitimacy – and the idea that legitimacy is *in* question – has been central to understanding policing since the foundation of the London Metropolitan Service Police, the first "modern" police organization, in 1829. Interpretation of the famous Peelian principles, the founding "mission statement" of the UK police (apocryphal as they likely are, Lentz and Chaires, 2007), has always revolved most importantly around what the relationship between police and policed should be, and how it should be maintained (Reiner, 2010; Reith, 1952). While early academic work on policing (e.g. Banton, 1964) stressed that this was an institution that functioned relatively well, a concern that relations with the police were strained among certain sections of the public was a continuous refrain: for example, the Royal Commission on Policing in 1962 described problems between police and younger people, on the one hand, and motorists, on the other. And earlier on, during the 19th and early part of the 20th century, police and politicians were explicit about the need for the new police powers and organizations to be justified to a sometimes sceptical public (Reiner 2010).

The word legitimacy did not, however, feature prominently in such debates, but was rather replaced with other, less loaded, terms such as approval, respect, support or confidence. One reason for this may have been the social and political charge of the very word "legitimacy" – policy-makers, practitioners and indeed academics may have shied away from suggesting the police could be *illegitimate*. The question of legitimacy was thus often addressed in a somewhat elliptical fashion – making the extent to which it has recently become explicit in police research, policy and indeed practice all the more striking. Consideration of legitimacy, both as a social science concept and arguably the central, defining, aspect of police/public relations, is largely a phenomenon of the last decade or so, but there can be little doubt it has become firmly embedded in all these arenas (as witnessed, for example in HMIC's (now HMICFRS – Her Majesty's Inspectorate of Constabulary and Fire and Rescue Services) 'PEEL' inspections, launched in 2014 – the "L" stands for legitimacy). The long history of scandal that enveloped the police from the 1970s onwards was, surely, a prime motivating factor for the decline in previous sensitivities. By the 1990s – and much earlier among some communities and parts of the population – it appeared all too easy to suggest that the legitimacy of the police was, to say the least, in some doubt, and it cannot be coincidence that the "Legitimacy turn" in policing scholarship dates from the last decade of the 20th century (Tankebe, 2015).

The social, political and academic history of police legitimacy in the UK is therefore framed by signal events and stories such as the Miners' strike of 1984/5, Hillsborough, the "inner-city" riots of 1981, the Guildford Four and the Birmingham Six, and the murder of Stephen Lawrence. But it is also and perhaps more importantly founded in the everyday interaction between police officers and members of the public, across the whole range of circumstances, situations and locations where such encounters take place: stop and search; community meetings; mass sporting events; serious crime investigations; road accidents; marches and demonstrations; neighbourhood patrols.

The question of legitimacy is implicated in and underpins all these events and interactions, and it is central to the way we understand policing. The police represent the coercive arm of the state, empowered to use whatever level of force necessary to deal with ruptures in the social order, whether these be crimes, disorderly behaviours or accidents. Equally importantly, they are charged with seeking to prevent such ruptures to order occurring in the first place. The police are thus central to the core duty of the state – to provide safety for its citizens – yet they are equally involved in actions that threaten those very same citizens, or at least their rights to assemble, to press for change, to be free from excessive state intervention (cf. Reiner, 2010). *Normative* concerns about the way police officers and organizations wield their power are unsurprisingly ever-present. It matters deeply how and to what ends police activity is directed. Equally, police in liberal democracies rely on the legitimacy they command and the public cooperation, deference and compliance it engenders, raising important *empirical* questions about how, why and to what extent the policed come to hold the police legitimate.

In this chapter we concentrate primarily on this second, empirical, concept (Hinsch, 2010) of legitimacy, and on two main sets of questions. Taking the perspective of those subject to (and beneficiaries of) police power, we first discuss the conceptual definition of legitimacy as a component of the relationship between police and public. On what basis can it be claimed that people believe that the police have the right to power and the authority to govern? We draw here most importantly on procedural justice theory and the mass of evidence that suggests fairness judgements are central to legitimacy. Second, we broaden out the discussion to consider the wider context of legitimacy, with a particular emphasis on how legitimacy can contribute to understanding the relationship between policing and the public good.

What is legitimacy?

At the most fundamental level, legitimacy concerns the justification of power by those subject to authority, and their obedience of that power (Coicaud, 2002: 10). Do we believe that those who govern us have the right to do so? Do we believe that those who govern us have the right to command us? At the threshold, then, legitimacy is constituted by assessments *of* and behaviours *in relation to* authorities able to direct and command, immediately indicating this is a complex issue deeply integrated into some of the central coordination problems of complex modern societies. Legitimacy can provide answers, for example, to questions concerning the ability of the state to garner willing commitment on the part of diverse groups (with different values and conflicting interests) who are nevertheless acting within the same structures of authority and right.

Discussing the legitimacy of institutional regimes, laws, norms and decisions, Wilfried Hinsch (2010) draws two useful distinctions that can serve to limit the terms of what would otherwise be an overwhelmingly complex debate. There are, first, *concepts* of legitimacy versus *conceptions* of legitimacy:

> A concept of legitimacy gives us the basic meaning of the term "legitimate" and tells us what we say about, e.g., a social rule or a political decision, when we call it legitimate. It also specifies the role of "legitimacy" in social theory and practical political deliberation. Conceptions of legitimacy, on the other hand, specify the criteria that have to be met by a rule or decision in order to actually be legitimate in the relevant sense.
>
> *(Hinsch, 2010: 39–40)*

Second, he distinguishes between two different concepts of legitimacy, "the empirical concept of the social sciences and the normative concept of political philosophy" (2010: 40); and notes the confusion that surround these concepts. This regularly leads to their elision – a discussion of one will blur very easily into the ideas more properly related to the other – a fact which Hinsch ascribes to the fact that both concern themselves with (a) normative authority and (b) the justification of state power. But what these all these terms mean can differ radically depending on whether one is discussing (a) what those subject to an authority actually think of it and how they behave in relation to it or (b) whether as a matter of law, practical ethics or moral philosophy that authority is behaving appropriately.

We are concerned here with the empirical concept of the social sciences, for which Hinsch (2010: 40–41) draws on Weber to provide an apt summary definition. On this view, an institutional arrangement such as "the police" is legitimate *as an empirical fact* when and to the extent that it finds support and approval from the group of people to which it relates, from which it is drawn and/or which it governs. To be constitutive of legitimacy this support must by definition be voluntary, since it is premised on the "sincere belief" of the governed that the arrangement in place is *appropriate* and *correct* (hence the concern with normative authority). If those subordinate to a particular institutional arrangement did not sincerely believe these things there could be no legitimacy within that relationship. Finally, "(s)ince no political regime or social order could persist without a fairly high level of unenforced compliance with its rules, the empirical understanding of legitimacy naturally occupies a central place in explanatory theories of social order" (ibid). Hinsch therefore concurs with a long succession of other authors who have stressed that organizations and institutions need legitimacy for their long-term survival. While in criminology legitimacy is often considered in terms of public perceptions of police, as, most often, an institution, it is important to remember that legitimacy is also a characteristic of police organizations, one upon which, in the long run, their very existence depends.

A two component model of legitimacy

Basic definitions in place, we can now turn to the ways scholars concerned with police and other criminal justice institutions have conceptualized legitimacy. In line with the distinction between normative appropriateness and relations with and to power, two aspects of, or constituent parts to, legitimacy judgements – the sincere beliefs people hold in relation to an institutional actor – form the basis of many such conceptualizations (cf. Jackson et al., 2014). The first component of legitimacy is normative appropriateness. Suchman (1995: 574) defines legitimacy as, "... a generalized perception or assumption that the actions of an entity are desirable, proper, or appropriate within some socially constructed system of norms, values, beliefs, and definitions". On this account, legitimacy is premised on a "fundamental accord" between rulers and ruled (Filiangeiri 1783–88, in Pardo, 2000: 5). It is founded in shared norms and values, and it is established by the "moral performance" (Liebling, 2004) of power-holders. Applied to the police, the claim here is that people: (a) judge the moral appropriateness of police behaviour (at the level of officer *and* organization) against specific norms of conduct; (b) draw lessons from such judgements in relation to the extent to which police represent and enact a set of aims, values and behaviours that they themselves share; and (c) come to an overall assessment of the extent to they and police are "normatively aligned" (Jackson et al., 2012a; 2012b; 2015).

As outlined by Suchman (1995: 579), such a sense of normative alignment with police – what he calls "moral legitimacy" – can be premised on evaluations of one or more of: outputs and consequences; techniques and procedures; categories and structures; and office-holders, leaders and representatives. People attend, that is, to what the police produce (the consequences of their activity), how they do it (the processes involved), the underlying aims, intentions, structures and values involved (which might be expressed in questions such as: "is this the right institution for this job?" and "is it trying to do the right thing?"), and the behaviour of individual police officers (or, in part, charisma in Weber's sense).

The second component of legitimacy is an internalized sense of consent to authority structures, and it can be considered to stem from these normative judgements. Here, legitimacy can be said to be present when people believe they have a *duty to obey* the instructions of power-holders (in this case, the police). When an individual recognizes the authority of the police, they feel a normatively grounded obligation to obey officers' instructions and the rules and directives operative within the space governed by police (Tyler and Jackson, 2014). Implicit (and sometimes explicit – Huq et al., 2017; Van Damme, 2017), therefore, is the idea that institutional normativity grants the right to dictate appropriate behaviour in certain prescribed circumstances – the former provides the basis for the latter. Legitimacy is not only a multi-faceted phenomenon: its different components exist in relation to one another. Evaluations of the moral rectitude of police – one's sense of normative alignment with police – flows into a sense of moral duty to obey police instructions (or not, if police fail to live up to normative expectations). This is why we suggest legitimacy can be thought of as an institutional virtue.

It is important to note that, as theorized above, the "duty to obey" is assumed to be characterized by *truly free consent*. If it is to be considered part of legitimacy, obedience should rest only on the willed acceptance of rules and instructions (an echo of Hinsch's insistence on the importance of sincere belief). The counterpoint is of course that people could believe that they should accept the decisions made by police for other reasons, for example because they feel powerless to do otherwise or fear the repercussions if they did not (Tankebe, 2009; Bottoms and Tankebe, 2012; Tankebe, 2013) – in which case such relationships could not be characterized as legitimate.

A word on trust and legitimacy

Believing that the police have the right to power has often been operationalized in survey work as institutional trust. This is based on the assumption that beliefs about legitimacy can be inferred as present when people believe officers can be trusted to act in ways that represent and enact their interests by being effective, fair and lawful (Geller et al., 2014; Sunshine and Tyler, 2003a; Tyler et al., 2010). The concepts of trust and legitimacy are, however, properly viewed as different from one another (Hawdon, 2008; Jackson et al., 2012a). Legitimacy is the property or quality of possessing rightful power and the subsequent acceptance of – and willing deference to – authority; trust represents evaluations and positive expectations regarding the intentions and capabilities of that authority (Bradford et al., 2017; Hardin, 2006; PytikZillig et al., 2016).

Yet trust and legitimacy are also plainly related to one another, most pertinently to the extent that trust can be considered as evaluation and expectation of normatively appropriate behaviour. Hardin (2006: 17) states: "To say we trust you means we believe you have the right intentions toward us and that you are competent to do what we trust you to do." These are normative judgements, relating to expectations about what police *should* do and the ways in which they *should* behave. To say that legitimacy emerges when people deem that the police tend to act in normatively appropriate ways, then, is equivalent to saying it emerges when they trust police. Figure 3.1 represents interrelationships across trust, deference to authority and normative alignment (see Bradford, 2011, 2014; Bradford and Jackson, 2016; Jackson and Bradford, 2009), linking them also to identity which we explore in more depth below, and to some of the potential antecedents of all three.

There is an important sense, therefore, in which trust flows into, or forms a precondition of, legitimacy. Yet, it is equally likely that legitimacy, in some situations, flows into trust, not least because a general sense that the police operate according to an appropriate moral framework will shape views of the likelihood of specific police actions. If one believes police generally do the right thing, then one is more likely to believe they will act appropriately if summoned to deal with a crime or incidence of disorder (see for example Hamm et al., in press). Trust and legitimacy therefore exist in close reciprocal relationship with one another, and while we

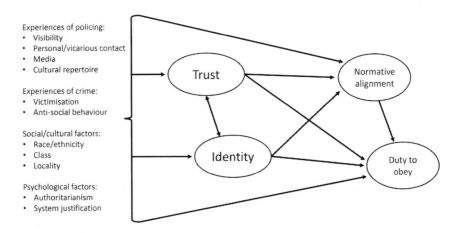

FIGURE 3.1 *A Model of Trust and Legitimacy*

concentrate here on legitimacy it is important to recognize that trust relationships are also at stake.

The role of fairness

Based on the two component concepts outlined above, people's sense of normative alignment with police is at the core of legitimacy. This immediately raises the question: "what norms?" How do people expect police to act, and what values do they expect officers to embody? Research conducted within the procedural justice paradigm suggests that when people are thinking about policing their normative concerns – the criteria they use to think about police activity, its outcomes and effects – revolve around questions of justice. This poses, of course, another question: "What constitutes justice?" What makes the legal, quasi-legal and extra-legal processes, interactions and experiences people have with the police fair and acceptable, both to those involved and to those who witness or come to hear about them?

Two sets of concerns are commonly identified. First are those related to outcomes. On this account, people essentially ask themselves: "Was the right outcome achieved?" and/or "Do I think the goods and/or impositions of this process were equitably distributed across relevant interest groups?" (distributive justice) (Leventhal, 1980; Folger, 1984). If the answers to these questions are positive, then favourable legitimacy judgements are likely to ensue, particularly perhaps in relation to the consequentialist evaluations outlined above. The second set of concerns relates to process. Here, the argument is that assessments of police processes, procedures and behaviours, and of the officers involved in them, are shaped in important ways by the nature and quality of the processes themselves: and specifically, by assessments of their fairness – what has become known as "procedural justice" (Tyler, 2017).

Procedural justice research presents two different ways of categorizing this concept. On the one hand, specific police behaviours are outlined, with a particular focus on four: (i) offering participation or voice; (ii) behaving neutrally; (iii) treating people with dignity and respect; and (iv) displaying trustworthy motives (see for example Tyler and Fagan, 2008; Mazerolle et al., 2013; Jonathan-Zamir et al., 2013). On these accounts, procedural justice has four components. When assessing people's assessments of an officer's behaviour (e.g. whether or not they felt they experienced procedural justice during an interaction), survey-based research tends to find that responses to items (questions) representing most or all of these different indicators collapse into one underlying psychological construct. In other words, there is one underlying factor, which represents a general sense of procedurally fair (or unfair) treatment on the part of the respondent (work in psychology labs is better able to distinguish between these different components – see for example Heuer and Stroessner, 2011). The implication is that people take a holistic view about the procedural fairness of a particular encounter or interaction, and indeed of the general way the authority concerned acts.

On the other hand, other research takes a subtly different approach. Here, the emphasis is on the "quality of decision-making" and the "quality of treatment" (Tyler and Huo, 2002; Reisig et al., 2007), with a further distinction sometimes drawn between formal and informal levels (i.e. those relating to formal rules and those relating to the behaviour of individuals – Blader and Tyler, 2003a; 2003b). Quality of decision-making refers to openness, consistency, neutrality and a lack of bias (and therefore, in general, the ability to make the right decision); quality of interaction relates to issues of respect, dignity, voice and trustworthiness. Work using this categorization tends to be better able to distinguish between these different components of procedural justice, although even here some studies have failed to find much distinction (e.g. Reisig et al., 2007).

In sum, procedural justice might be considered, at least in the first instance, as an over-arching psychological evaluation and response people experience during and after an encounter with a police officer or officers, which reliably includes some or all of the characteristics outlined above. In whatever particular way it is categorized, research across a wide variety of contexts has shown that procedural justice is a more important predictor of legitimacy and related outcomes than either outcome favourability or distributive justice (Tyler and Huo, 2002; MacCoun, 2005; Tyler, 2006; Jackson et al., 2012a; Murphy et al., 2016; Tyler, 2017).

The idea that fairness is central to normative judgements of police, as, perhaps, the core component of legitimacy, is thus well supported, as is the idea that the most important aspects of fairness relate to process, rather than outcome. Procedural justice can often appear a rather abstract concept, divorced from the practice of everyday officers and, in particular, the structures and institutional processes within which they operate. However, procedural concerns can be identified in almost all judgements people make of police. They are bound up not solely, or indeed primarily, with the ability of officers to provide "tea and sympathy", but with all the formal and informal processes of police work, which can open up or close down the possibilities and quality of interactions between police and public. Take, for example, the accounts of victims of hate-crime recently collated by Neil Chakraborti (2017). His respondents indicated not only the need for trust, empathy and kindness at the individual level (in particular the need to be listened to), but also that:

> problems encountered at the pre-reporting and initial response stages were compounded by what they perceived as a slow, intimidating and at times incomprehensible criminal justice system. Many spoke at length about the difficulties that they had encountered when trying to make sense of what police officers were telling them to do; or the complex, unfamiliar terminology used in reference to hate crime and accompanying legislation; or the seemingly endless delays in waiting to receive any form of communication or follow up.
>
> *(Chakraborti, 2017: 11–12)*

"Procedure" means here something much more than "a process of face-to-face interaction". It relates perhaps most importantly to the journey that this particular group of victims, and many other of "clients" of police, take through the criminal justice system.

Complications to the two component model of legitimacy

As might be expected, the two component model proposed above is subject to some significant complicating factors, of which three are of particular relevance here. First is the question of legality. The notion that legitimacy is bound up with "following the rules" (Beetham, 1991) is so central that this is often included as a distinct component of the underlying concept. However, it seems plausible to suggest that questions concerning whether police follow the rules intended to govern their behaviour form part of larger judgements about normative appropriateness. At the simplest level, one might suggest that "legality" provides a ready heuristic for people when making judgements about the normativity of police activity. If police are obeying the rules they are doing the right thing. Equally, though, the category of law does not exhaust the set of norms and values those subject to police power expect officers to live up to and enact, not least for the reason that police spend so much of their time dealing with issues not directly (or even indirectly) to do with law-breaking and illegality (Brodeur, 2010). The implication here is that while rule-following and/or legality might be seen as simply a special case of normative appropriateness, the latter is a far larger category. Normative appropriateness may include some judgements that are only tangentially related to the law and legal categories.

Picking up this last point, the second complicating factor is that norms and values beyond fairness are at stake in people's judgements of police. As Suchman might suggest, these include a more or less narrowly defined instrumental effectiveness – what the police achieve in terms of professed aims of controlling crime and disorder is important, not least because an ineffective, inefficient police service seems unlikely to live up to normative expectations about how police *should* behave (cf. Tankebe, 2013). The extent to which police respect the boundaries of their authority may also be an important factor relating to "performance" more widely construed (Huq et al., 2017, Hamm et al., in press). Yet, equally, there is an emerging body of work that suggests a whole range of factors beyond police activity come together to influence the normative judgements of the policed (see Figure 3.1). These include assessments of the nature of order in society, who is regulating it, and the types of behaviours needed to assert it (e.g. Bradford and Jackson, 2016; Jackson et al., 2012a); community and neighbourhood context (e.g. Antrobus et al., 2015; Kwak and McNeeley, in press); and wider psychological needs, preferences and motivations (e.g. Mehozay and Factor, 2016; Gerber and Jackson, 2017). In short, the empirical legitimacy of police is a product not just of fairness judgements but a whole set of complex, and likely interacting, psychological, social, political and economic variables.

Looming large enough in this set to constitute on its own the third complicating factor is the concept of social identity. The idea that legitimacy is closely related to identity and shared group membership is a consistent theme in the literature (see Bradford, 2014 for a review). One important aspect of this is the extent to which identification and identity judgements moderate and mediate the links between procedural justice and legitimacy. On some accounts the moral performance of power is central to convincing the public that the police share group membership with them – or are valid partners within an intergroup relationship – and are the appropriate authorities to deal with issues of crime, disorder and accident, either in particular situations (Stott et al., 2012) or in a general sense (c.f. Pardo, 2000). Identity can here be positioned as a *moderator*, calibrating judgements of police activity and modulating the strength of the relationship between procedural justice, legitimacy and other constructs (Radburn et al., in press; Sargeant et al., 2016). Other accounts treat some level of shared group membership as a given, and stress the extent to which shared social identities *mediate* the link between fairness judgements and legitimacy (Bradford, 2014; Bradford et al., 2014; Blader and Tyler, 2003, 2009). Key here is the idea that police represent social identities that are salient to many people (and within which they recognize the figure of the police officer as an important group representative) – something that chimes well with sociological accounts that position police as representative of nation, state and community (Loader and Mulcahy, 2003; Manning, 1977). The experience of procedurally just policing strengthens the bonds between individual and group, generates, encourages and/or enhances a sense of inclusion and value within this group, and promotes identification with the authority figure concerned, with the values it represents – and hence legitimacy.

All three of the complications outlined above have important implications for the argument we wish to advance in this book, and we return to them in more detail in the pages that follow. First, though, it is important to consider what legitimacy "does". To extend the normative/empirical distinction outlined above, is clear that the *empirical* legitimacy of police is important in the sense that it is *normatively* desirable that people are governed by institutions whose values broadly align with their own, and which they believe are thus entitled to be obeyed. Criminological research has tended, however, to concern itself primarily with the effects of legitimacy on behaviours within the public, and consideration of these illustrates other important aspects of the phenomenon.

The motivating power of legitimacy

One of the most consistent findings in the procedural justice literature is that legitimacy is a relatively strong positive predictor of people's willingness to cooperate, work with and defer to the police (e.g. Sunshine and Tyler, 2003a; Murphy et al., 2008; Wolfe et al., 2016). Equally, there is much to suggest that police legitimacy is linked to compliance with the law (Paternoster et al., 1997; Tyler 2006; Jackson et al., 2012a; Murphy et al., 2016). This research suggests that the police, and indeed society, have much to gain from efforts to enhance legitimacy, and it has triggered significant policy interest in recent years (e.g. the Obama administration's President's Task Force on 21st Century Policing).

From a social psychological perspective, legitimate authorities can affect individual's behaviours in a number of distinct ways (Kelman and Hamilton 1989). One route is via *internalization*. On this account, our value systems are shaped in large part by the institutional context into which we are born and socialized (Berger and Luckmann 1966). The institution of police is part of this context, and legal socialization promotes internalization of the idea that it is right and proper to follow the diktats of authorities operative within it (such as the police). In other words, people internalize the moral value that they should obey the rules associated with and orders coming from the police because they form part of the institutional framework through which those individuals understand and make sense of the world. This sense of reciprocal civic obligation to respect authority and abide by the law is not static, however, but is at least part emergent from ongoing experiences. Perhaps most importantly, it is shaped by encounters with police (whether personal, vicarious or mediated). When officers use their power and authority appropriately, they demonstrate that this authority is properly – i.e. morally – constituted, reinforcing established norms and motivating in response appropriate behaviour (e.g. compliance with the law or with the dictates of legal authorities).

Legitimate authorities can also influence people's behaviour via the mechanism of *identification*. As noted above, the ways authorities act – particularly in relation to the procedural fairness of their behaviour – can activate and strengthen individual's roles within important self-satisfying, and often self-defining, social relationships. Given that the police powerfully represent nation, state and community, the roles so activated may include that of "citizen": not simply in the narrow, legal sense this label may have (a recognized subject with certain entitlements), but in the sense developed by the perspective of virtue ethics – of being a full member of society with a set of duties as well as rights. This role should, in turn, motivate particular behaviours. Important here is the idea that encounters with police officers not only *activate* processes of identification but also serve to construct the categories concerned and patrol their boundaries. To switch the argument developed so far, it is not only the case that people judge the police. Both instrumentally and expressively, police officers serve as arbiters of moral conduct, defining respectable and disrespectable behaviour and delineating the normative from the deviant. This means it is just as true to say that the police judge the public (Choongh, 1997; Fassin, 2015; Waddington, 1999), and the form such judgements take, and the way they are communicated, can have important effects.

Encounters with officers can therefore influence how those involved see themselves in relation to a range of important social categories (an argument this approach shares in common with labelling theory – Bradford et al., 2014). Feelings of inclusion, recognition and shared values in one's relations with police – the experience of being placed on the 'right' side of these categories – may activate attendant expectations for behaviour and, all else equal, we can expect that cooperating with the police and abiding by the law to be among those expectations (being a 'good citizen' involves adhering to properly established norms of conduct) (Bradford et al., 2014, 2015; Jackson, 2015; Murphy et al., 2016). To do otherwise – to act contrary to role expectation – risks undermining self-image and damaging the relationship between individual and group. This process is likely to be symmetrical, of course. An illegitimate police force may activate different roles that do not discourage, and may even promote, law-breaking behaviour. People who feel they do not share norms and values with police are less likely to believe they should behave in ways that support this authority, and are less motivated to comply with the norms of the wider group it represents. Moreover, negative or unfair treatment can incite existential anxiety and uncertainty as to one's status and social value or one's membership of a group, further weakening the pull of behavioural norms – a process akin to Matza's (1964) concept of "drift".

Finally, legitimate authorities may exert influence by creating situations wherein certain actions are encouraged or precluded in order that individuals maintain congruence with their own internal value systems. The sense that crime is wrong is very widely shared (Robinson and Darley, 1997), but people are more likely to act in accordance with their personal moral judgements concerning criminal acts if they feel the social context they inhabit is integrated and functions in accordance with their own values. To return to the arguments of legal socialization, a legitimate police force may provide one element of a strong normative framework toward which people orient themselves and through which they experience and understand the world.

Wikström's Situational Action Theory (SAT) provides one way of understanding how such a process might work (Wikström et al., 2012). SAT is an attempt to develop a theoretical model capable of encompassing within its explanatory framework all intentional criminal acts, defined as a subset of a wider universe of moral rule-breaking acts (Wikström, 2006). Central to SAT is the positioning of individuals in specific and potentially criminogenic contexts. For a person to commit a crime in a given context, it must first offer the objective possibility of such an act: the individual must then perceive this criminal act to be an option; they must make a judgement about that option; and finally they must choose to act based on that judgement. At each stage separate but interrelated factors may come into play that can encourage or inhibit offending.

At the most basic level, the key question is whether an individual sees crime as an option. Whether they do so or not may be related in large part to habitual, routinized and indeed normative behaviours. If one complies with the law because such compliance is 'ingrained in everyday life' (Robinson and McNeill 2008: 436) it is unlikely that one will perceive offending as an option even when confronted with a situation which, objectively, offers such an opportunity. If and only if an actor perceives committing a crime to be a possibility, they must then make a judgement based on this perception: the possibilities of action will be evaluated against their moral rules and principles. If the judgement is made that committing the crime is a viable and/or desirable option, the individual must finally choose to act. This choice will be influenced by their personal characteristics, such as their level of self-control, and external contingencies, such as the level of informal social control evident in the situation or the probability of getting caught by agents of formal social control.

On the face of it the decision (choice) to act will be influenced by factors favoured by rational choice inflected theories of compliance. In other words, individuals who see crime as an option will choose not to break the law when and if they think they will be apprehended or interdicted for doing so. But values, feelings and motivations are also implicated in decisions to offend – most pertinently, social and moral assessments of the situation may play a vital role. Individuals who see crime as a possible or even desirable option may choose *not* to act, and this choice will be influenced not only by the risk of sanction but also by a wider set of 'moral norms' (Wikström et al., 2012: 24) that pertain in the action setting. These moral norms will act as a filter, delimiting and circumscribing which actions are seen as appropriate or correct and which are not (ibid.). SAT therefore suggests both internal motivations and the nature of the social environment influence individual's acts of crimes – indeed this is the central claim of the theory. Crimes are most likely to occur when an individual's propensity toward crime is high, when they make a moral judgement that offending is a viable and desirable option, and when the nature of the setting in which they are acting appears to encourage, or at least not preclude, acts of crime.

Police activity obviously hopes to exert pressure at the end of this chain, for example by providing a risk of sanction or the presence of a capable guardian. But internal drivers to obey the law and cooperate with the system may be more powerful than external factors involving deterrent threat – because they are part of an individual's way of seeing the world – so the effects of procedural justice, identity and legitimacy on individual's decision-making in relation to crime seems therefore most likely to occur at the early to middle stages of the SAT process. People who perceive the police and other legal authorities to be legitimate are less likely to see crime as an action alternative: legitimate legal authorities form part of the general moral framework within which individuals are socialized and toward which their own moral values are oriented. Equally, however, even when crime is perceived as an option those who hold the relevant authorities legitimate should, all else equal, be less likely to commit an offence because they desire to uphold group rules and wish to maintain roles appropriate to their relationship with those authorities. On this account, policing forms part of the moral framework of everyday life, shaping the way people read and react to particular situations – and if *legitimate*, contributes in multiple ways to the maintenance of desirable forms of social order within those situations.

Policing and the "good citizen"

Police activity can therefore influence not just the legitimacy judgements of the policed but also the way the latter think about themselves and others around them and also, it seems likely, their behaviours. Legitimate – fair – policing therefore creates the possibility for a particular kind of relationship between police and public, and in doing so it comprises a mode of state action that enables the "citizenship" behaviours of the policed. In this section we explore these ideas in a little more depth, and tie them back to the notion of the public good developed in Chapter 1. We consider, that is, the extent to which policing can contribute to the ability of citizens to live the good life, not simply by limiting harm but by providing conditions that allow people to flourish.

To be clear, this is not the same as "making good citizens" – with all the potentially troubling implications that phrase invokes (cf. Neocleous, 2000) – but there is a possibility that it might. There is a danger, that is, that the kinds of processes described above might create a kind of false consciousness among the policed, resulting in acquiescence to structures of power and dominance and producing the kind of "docile bodies" imagined by Foucault. Procedural justice, in particular, might give a veneer of fairness to police activity that masks underlying injustices and inequalities while, at the same time, motivating people to legitimize power structures implicated in their oppression (MacCoun, 2005). It probably goes without saying that this is not what we envisage here. But we recognize the danger, and indeed our broader aim in this book is to think about a way of doing policing that, at least in theory, avoids such potentialities because it is tied to an appropriate ethics.

The work of Ian Loader and colleagues provides our starting point here (see, in particular, Loader and Mulcahy, 2003, and Loader and Walker, 2007). In *Policing and the Condition of England*, Loader and Mulcahy argue that policing acts as a condensation symbol (Turner, 1974), a means by and through which people make sense of their past and their potential future; particularly in relation to the articulation of collective identities and a sense of belonging embedded in local community *and* the wider national context (Girling et al., 2000). Because police represent dominant social categories, police activity functions as an explanatory tool for people seeking to understand their place within these categories, the trajectories of change shaping the groups concerned, and their success in maintaining normative social order and in the provision of solutions to other collective social dilemmas. Particularly relevant is the extent to which officer behaviour creates and reproduces such feeling. Police are not just part of the story people tell about themselves, but are actively involved in its emplotment, especially in relation to the ability of officers to communicate messages of inclusion or exclusion to the populations they serve. Waddington (1999) argues, as noted above, that police patrol the boundaries of respectability, and officers' bureaucratic activity names, delimits and transcribes the identities of the individuals with whom they interact (Ericson and Haggerty, 1997; see also Bradford, 2017). Police activity "does things" to people, shaping their objective and subjective positions in the structures of power and affect within which both parties are embedded. And police *officers* are active agents in this process (Fassin, 2015).

These understandings of the power of police to define and patrol the boundaries of identity correspond closely with the place of social identity in procedural justice theory (Tyler and Blader, 2000, Tyler and Huo, 2002, Blader and Tyler, 2009). Individuals construct their identities around and in relation to groups (Tajfel and Turner, 1986), and assessments of inclusion and status within a group are based, to a significant extent, on fairness judgements made in relation to the behaviour of group members and, in particular, group authorities. When people feel fairly treated this indicates (1) that they are included and have status within the group and (2) that the group itself is worthwhile and something to be proud of. The procedural justice literature therefore recognizes identity as an aspect of the social self that links individuals to groups (Tyler and Blader, 2000). This could be almost any group – a work organization, a leisure group, a pressure group or a nation – and the fact that people have multiple group memberships is explicitly accepted in this body of theory. Strong social identities in relation to a particular group are marked by a sense of pride in its status, and in a positive evaluation of one's position within it. Social identity thus comprises a cognitive component, a sense of belonging, and an evaluative component that captures the worth people place on the group and their membership of it (Blader and Tyler, 2009: 448).

Processes that generate legitimacy are therefore intimately linked with identity. Indeed, viewed from some perspectives legitimacy and identity collapse into one another. Relational identification with police, people's sense that police officers are "like them", is a vital factor in the hypothesized social psychological processes linking fair procedure to group identification. Such identification relies in large part on people's assessments of the extent to which police share their own values (Sunshine and Tyler, 2003a, b; Radburn et al., in press) – that is, on their sense of normative alignment with police. There is thus considerable conceptual overlap between legitimacy and identification.

What is important for current purposes, though, is the idea that legitimate policing can be central to producing the "ontological security" described by Loader and Walker (2007), who use this term in Giddens' sense as a feeling of trust and stability that itself revolves in an important sense around identity: "A sense of dignity and authenticity, of ease with and acceptance within one's social environment" (Loader and Walker, 2007: 166). This aspect of identity, or perhaps way of being, is closely associated with self-feeling and self-confidence and is characterized as a secure sense of belonging within a viable political community. It reduces subjective vulnerability, and provides a resource people can draw upon to reduce fear and anxiety in the face of, most obviously, crime and security threats (ibid.). In line with Giddens' wider theorization of the late modern condition (e.g. Giddens, 1990), this sense of belonging is seen as enabling, allowing and even promoting actions and interactions premised, crucially, on an absence of fear and the safety of inclusion and fellow-feeling. Basic, lived feelings of belonging and being safe and secure allow us to act, opening up avenues of possibility that would otherwise be closed or obstructed by fear or uncertainty.

Naturally, and to reiterate Suchman's argument above, process-based concerns are not the only things that give rise to legitimacy, and the outcomes police deliver will also be important here, particularly, it seems likely, to people living in high-crime or otherwise socially fragile environments (Tankebe, 2009; Bradford et al., 2014). Our sense of security more traditionally defined is also linked to our perceptions and understandings of police and policing, and legitimacy – a perception that the police do the right things for the right reasons – can in this narrower sense contribute to a sense of safety.

Legitimacy, and the processes which sustain it, can thus be linked to the "crime-related" behaviours of the policed – but also to a much wider set of attitudes and orientations relating, ultimately, to people's sense of themselves and their place in the world. Relationships with police, perhaps particularly among those who have frequent or at least recent contact with officers, may exert a profound influence on peoples' security, not only in the narrow sense of "freedom from" but also in the deeper, enabling, sense of "freedom to" (Loader and Walker, 2007). This is an important idea for our main argument in this book – that policing should be seen as contributing to the public good – because it shows how policing can contribute to flourishing and is not only about limiting harm or response to crisis.

Needless to say, the most obvious way these ideas find empirical expression is when police fail to live up to the "promise" of procedural justice – something which, although rarer than many might imagine, happens on an all too regular basis. Victims who fail to receive appropriate (i.e. procedurally fair) response from police can experience an accentuated loss of self-worth and emotional trauma (Elliott et al., 2012; Jordan, 2008). Individuals stopped and/or searched by police and other security actors come away feeling denigrated, marginalized and often traumatized (Parmar, 2011; Blackwood, 2015; Bradford 2015; Geller et al., 2014). Those who are arrested can have a magnified version of the same experience (Choongh, 1997). Even the most mundane encounter between police and public runs the risk of undermining the kind of positive social identities outlined above (Bradford et al., 2014), thus weakening the subjective security and sense of social embeddedness of those involved.

It is important to note, though, that procedural fairness, when it is displayed, can have important positive effects. Elliott et al. (2012) argue, in their study of the experiences of victims of crime, that officer procedural justice – listening to victims, empathizing with them, acknowledging their experiences, and relating to them as people – can have profound effects on their ability to begin the process of recovery and reintegration. As one of their respondents put it

> They (*police*) acknowledged it was crime as before everyone including my family ignored that, and although [the] case did not proceed, I got closure because of the way police treated me: my nightmares gone, I have started exercising, eat better, my social relationships improved, I feel happy that I can go on with my life (#15, victim of child sexual abuse).
>
> *(2012: 597, emphasis in original)*

Similarly, in a study focused more on those likely to "come to the attention of police" (many of whom will also have been crime victims, of course), Bradford (2014) found that among a sample of young men from ethnic minority groups in London, experiencing policing as procedurally fair was linked to a stronger sense of "belonging" – to one's local area, London and the UK. Notably, this effect was stronger among those who self-identified as non-British, who, it might reasonable be surmised, felt more insecure about where they "belonged". Procedural justice has a real integrative potential, then, even if we tend most often to think of the alienating effects of *in*justice.

Conclusion

Legitimacy, as described above, is a rich concept, which draws together multiple strands: not just the behaviour of police, but the ways people experience that behaviour; the contexts within which it occurs; wider social, cultural, political and economic forces; and the multiple antecedents and consequents involved. For all that, though, the argument is at its root quite simple. The legitimacy of the police is founded in public judgements of the normativity of police actions, and the most salient – although by no means only – norms involved are those of fairness, and particularly of fair process. Not only does police legitimacy flow from positive judgements relating to criteria of fairness, but so also, and relatedly, does a secure sense of belonging, inclusion, and an ability to act in the world among the policed. Placing legitimacy at the heart of our consideration of policing therefore presents us with a clear view not only of what 'good' policing looks like but of how policing can contribute to the public good. Or to put it another way, *legitimate* policing is the founding institutional virtue that underpins "good policing". It explains how the police should contribute to the production of order, consistent with pursuit of the public good.

There are two important qualifiers to this argument, which together motivate the chapter that follows and indeed much of the rest of the book. First, as we have made clear, fairness is not the only factor that generates legitimacy. Other norms and values are involved, and some of these may be inimical to any justifiable notion of the public good. Second, and relatedly, the argument above rests on the question as to whether police organizations, and individual police officers, can indeed be "virtuous". This is a question that can invoke quite different responses depending on the personal experiences and social and political inclinations of those to whom it is asked. These provisos return us directly to the question of what governance means and that we explored in Chapter 1 (please see also Figure 1.1).

This chapter has provided answers to some of the "why" questions of governance based on an in depth, rigorous overview of legitimacy. It may be less important to focus on the "how" outcomes of policing than to understand why legitimacy could be a foundational virtue in good policing. To build a picture of policing as contributing to the public good, we need to move policing more in the direction of greater procedural fairness. This helps with thinking through the "why" and "how" of governance. But then the focus on legitimacy also highlights potential tensions and incoherence if we return to the question of governance modes. This is because market modes of governance are often advocated on the basis they produce the best outcomes (competition – rightly or wrongly – is seen as the best way of encouraging optimal allocation of resources). Hierarchical modes are concerned with principles. Contemporary governance reforms that try to displace hierarchical modes in policing (see Table 1.1) may therefore be running counter to the basic logic of concern with principles that underpins legitimacy. As well as considering legitimacy as a founding institutional virtue, we also need to think of whether the environment for policing supports the development of legitimacy. What organizational and institutional structures, processes and pressures are in play, and how do individual officers, as actors and agents in the field of policing, navigate them?

4
IDENTITY

This chapter focuses in particular on ways normatively appropriate – i.e. "good" – policing might be encouraged, and on the challenges posed by the social and operational context of policing. The discussion therefore motivates much of what follows in the rest of the book, and forms an important link between our beginning chapters on governance and the policing good, and chapters in the following sections which look at particular aspects of police practice. To make this link stronger, we can usefully begin by reviewing the discussion of police legitimacy in the previous chapter.

Police legitimacy

In the previous chapter we described what police legitimacy "is" and what it "does". We paid particular attention to the many associations between those processes that build and sustain police legitimacy on the one hand, and the sense of security and belonging they can foster among the policed on the other (see Figure 3.1). We argued that legitimacy is not only a normative requirement for democratic policing (not only something policing "should" do), but that it also has important generative aspects. Legitimacy produces a certain type of relationship between police and public, and enhances the potential for the "good life". Central to all this is the way people experience, read and respond to police activity – as well of course as the actual content of that activity – with dimensions of fairness of paramount importance. Policing that generates and reproduces legitimacy is, seen in this light, both good policing and policing for the public good.

If legitimacy and the broader set of concerns it encompasses is so important, then we also need to ask a set of supplementary questions relating to the "where", "what", "who" and "how" of legitimacy. For example:

1. Where and when can appropriate police behaviour be identified?
2. What makes the police behave in ways that are antithetical to sustaining and enhancing legitimacy?
3. Who can deliver the forms of policing the procedural justice literature suggests are so important?
4. What organizational or other barriers are there to policing with legitimacy?
5. How can these barriers be overcome?

Controlling the police

The essence of the "where", "what", "who" and "how" questions posed above is the question of how to control the police. How can the power of this foundational state institution be channelled in desired directions, and who should be involved in such processes? In much of the criminological literature this question is covered, often in rather in broad-brush terms, by the notion of "democratic policing". The rather voluminous literature on this issue is summarized by Manning (2010: 65–66), who identifies the following principles of democratic policing – or perhaps more accurately, distils the behaviours and structures of "democratic" police agencies:

- Constrained behaviour and the use of fair process, and the exclusion of illegality, mass coercion, and the policing of thought.
- Fundamentally reactive to the demands, needs, and priorities of citizens, and only "proactive" in a lesser and more restrained sense.
- Fair in the distribution of coercion, where the level of coercion used is based on "minimalistic" (p. 66) criteria.
- Fair in internal procedures (e.g. hiring, promotion, discipline etc.).
- Competitive in a 'mixed economy' of policing, which involves "formal and informal modes of cooperation rather than unified and unrelenting" (p. 66).
- Accountable and responsible to individuals and a range of other agencies and organizations, both state and non-state.

This list is one that is often added to and elaborated on. For example, the "British model" of policing, at least, would refer to the appropriate use of force, rather than minimal coercion, to reflect the extent to which the term "minimal" might not be appropriate in some circumstances, and that the use of force (coercion) is so central to the role of the police that the term "minimal" might even be a misnomer. Others would be more expansive in relation to issues of accountability and responsibility, referring specifically to principles of citizen participation, equity, responsiveness and the prioritization of service, a wide distribution of power, the provision of information, and clear avenues for redress (Jones et al., 2012).

There is little to disagree with here, particularly in the light of the qualifications Manning (2010) and others (e.g. Jones et al., 2012) have added to these lists, which make them more alive to the operational and institutional demands of police practice. Perhaps most importantly there is an inevitable tension between the different components of "democratic policing". Manning notes, for example, that police are increasingly pushed towards surveillance, and the monitoring and tracking of suspects and non-suspects alike, which would seem to contradict several of the principles outlined above, but which is equally a response to calls for police action, from the public, policy actors and others, in the face of new crime and security threats. Increased police surveillance therefore *meets* some of the other criteria of democratic policing (e.g. responsiveness). However, often missing from this debate is consideration of how such principles can be put into action, particularly at the level of individual officers and their practice (for exceptions see Sklansky, 2008, and some of the work cited below). How can police organizations, and officers, be encouraged to behave in these types of ways? What can be done when they do not? What level of control can be asserted? The idea of controlling the police is a challenging one. As an institution "the police" have such unique power, and play such a role in producing order that "democratic policing" could almost seem a contradiction in terms. Indeed, even if democracy is not antithetical to policing at the least it renders it inevitably problematic. To understand this we need to look more closely at the nature of police power itself.

Police power

Markus Dirk Dubber (2005) describes this power as regulative, productive, diffuse, non-specific and relating in a fundamental sense to the "self-preservation" of the state: and as such, unlimited. He uses a concept of police much broader than the bureaucratic state agency that concerns us here, referring in a more general sense to the system of regulations, practices and state agencies that revolve around the idea of order, properly maintained. Yet one does not have to accept every detail of Dubber's argument to recognize the importance of its general thrust: the institution of "police" is that which is tasked with doing whatever is necessary to maintain the integrity and continued existence of the state; and the uniformed state police is the key actor within this institutional field. Thus construed, notions of minimalism, responsiveness and distributive equity might appear rather puny in comparison to the underlying purpose of police. On a more practical level, we might note that the magnitude and variety of the powers vested in police – the extent of officers' ability to insert themselves into the lives of the public, the fact that police tactics and techniques are often only loosely constrained in law and/or are unavailable to other actors (Brodeur, 2010), and the nature of the powers and discretion invested in street-level officers – serves simply to make questions of direction and control more pertinent and more pressing.

One obvious potential solution to this challenge is recourse to the law, and the use of legal regulation to restrict, restrain and in effect coerce police practice. But the fact that officers need to be able to deal with a huge range of problems limits this possibility significantly. Police are the first and often only responders to a huge variety of situations and events; they require an ability to react to and (re)direct these events and the individuals present that is – due to the freedom and discretion required to meaningfully enact these roles – by definition difficult if not impossible to codify within a set of legal rules. The task of policing is so diffuse and wide-ranging (and difficult) that is impossible to come up with an a priori list of possible problems, and potential solutions might be applied in an almost limitless set of circumstances (Bittner, 1974; Reiner, 2010). Discretion in identifying and applying solutions is fundamental to the practice of police, and to limit it would not only fundamentally alter the nature of policing but would also make it less effective.

This is not of course to claim that the law is unimportant or unnecessary, merely that it is insufficient in terms of controlling the police. The same is true for other processes of legislature, executive and inspectorate. "Democratic oversight" of police, whether by Police and PCCs, the Home Office, Parliament, HMIC or the IPCC is vital, and each of these bodies has, or at least has the potential, to contribute much to maintaining democratic policing as outlined above. But it takes no more than a moment's reflection to realize none of this is or ever has been enough. Relating this to the discussion in Chapter 1, these mechanisms are only likely to be a partial solution because they rely on a logic that sees governance primarily, and often solely, in terms of the management and control of individuals and individual choices. This contrasts with a virtue ethics perspective which seeks to understand governance in terms of broader, system-wide features such as tradition and context. Rather than being seen as individuals whose choices need to be kept in check, a virtue perspective emphasizes the continually unfolding character of people and institutions in complex and interconnected social worlds.

Despite the presence and activity of these and other actors and agencies, police officers and organizations all too often fail to live up to the (admittedly sometimes rather lofty) ideals codified not only as democratic policing but in the "mission statements" of the forces themselves (see for example Evans and Lewis, 2013; Whyte, 2015; Hales et al., 2015). To use the terminology of the previous chapter, police can and do behave in ways that communicate a lack of normative alignment with those they serve, whether this is via procedural injustice during individual encounters, organizations covering up their mistakes, corrupt practices, or the unjust targeting of individuals and groups.

The central issue here is that most if not all the directive and accountability infrastructure that sits around policing relies to a greater or lesser extent on the threat of sanction and bribes for compliance. Yet, like anyone else, police officers cannot be *forced* to do the right thing in any consistent or sustainable fashion. The extent to which legitimacy-oriented policing is part of the everyday practice of individual and organization cannot be determined by external pressure. Rather, it must more importantly spring from internal motivations. To outline the implications of this, it is useful to compare and contrast the relative importance of extrinsic and intrinsic motivations for conduct (see Bradford and Jackson, 2016 for a fuller treatment of these issues).

Extrinsic motivations

A whole range of authority structures and processes sit either inside police organizations, intended to direct officer practice (e.g. the reward and disciplinary processes of individual forces); or outside police organizations, intended to direct the activity of the organization as a whole or classes of its employees (e.g. PPCs, HMIC, etc.). Some bodies take on special or difficult cases (e.g. the IPCC), or provide other forms of democratic oversight (e.g. local councils, the Equality and Human Rights Commission). All these offer extrinsic motivations for behaviour – they exist external to the individual and/or organization and they seek to exert pressure of various kinds to produce change. Criminal and civil law comprise further motivating factors largely construed as extrinsic, at least in terms of organizational behaviour – organizations, that is, comply with laws because of the consequences of non-compliance, not because they have somehow internalized the values those laws represent. These and related structures can be utilized to motivate individual officers and police organizations to behave in line with norms established by the notion of democratic policing outlined above, and procedural justice, as discussed in the previous chapter.

This is, by and large, the "traditional" approach to constraining the power of the police and directing it in normatively desirable directions, and it would be foolish to argue that it has not had some success. In a general sense, police practice has changed for the better over the years as a result of regulatory change and enforcement, the Police and Criminal Evidence Act 1984 (PACE) being perhaps the most famous UK example (although as Reiner (2010) notes, while it certainly increased accountability it is less clear PACE constrained the power of the police). Equally, there are many examples of successful efforts by HMIC and others to enforce new norms and place pressure on poorly performing forces to improve standards; one recent example might be the change in police practice wrought by the welter of enquiries into the failure, by multiple forces, to deal properly with cases of child sexual exploitation (see HMIC, 2015a,b).

Despite such successes, though, it is unlikely that extrinsic motivators will ever be enough on their own to maintain an appropriate level of legitimacy-enhancing practice. For example, as have others before them Bradford and Jackson (2016) note that there was a reduction in the use of stop and search, and the accompanying ethnic disproportionality, in England and Wales around the time of the Stephen Lawrence enquiry in 1999; a result, it is claimed, of change in police practice in the face of significant public and political scrutiny in the wake of the scandal the enquiry uncovered (e.g. Delsol and Shiner, 2015). Here, the extrinsic pressure was policy-related, in terms of the recommendations of the Lawrence enquiry, but perhaps equally importantly reputational. Police risked losing public support for, and over, a key power, which served to moderate their behaviour. However, as the political and media agenda changed and shifted focus in the years that followed the Lawrence enquiry use of stop and search, and ethnic disproportionality, increased significantly, and indeed soon surpassed previous levels (Bradford, 2017; although it has of course since fallen again).

Another example of a potentially successful extrinsic motivator is provided by the recent, and rapid, uptake by police of body-worn video (BWV) cameras (Jennings et al., 2014). Part of a wider trend towards increased police visibility (e.g. Goldsmith, 2010), BWV has been presented as something of a panacea (Ariel et al., 2016: 747) that will resolve deep-seated issues in the relationship between police and various "publics" by providing an immediate deterrent to officer malfeasance on the basis of threat to reputation or risk of punishment. Moreover, in this instance, and given that in theory the vehicle of deterrence is ever-present (i.e. unlike media attention the camera is always there), BWV might be expected to trigger a longer-term shift in the "rules of engagement" between police and public, as officers and public internalize new norms of behaviour (Ariel et al., 2017). These arguments are prima facie compelling – yet the empirical evidence behind them is surprisingly rather mixed. While some studies have identified pronounced positive effects on, for example, use of force and complaints against police (Ariel et al., 2015), others have reported null effects (Ariel et al., 2016a), and yet others an increase in recorded assaults on officers (Ariel et al., 2016b). While these less positive findings may be largely methodological artefacts, a result of less than perfect methods or perverse outcomes such as BWV increasing officers' propensities to report assaults, the underlying point is perhaps that this technology, while promising, is indeed unlikely to be a panacea. Most fundamentally, BWV cannot change the underlying dynamics of police power – the ability of officers to insert themselves into people's lives, to order and direct, and to define what is and what is not proper and allowable – or shift their motivations beyond a deterrence-induced minimal norm compliance. Being recorded – in any format – seems likely to constitute only a "thin" governance which prioritizes the form of an interaction (being seen to do the right thing in a particular moment) over its substantive content (what police were trying to achieve and why – answers to the question "what are we trying to do here").

In sum, extrinsic motivations are by nature short-lived, even transitory, and can be disconnected from the kinds of underlying norms and values that virtue ethics emphasizes. Deterrence, by definition, works primarily in the here and now. Insofar as they are noticed at all, the effect of deterrent factors soon wears off once the threat of sanction is alleviated, removed or becomes less salient (Nagin, 1998). Rewards are equally effervescent in nature, failing to motivate behaviour beyond the immediate time horizon – and often not even then (Kohn, 1999). And in both cases the behaviour change purchased, sometimes literally, is likely to be only surface deep, leaving underlying motivations untouched (although, as noted, short-term change in behaviour can, over time, become long-term internalized norm). Quite aside, then, from the implausible claim that truly ethical behaviour can be coerced or cajoled, it seems that the governance of police – efforts to formulate, direct and make right police activity – cannot be achieved solely by the threat of sanction or the promise of reward.

Intrinsic motivations

Tyler (2011) joins a long history of research that contrasts extrinsic with intrinsic motivations – those which are derived from the moral values, cognitions and practices of people (as individuals and as members of social groups). Consideration of the intrinsic motivations of police officers to conduct themselves in an ethically and normatively desirable manner offers a counterpart to the arguments above and provides for a new way of looking at the notions of democratic, or legitimacy-based, policing.

If extrinsic motivation refers to doing something because it leads to a separable outcome (Ryan and Deci, 2000) – such as avoiding sanction, maintaining reputation or receiving a reward – intrinsic motivation refers to doing something due to its "inherent satisfactions" (2000: 56). People who are intrinsically motivated to undertake or attempt a particular task do so not because they expect to receive or avoid something else upon completion, but because they find enjoyment, meaning and/or self-actualization in the task itself. Classically, intrinsic motivation is seen to stem from a sense of autonomy and an "internal perceived locus of causality" (i.e. self-determination) – people have to believe, that is, that they are determining their own behaviour. But perhaps more importantly for our purposes here, intrinsic motivations are also seen as stemming from individual's social environment, their location within it and, in particular, the extent to which organizational policy and practice is configured in such a way as to encourage employees (i.e. police officers and police staff) to act according to their values (Tyler and Blader, 2005).

On this account, the moral values of adults are difficult (although not impossible, as we discuss below) to change. It is hard to shift people's underlying sense of what is or is not "the right thing to do". A more fruitful way for employers and managers to proceed is to structure their organizations in such a way as to encourage those working for them to behave in a fashion congruent with their own values. Two key assumptions underlie this argument. First, that these values are more likely than not appropriate (i.e. that people tend to want to treat others in normatively desirable ways). Second, that people acting according to their own values are intrinsically motivated, meaning they obtain satisfaction from the act or task itself and do not attend to the structures of risk and reward that sit around it. This is important from an organizational perspective because intrinsic motivations have a stronger, more consistent and longer-lived effect on behaviour than extrinsic motivations (Tyler, 2011).

Identity and change in policing

The notion that police officers should be encouraged to follow their own values is likely to make some academics, and many political activists, nervous. Surely the power of police, as sketched out above, is such that a more rigorous way of controlling the police is needed? Left unchecked, is not damage to legitimacy and the ideals of democratic policing inevitable? But there is a danger in over-stating the extent of police misbehaviour and malpractice in discussions such as this. A wealth of research, based on observations of police officers in the field, and interrogation of the views of the policed collected from a variety of sources (e.g. Quinton, 2011, 2015; Bradford et al., 2009; Bradford 2017) has found that most police officers behave in a broadly procedurally fair manner that is likely to at least maintain, and perhaps even enhance, trust and legitimacy. As is often the case, of course, the devil is in the transgression – the relatively small number of occasions where officer and organizational behaviour does not live up to the values of democratic policing, and when trust is lost and legitimacy undermined. These instances can have an effect out of proportion with their number, most obviously captured by the well-known 'asymmetry effect' of everyday police contact on public trust – good quality contact judged satisfactory by the public (the norm) has a much smaller *positive* effect on public trust than the *negative* effect arising from poor quality contact judged unsatisfactory (the exception) (Skogan, 2006; Bradford et al., 2009; Myhill and Bradford, 2012). And more significant transgressions, or those that relate not to mundane policing but higher-profile investigations or events, can have an even larger effect.

All this means that running alongside the pressure to *maintain* police behaviour within acceptable moral and ethical boundaries there is also a constant and significant pressure on police organizations, and officers, to *change* – to police better, to engage more with communities, to be more 'evidence-based'. Consideration of the success or otherwise of such efforts, and the social and psychological pressures involved, shows how intrinsic motivations can be encouraged and what the likely consequences are. It also foregrounds the role of individual's identities *as police officers* in shaping both receptivity to change and their wider willingness to engage in legitimacy-oriented policing.

Achieving change within police organizations has, of course, traditionally been seen as difficult, fraught with tension, and hard to sustain. Resistance to new developments, programmes and ways of working is often spread right across the organization, particularly in cases were reforms diverge significantly from accepted operational norms and/or stem from sources outside the police (e.g. academics or policy entrepreneurs); which is indeed often the case (Bayley, 2008). Senior managers worry about losing control and the possibility of adverse publicity (a fairly constant concern across all areas of present-day policing), middle-managers and supervisors see a challenge to their authority, and street-level officers are frequently cynical about "yet another new programme" and resentful of outside interference in their work (Chan, 1996; Skogan, 2008; Reiner, 2010). The idea of "police culture" is central to this picture (Chan, 1997; Cockcroft, 2012; Fielding, 1994; Glaeser, 2000; Harris, 1973; Loftus, 2010; Myhill and Bradford, 2013). Studies over a wide range of contexts have found that the internal culture of police organizations is marked not only by cynicism, but also by currents of pessimism, conservatism, action-orientation and inward-looking mentality (Foster, 2003; Loftus, 2010; Reiner, 2010) – many which seem a priori inimical to change and, indeed, to the wider effort to corral policing within "democratic" norms.

There is a danger, though, in over-stating how different police organizational culture is from other organizational cultures, and, connectedly, there are other compounding factors, generating resistance to change, that might be found in any large-scale bureaucracy staffed by empowered professionals. First is the frequently "top-down" nature of reform, which is usually initiated at behest of senior management but must be implemented by the front-line (Gau and Gaines, 2012), and which can have a disproportionate impact on the middle layers of police organizations (we consider this in more depth in the next chapter). Police officers can be cynical and suspicious not only about outsiders but also their superiors (Reiner, 2010), making them unwilling to implement change programmes they perceive as being "handed down from on high" (MacQueen and Bradford, 2017). Second, the discretion granted to street-level police officers, and the extent to which they operate outside direct supervisory control, means that not only can they often disobey the instructions of senior managers with a sense of impunity, but that they are specifically enabled to make their own decisions about what is the correct way to proceed in a specific situation.

In sum, it is hardly surprising that accounts of the differential uptake, troubled delivery and indeed outright failure of change programmes are common in the academic and policy literature (Boba and Crank, 2008; Cordner, 2000; Skogan, 2008). Recent research within criminology has started to explore ways to work round this apparent impasse. An emerging body of work has suggested that the best way to promote change within law enforcement agencies is by changing the ways officers relate to their organization (Trinkner et al., 2016; Tyler et al., 2007). Specifically, it has been suggested that by adhering to principles of procedural justice within law enforcement agencies, senior managers and supervisors can encourage front-line staff to adhere to rules and regulations (Bradford et al., 2014; Haas et al., 2015; Tyler et al., 2007; Wolfe and Piquero, 2011), take on new ways of working and extra-role activity (Gau and Gaines, 2012; Trinkner et al., 2016), and modulate their attitudes towards those they police (Bradford and Quinton, 2014; Myhill and Bradford, 2013; Trinkner et al., 2016; Wolfe and Nix, 2016).

At the centre of this research lies the insight developed in the wider field of organizational justice research that, just as in the relationship between police and public, people working within organizations are sensitive to way those senior to them wield power and authority. This process mirrors exactly the thrust of procedural justice theory described in the previous chapter. When managers and supervisors behave in a procedurally fair manner – making decisions in an equitable, open and transparent manner, behaving in an unbiased fashion, treating staff members with dignity and respect, and maintaining good quality flows of information up and down organizational hierarchies – staff members feel that their superiors are trustworthy, that they are supported by their organization, that they have a stake within it, and that the organization is legitimate (Colquitt, 2008; Colquitt et al., 2001; Greenberg, 2011; Tyler, 2011; Tyler and Blader, 2003). Feelings of trust, support, inclusion and legitimacy promote, in turn, compliance, cooperation, extra-role activities and "organizational citizenship behaviours".

Notably, the association between procedural justice and organizational outcomes appears stronger and more consistent that the association between instrumental concerns and outcomes. While promises of reward and threats of sanction do seem to motivate compliance and other behaviours within organizations, studies have consistently found that effect sizes tend to be smaller than those associated with procedural justice concerns, organizational commitment and legitimacy (Blader and Tyler, 2009; Bradford et al., 2014; Tyler, 2011; Tyler and Blader, 2000; Tyler and Trinkner, 2016).

There are, again, a variety of psychological mechanisms that link the experience of procedural justice within organizations with positive outcomes such as compliance and extra-role behaviour; and two, in particular, concern us here. One is legitimacy. On this account, feeling fairly treated within and by an organization promotes a sense that its structures of authority are legitimate and therefore worthy of obedience. Specifically, fair processes and interactions indicate to people working in an organization that power within it is wielded in a normatively justifiable manner. This sense of normative alignment motivates in turn a feeling that the orders and instructions of power-holders within the organization should be obeyed (Tyler et al., 2007; Trinkner et al., 2016) because such obedience is experienced as the right thing to do in and of itself. One implication here is that people experience a feeling of self-worth and self-actualization when following the instructions of legitimate authority. This is a concept of legitimacy within police agencies that is therefore entirely in accordance with that used in the wider procedural justice literature, where the concern is with legitimacy in the relationship between those agencies and those they police.

The second mechanism thought to link "internal" procedural justice and the outcomes outlined above relates to identity. This is the process of identification – more specifically organizational identification (OI). OI is one kind of social identification, which can be seen as a process or set of processes whereby we make sense of the social world through comparison and classification. Identification explains how we locate our self and others in these contexts (Cooper and Thatcher, 2010). As well as providing a basis for coordination and communication, identification reduces uncertainty (Hogg and Terry, 2000), helping us to clarify complex social contexts. It can also help to establish a stronger sense of self (Chattopadhyay et al., 2004), where the self is understood in relation to a broader group.

The main way we establish this belonging is by using categories, abstractions and prototyping schema that express themselves in terms of different social identities (Ashforth and Mael, 1989). These can overlap and intersect. Social identity is a bundle of such classifications: perceptions of belonging to, membership or oneness with meaningful referent groups (or conversely, a distancing from or sense of exclusion from such groups). In management studies, organizational identification is a "root construct": something that is necessary for any organization to function (Albert, Ashforth and Dutton, 2000; Ashforth, Rogers and Corley, 2011; Hogg and Terry, 2000). Many management scholars (see Table 4.1) have set out a view of organizational identification anchored by the principle that the self and group are related, experienced and expressed as a kind of membership (Albert and Whetten, 1985; Ashforth and Mael, 1989; Ashforth et al., 2008; Brewer and Kramer, 1985; Haslam and Ellemers, 2005; Hogg and Abrams, 1990; Mael and Ashforth, 1992; Tajfel, 1978, 1981).

If we think how this might apply to policing, an interesting example comes from an interview with a female officer (taken from the empirical work described in Chapter 6 – see Table 6.1). The question of memberships featured because at one point (since she was the only woman training that day as part a specialist public order unit) we asked if she was ever made to feel conscious of her gender (see: Davies and Thomas, 2003; Dick, 2005, 2010; Dick and Cassell, 2002; Holdaway, 2010; Silvestri, Tong and Brown, 2013). As would be the case with other officers there were different layers to her social identity – as part of her unit, part of her

TABLE 4.1 *Organizational Identification and Membership*

James (1890/2007: 294) (credited as the original source for this view of identification).	*A person has "as many social selves as there are individuals who recognize him [sic] ... as the individuals ... fall naturally into classes, we may practically say that he has as many different social selves as there are distinct groups of persons about whose opinion he cares".*
Tajfel (1978: 63; also Tajfel 1981: 255).	Social identity is, "that *part* of an individual's self-concept which derives from his knowledge of his membership of a social group" (original emphasis).
Tajfel (1982: 2).	For, "… 'identification', two components are necessary [first] awareness of membership".
Ashforth and Mael (1989: 21).	"Social *identification*, therefore, is the perception of … belongingness to some human aggregate" (original emphasis).
Brown and Starkey (2000: 650).	"Identification … refers to a perception of oneness with or belongingness to a social category."
Ashmore et al. (2004: 81).	"Identification is first and foremost a statement about categorical membership."
Cole and Bruch (2006: 588).	"[O]rganizational identification … reflects the specific ways in which individuals define themselves in terms of their membership in a particular organization."
Meyer et al. (2006: 666).	"[S]ocial identities have been defined in many ways, the common element in these definitions is inclusion of group membership as part of one's self-concept."
Ashforth et al. (2008: 327; 328).	"Social identities are shared by members and distinguish between groups"; "an individual's identities inside an organization [emerge] from the central, distinctive and more or less enduring aspects – in short, the essences – of the collectives and roles in which he or she is a member".
Zhu et al. (2017).	"Individuals who identify with a social unit have a more positive and clearer sense of self (i.e., a positive and clear social identity based on organizational membership) and a greater sense of belonging."

force, as a police officer and (when confronting disorder) as someone representing the state. However this was made more complex because of gender. Something we return to in Chapter 7 is that her uniform itself influenced this identity. In what we would colloquially be called full riot gear, police officers can appear anonymous, and even their gender may be obscured, but in her case the police force she belonged to used uniforms with named epaulettes. This affected relationships with other forces who did not have names on their epaulettes and also with the public in some situations where she could be targeted as a woman:

> whenever we go to do mutual aid [joint operations with other forces] the other forces more or less laugh at us because we've got names on our shoulders which does lead to people shouting your name or people being over-familiar with you because they think they know who you are because your name's written all over you. Which then, you know, as part of public order at the lower part [can be helpful] talking to people. But once you put the helmet on, once you put the face coverings on I don't see that purpose, you're there for a reason if you've got everything on like that. So I don't think names are important then or shouldn't be on your shoulders then because it does identify you as a female.

In police organizations we can furthermore make some useful connections between identification and legitimacy. In doing so, the main idea would be that the experience of procedural justice in workplace processes and procedures can motivate these feelings of membership – of being part of the organization (Bradford et al., 2014; Bradford and Quinton, 2014; Tyler and Blader, 2003). When people feel fairly treated by managers and supervisors they are more likely to feel proud of their organization and their role within it, and to feel that they are accorded a high status by co-workers and superiors. Identification and the associated feeling of self-worth linked to such experiences (De Cremer and Tyler, 2005) activate in turn a sense of duty towards the organization and a merging of self and group and internalization of organizational ends and values (Ashforth and Mael, 1989; Tyler and Blader, 2000). Put simply, people who identify strongly with an organization follow its norms and values because they have adopted (internalized) these as their own – a counterpart to the argument that it is hard to change people's values once they have reached adulthood. Here, the values of police officers can be actively shaped and re-shaped by the organizational context within which they are operating.

These two mechanisms, legitimacy and perhaps particularly identification, provide for a more nuanced picture of police culture than that often described in the criminological literature. First, they serve to underline the fact that while unique in many ways police agencies also have a great deal in common with other large, bureaucratic organizations, not least in the way that the police as employees experience similar basic processes of identity formation and reproduction as those experienced by other types of organizations. Police agencies can thus usefully be viewed and understood using the same kinds of tools and concepts that have been developed in relation to other organizations. Second, they underline that there is no one police culture but rather a range of police cultures (Fielding, 1989). Crucially, these are linked to processes of legitimation and identification within the organization that are founded in the relationships between individual officers, between those officers and their superiors, and between human actors and wider organizational configuration and process. Policing identities, embedded in and reflecting structures of authority and affect, are formed and re-formed by organizational structures, and by the ways individuals, groups and types of officer understand and navigate those structures. This complex picture produces a range of "ways of being" police, associated with different behaviours or "ways of doing" police work.

Take as a brief example a recent study of an English constabulary (Bradford and Quinton, 2014). Here, two distinct organizational identities were associated differentially with perceptions of organizational justice, on the one hand, and with officer's sense of their own legitimacy, on the other. Those officers who felt emotionally attached to, and proud of, the force tended to experience just and fair organizational processes and to have a strong sense of their own legitimacy – a confidence in their own power and authority founded in a feeling of security within the organization and finding expression in a stronger commitment to, notably, democratic policing norms such as willingness to protect suspect's rights. Those officers who felt less emotionally attached and proud tended rather to express a cynical (sub)cultural adaption associated with a negative in-group solidarity. This group experienced less organizational justice, were less confident in their own legitimacy, and expressed less commitment to democratic policing norms. It seems that differential experience of organizational processes moulded commitments to "doing" policing in quite different ways, which tapped directly into the concept of democratic policing outlined at the beginning of this chapter.

This literature is, within criminology, still in its infancy, and a number of potentially important factors remain under-explored. Four issues, in particular, can be identified. First, the recent move towards the concept of organizational justice has not been accompanied by consideration of the ways organizational practice and process beyond questions of fairness shape the organizational – and operational – identities of police officers (ideas covered well in some of the classics of police sociology, e.g. Van Maanen, 1975). For example, how do the messages encoded in training and development processes influence the way officers see themselves as "police" and as enactors of a set of norms and values? Second, little attention has been given to the ways officers reflexively consider their own positions, and how they categorize themselves as different "types" of police. Third, and relatedly, there has been little thought given to how "identity" embeds itself in and motivates behaviour. How, for example, do officers internalize and then enact a set of norms associated with a particular "police identity"? Finally, much of the extant literature considers front-line officers, with relatively little thought having been given to "management cops" (Reuss-Ianni, 1983). We turn to these questions in the chapters that follow.

Conclusion

In this chapter we have considered the vexed question of how to ensure policing is conducted in an ethical manner as possible. How, that is, can police organizations and the architectures of governance that sit around them shape the behaviour of officers? While by no means discounting the efficacy of extrinsic motivations of behaviour, we have drawn on the organizational justice literature to suggest that the most long-lived, deeply embedded and consistent motivations for behaviour are likely to stem from officers' intrinsic motivations – their readiness to enact their own values, which it itself deeply bound up with their identity (or rather identities) as police officers. As we discuss in subsequent chapters, the interaction between individual, organization and context is thus central – we cannot think about how people "do" policing without considering where, with whom and under what conditions they do it, but, equally, we cannot think about how police organizations function without considering the practice of individual officers and the way they navigate the organizational, social and political contexts within which they find themselves.

5
WORK

As well as considering institutional virtues, looking at individuals is important in understanding virtue. This chapter focuses on one understudied aspect to police work – namely that many police officers carry out managerial work. We discuss a case study of change in a police force that had an effect on several managers. Using virtue ethics, we explain how they experienced and coped with this change drawing on the concept of character – which is partly expressed through individual virtues.

Why "policing as work and management"?

One advantage of considering the role work plays in producing order is it brings in a range of tools and ideas from management studies. This usefully complements the focus of the previous chapter on policing and social identity. From a management studies perspective, it seems there is a great deal of literature on what policing involves at the front line or "street-level", and there is also a great deal on the role "the police" play in society – but it does not always seem policing is thought of in theoretical terms as "managerial work". This seems an important consideration in relation to governance because whereas there are almost inevitable constancies to front-line policing, governance changes and reforms dramatically affect managerial roles, particularly for middle managers. (By middle managers we mean those with at least two layers of organizational hierarchy below, and at least two layers above – Currie and Proctor, 2005).

People who study management are also concerned with the production of order – because institutions and processes, organizations depend on producing order and a large part of management is about control. However, particularly to more critically oriented management scholars, "work" is not just about an institutional role or set of practices (Noon, Blyton and Morrell, 2013). Work is both these things, but it is also a process and a place. It is often characterized by exchange or transactions, but it is also the intersection of social relations, interactions and solidarities (Bain, 2005; Doherty, 2009); a source of membership and affiliation, and – potentially – of divisions and "othering" (Collinson, 2006). Whilst work provides a source of meaning and sense of self (Glaeser, 2000), changes to work, or particular jobs, can erode the stability of a self-concept or character (Sennett, 1998). It is this in particular that interests us in relation to policing governance because character is the main way virtue ethicists understand the cultivation and expression of individual virtues.

Why middle managers?

Many initiatives that try to reform how order is produced in organizations have the biggest effect on "middle managers" (Balogun and Johnson, 2004; Floyd and Lane, 2000; Lüscher and Lewis, 2008; McKinley and Scherer, 2000; Westley, 1990). Examples include business process engineering, downsizing, delayering and restructuring; as well as programmes of culture change such as professionalization, continuous improvement, Total Quality Management, "lean" initiatives, employee empowerment and team-working (Redman, Wilkinson and Snape, 1997). These were initially private-sector initiatives, but as part of New Public Management (NPM), many have formed the template for change in public organizations (Currie, Finn and Martin, 2009), including police forces (O'Malley and Hutchinson, 2007). As well as organization-level structural and cultural changes, a raft of service-wide governance reforms have had impacts on the job of middle managers in public services (Reed and Anthony, 1992, 1993; Dawson, Mole, Winstanley and Sherval, 1995). Such changes (discussed in Chapter 1) include marketization, personalization of services, new forms of accountability, audit and inspection, pressure to cut costs and – more particularly in policing – the need for collaborative, multi-agency working, demand complexity, civilianization, drives towards professionalization, the influence of the College of Policing, and initiatives such as evidence-based policing (see Holdaway, in press).

In policing, the middle manager is a revealing focal point to understand the production of order because they personify some of what is happening to the contemporary governance of policing. Some of the problems they have to deal with arise from NPM-like reforms including cuts and the introduction of professionalization. Others result from the interplay between different sources of authority and power – the professional bureaucracy (Mintzberg, 1979, 1995). "Professional bureaucracies" combine two sources of authority – professional power (where individuals have status because of their expertise and knowledge) and bureaucratic or organizational power (where they have status because of their seniority in the organizational hierarchy) (Finn, Currie and Martin, 2010). Especially during large-scale change, professional bureaucracies pose challenges to middle managers, who have to cope with tensions between these two kinds of power (and forms of resistance to change) (Brooks, 1999; Currie and Proctor, 2005; Holdaway, in press; Huby et al., in press; Reed, 2011).

Professional bureaucracies create a more complex picture for the middle manager who, "straddles the two worlds of the professional or service domain and the managerial domain" (Forbes and Prime, 1999: 112), and needs the "ability to inhabit two worlds" (Mo, 2008: 412). This also needs to take into consideration effects on identity. Middle managers continue with different identities in parallel: "[d]octors are taking on managerial responsibilities and, *at the same time*, maintaining both clinical autonomy and professional identity" (Exworthy and Halford, 1999: 122, original emphasis); or when they combine in an altogether new form, "the fusion of value systems or ideologies, rather than merely of role" (Brooks, 1999: 50).

A central question then is whether they combine two identities (manager/ professional) into a new form (e.g. Brooks, 1999) or "breed" (Fitzgerald and Ferlie, 2000: 731), or whether they somehow run both in parallel (e.g. Exworthy and Halford, 1999; Forbes and Prime, 1999). One way to understand this could be in terms of Reuss-Ianni's (1983) older but well-known distinction between management-cop and street-cop (see also Holdaway, 1977). One interpretation of the management-cop label is this is someone who is no longer a professional, but is now a bureaucrat: a "desk-jockey" (the origin of bureaucracy is *bureaux* or desk). One can imagine that this kind of derision could be traumatic and even be experienced as a form of social death.

But if we open up the category of middle manager a little, it prompts some subtler questions. Instead of no longer being a "proper copper", is it more accurate to think of middle managers in policing as a new kind of worker who is not just manager or cop but something new – combining elements of both? Or are they someone who is part-manager and part-cop? Or are they people who switch between manager and cop? A helpful analogy for these is the difference in chemistry between a mixture and compound. A mixture, like a jar of blue marbles and red marbles, combines two or more substances that are not joined chemically and separable. A compound, like water, is a single substance made of two or more elements that have undergone a chemical reaction (and whose proportions are also fixed). We will return to this analogy discussing the case we introduce below. First we want to develop our suggestion that part of becoming a police officer is to do with character.

Police work and character

Character is central to virtue ethics and we argue it is extremely relevant when understanding policing. This is partly because of the effects of social identity which we discussed in the previous chapter and partly because from a virtue ethics perspective, character is made up of individual virtues (or vices). As we emphasize many times in the book, police officers have unique powers among public servants. Seen as a kind of work or occupation then, one thing interesting about the police is they undergo intense, character-forming experiences in terms of socialization, induction and common exposure to danger (Cockcroft, 2013; Dick, 2005; Dick and Cassell, 2002; Fielding, 1988, 1994; Glaeser, 2000; Loftus, 2010; Reiner, 2010; Skolnick, 1966; Van Maanen, 1975). In the following chapter we discuss the role of training and habits in forming character, here we want to look at how change can create conflict with character in middle managers in policing.

The meaning that people attach to their work is often anchored in terms of the identity of an occupation, and associated expectations: the content or processes of the work in that occupation; perceived status, and status relative to other occupations; traditions, history and kinds of jurisdiction (Beadle and Knight, 2012; Glaeser, 2000). More broadly, and without straying too far into the topic of social identity (the previous chapter's focus), there are different ways of seeing the relationship between work and character. These include "over-socialized" accounts – almost wholly reliant on structures as an explanation for what work means for individuals, and "under-socialized" accounts – almost exclusively emphasizing agency, with an array of positions in between (for a relevant review see Marks and Thompson, 2010).

People sometimes compare occupational roles to acting out scripts (Goffman, 2002). Using this metaphor, over-socialized accounts of the relationship between work and character would see work as following instructions, under-socialized accounts would see work as continual improvization. We develop an intermediate position – police work is, in part, the formation of *character*, where character refers to our "connections to the world [and] personal traits which we value in ourselves and for which we seek to be valued by others" (Sennett, 1998: 10). MacIntyre (1999: 315) helps us understand the metaphor of role-playing in relation to moral agency:

> I have to understand myself, and to present myself to others, as someone with an identity other than the identities of role and office that I assume in each of the roles that I occupy. I have to understand myself as someone who brings with her or himself to each role qualities of mind and character that belong to her or him [as] individual and not [as] role-player.

Applied to this setting, being "a police officer" is more than simply inhabiting a collective identity, following instructions or wearing a common "mask" it involves discretion and choice. This is well understood in relation to the front-line and street-level dilemmas of policing (Brown, 1988; Klockar, 1984; Lipsky, 2010; Mastrofski, 2004; Skolnick, 1966), but it is not often acknowledged that police in managerial roles continue to have dilemmas – if anything they may be more pronounced and aggregated. This is because police middle managers have to navigate the identities of cop and manager, whilst supporting those below who are grappling with dilemmas, and being responsible for implementing change they may disagree with.

MacIntyre's point is that we sometimes occupy roles but we are not responsible as role-players we remain responsible as individuals. Responsibility is about how we discharge these roles and it is in doing this that we can exhibit virtues and display character. Character is something we recognize in others through their behaviour (or discourse). It is a social expression and realization of the self, "read through the medium of individual acts" (Dewey, 2007: 38). Elements of constancy and habit are important in evaluating character because without these a person would be, "simply a bundle, an untied bundle at that, of isolated acts" (Dewey, 2007: 38). Wright and Goodstein (2007: 932) suggest character comprises "interpenetrable habitual qualities", interconnected elements developed over time and that have some constancy.

For virtue ethicists, character is not just a neutral or analytical concept, like an analysis of personality might be. Because character is about social conduct, and the legacy of conduct, it is normative. Character – the self or I – is the source of moral agency (MacIntyre, 1999). This agency has a social aspect, it is tied to attributions by others because we read character in others through individual acts. But character is also about individual integrity, "composure of the senses necessary to care of the self: an internal equanimity in the midst of experience" (Augst, 1999: 99), with "the impossibility of being displaced or overset" (Emerson, 2002). There is a constancy to character that connects with long-established traditions in Homeric, Socratic and Aristotelian accounts of virtue ethics (MacIntyre, 1997; Morrell, 2012a; Shotter and Tsoukas, 2014). Linking this to foundational contributions to the policing literature, character is useful because it builds on Skolnick's (1966) seminal account of police culture in terms of the "working personality" of the police officer – whose role has two essential characteristics: danger and authority (Reiner, 2010). As Reiner identifies, Skolnick is not really describing "personality" because this account brings out relational and socially enacted aspects to policing, however at the same time it does not take sufficient account of, "political dimensions to police culture" (Reiner, 2010: 119).

Being something (characteristics) or becoming someone (a character)?

Often reform is focused on outcomes and targets and making changes as quickly as possible to achieve those outcomes. One reason a virtue ethics perspective can enhance conversations about policing is that encourages us to think over much longer timeframes and about what is ultimately important. Character is developed over time and it takes time. Townley (1995) draws a nice distinction between two very different kinds of projects that can help us understand this: (i) *self-awareness* – based on looking inwards and individualism; and (ii) *self-formation* – cultivation of the self in the context of an appreciation of culture and rules of conduct. To be self-aware is to have greater individual access to insights about that make you who you are. One can imagine that with the right tools and techniques one could quite quickly start to say something about self-awareness from the perspective of applied psychology. This could be helpful of course, we are not denying the value of this at all (see e.g., Morrell and Hartley, 2006b). But it also reflects certain assumptions about what it is to be human.

Now imagine you are interested in self-formation. This is an ongoing, never-ending process, where becoming who you are is a continual journey and depends not just on looking within but on seeing how you relate to others and how you act in certain situations. It is learning over time, where you carry your choices with you through life. To understand character in relation to policing, we suggest that this often about self-formation. For instance, as the previous two chapters show, policing is often about a kind of membership and about the production of membership categories in others ("good person", suspect, witness, victim, arrestee). It often involves expressions of solidarity or, conversely, othering.

Holt (2006) draws a comparable distinction that helps us recognize the difference between the self as something objectified and interior, versus the self as embodied and related to context. This is the difference between (i) "being *something* (a *characteristic* possessed by oneself)", and (ii) "becoming *someone* (a *character* recognized by others)" (Holt, 2006: 1662, emphasis added). Character signals something that expresses and instantiates the self, that is developed over time, rooted within in a context or place and set of associated practices and traditions, and is partly embodied and habitual (Dewey, 2007; Emerson, 2002; Holt, 2006; Sennett, 1998; Wright and Goodstein, 2007). This is where we can now begin to make useful connections to virtue ethics and also scale up from the character of the police officer as a middle manager to policing governance as a whole.

Police reform

To consider why this is helpful in relation to police work, it is necessary to consider the context in more detail. In common with other parts of the UK public sector, policing has been undergoing dramatic change, and has been subject to reform by successive administrations (Bridges, 2011; Lister, 2013). The details of particular reforms are not as significant as the broader point that reforms to policing raise particular considerations central to democracy (Cole and Smith, 2006). Police forces are also totemic institutions and alignment with the police force is politically desirable for parties wishing to be seen as "the" party of law and order. As discussed in Chapter 4, perennial themes in studying police work relate to the adequacy of police supervision, the extent to which there is a legal basis for some police actions, and the limits to the power of individual officers and the police force as a whole. These touch on wider debates about the politicization of the police, the difficulty of reconciling individual liberty and national security, and the issue of how the police are themselves policed (Fleming, 2008).

These complexities can be understood in terms of a broad institutional environment and what we call "institutional virtues", but, importantly for our understanding of character, they also stem from basic tensions involved in enacting police work (Waddington, 1999). The police have the unique authority to use coercive force against the public, and this leads to dilemmas and ambiguities. How individual police officers negotiate these dilemmas is part of their self-image (Dick, 2005). Police officers have a duty to uphold certain rights but also experience complex accountabilities and imperatives (Wicks and Carney, 2009). Conflicts between these, and the unpredictable nature of policing, produce dilemmas. Some are resolved through recourse to the law, but at heart police work involves problem solving and exercising discretion (Bayley and Bittner, 1984; Brown, 1988). Discretion comes about because of their unique powers and roles (Waddington, 1999). It is an inevitable by-product of resource constraints, and the need to navigate ambiguity and exercise judgement in the face of constraints. Davies and Thomas (2003: 683) describe:

> a key control dilemma facing policing organizations, that of the need for both rules and procedures for operation, in conjunction with high levels of individual discretion.

When thinking about governance as the production of order, the interplay between standardization and discretion means police work is often taken as a paradigm example of "street-level bureaucracy" (Lipsky, 2010). Lipsky's idea is that the street-level bureaucrat constantly faces dilemmas. These come about because the irreducible complexity of the individual case (in policing this relates to criminality, risk or liberty), has to mesh somehow with the machinery of the state (Hudson, 1997). In everyday talk, rather than "bureaucrat", "professional" is usually used to describe police officers (e.g. Walker, 2012). Even though there are similarities between the police and "archetypal" professions (Ackroyd and Kirkpatrick, 2003; Ackroyd and Kirkpatrick, 2003) – occupational closure; jurisdiction over particular kinds of activity; a common, specialist language; shared standards of training and accreditation; institutional membership – policing does not fall neatly into the archetypal categories used to describe "professionals" (Dick, 2010).

One important point of difference is that whilst police officers (like other professionals) undergo formal training associated with accreditation, learning how to do police work is very much a mixture of formal and informal training. Of course on-the-job training and situated expertise applies in other professions (Schön, 1983), but in policing its importance is more pronounced – notwithstanding that some argue this potentially sets up a false dichotomy between policing as craft and science (Bayley and Bittner, 1984). Learning about policing has been described as more like socialization than any conventional instruction in a trade, or induction into a profession. At the same time, this is not simply indoctrination because policing comprises many sub-cultures and paradoxes (Fielding, 1988). Van Maanen's classic study of US urban policing describes, "the gradual development of an 'in the same boat' collective consciousness" (Van Maanen, 1975: 220). This is in part what we signal by using character to describe police work. Rather than acquiring individual characteristics, becoming a police officer is about developing character. This is a personal project, but understood in relation to a collective social identity as well as different sets of expectations within policing and in relation to multiple publics. It is a continual struggle to make sense of identity and meaning given the nature of police work.

A number of related factors combine to influence the development of character among officers. Alongside the street-level, dilemmatic nature of police work, there is also common exposure to risk, shared induction and socialization, common training (Fielding, 1988). Police culture (Chan, 1996, 1997), and facets of this like "canteen culture" (Fielding, 1994), have received much attention in the policing literature (for a review see Cockcroft, 2013). Some features of police culture are remarkably endurable across different time periods and in different jurisdictions; for instance a recent ethnography of a UK police force (Loftus, 2010: 17) corroborates work from a comparable US ethnography conducted almost 50 years earlier:

> Skolnick (1966) argued that police culture arises from the common tensions that are inherently associated with the job of being a police officer … officers continue to derive their self-identity from their work and the basic challenges of that work identified by Skolnick all those years ago … the durable occupational and organizational demands create and sustain the culture today.

As we show in the case study below, these considerations are crucial in understanding reactions to change.

Case study

Our case study is based on that of a UK police force; we use the pseudonym "Sunnydale", and to preserve anonymity we have altered some details (such as exact dates) slightly, but not in a way that compromises our ability to study police work and character. Sunnydale was subject to dramatic change over the seven years prior to our research. Its structure at the time of interviews (2008–10) was the result of radical restructuring beginning in 2001, which involved splitting the force into five territories – Basic Command Units (BCUs). Each BCU was headed by a police officer (a Divisional Commander) and supported by eight specialist departments, also headed by police officers. We will refer to these police officers in managerial roles as "cop-managers" to differentiate from the slightly different meaning that is implied by the term "management-cop" (which sets up an inevitable contrast with "street-cop"). In 2003, a new role of Business Manager was created and appointments to this role were made in each BCU to cover the specialist departments. Business Managers were civilian entrants. Each had a finance qualification and experience in another sector(s). Here we will refer to these as "civilian-managers".

Following external scrutiny and with the oversight of the Police Authority, an independent body charged with ensuring effective policing, Sunnydale published a pivotal policy document: *Your police, your community* (re-titled to preserve anonymity). This set out a vision for policing, translating national priorities into local ones. During 2001–8, for all UK forces, the Home Office increased emphasis on public satisfaction, moving away from targets and measures towards more nebulous goals like public confidence (Jackson and Bradford, 2009). The vision *Your police, your community* created was a force focused on improving public confidence and satisfaction, in partnership with other agencies: local authorities, the probation service, community groups. This was a shift from hierarchical governance modes to networks. Change was also based on moving senior managers away from a model where they oversaw resource spend, to a model where they had to make most effective use of resources.

Comparisons could be drawn with the context for Davies and Thomas' (2003) research on the enactment of New Public Management (NPM) within the UK police service. They identify analogous sweeping changes associated with NPM-like reform, in moves, "away from the traditional authoritarian style of policing to a more open, democratic and intelligence-led style" (Davies and Thomas, 2003: 687).

To balance breadth and depth, we focused on three organizational units at Sunnydale: Operations Delivery; Organizational Support; Corporate Support. Within these, we looked at middle managers' work. Our principal data source is 49 interviews with middle managers who were police professionals ("cop-managers") or who were civilian entrants ("civilian-managers"), and stakeholders. In stakeholder interviews the focus remained on middle managers: eliciting stakeholders' perspectives on how change affected work at middle level (rather than in how they personally experienced change). Table 5.1 shows basic detail about these interviewees.

Interviews typically lasted between 45 minutes and one hour; several were longer. They were taped and transcribed, face-to-face (except two telephone interviews, necessary because of last-minute changes in interviewees' schedules). Interviews explored change in terms of two broad areas: (i) how change had affected the force, and (ii) how change had affected the work of the managers themselves (or, with stakeholders, how they felt it affected this middle level). To encourage natural conversation and allow more extensive probing, initially, interviews were otherwise unstructured. These did not use schedules, or specific, set questions. To inform understanding of the context, relevant national and force-specific policy documents were also analysed.

Later interviews incorporated recurring themes emergent from the raw data into semi-structured topic guides. These were also developed in relation to the extant literature on change in public management in an iterative, continuing comparison between data and theory. The goal was to seek the most plausible explanation for change in this setting, following an approach to theory development that utilized what Parlett and Hamilton (1976) call progressive focusing. Progressive focusing aims for gradually more specific, contextualized explanations of social phenomena that attempt to link a richly detailed research setting to more general theory (Stake, 2010). Throughout the research, in theorizing about the data, a central aim was to see whether it was possible to identify precedents in the literature for attempts to

TABLE 5.1 Cop-managers, Civilian-managers and Stakeholders

Police (descending order of rank)	N	
Chief Superintendent	7	Cop-managers
Superintendent	7	
Detective Superintendent (equal to Superintendent rank)	1	
Chief Inspector	3	
Inspector	1	

Paraprofessional (approximate descending order of seniority)		
Business Manager	5	Civilian-managers
Heads of Service	3	
Directors (of Information and HR)	2	
Heads of HR	2	
Chief Officer Team (Accountant, Solicitor, Resource Manager)	3	
HR Managers	5	
Heads of Strategic Support and/or Business Development	2	

Other		
Deputy Chief Constable (Senior Management)	2	Stakeholders
Assistant Chief Constable (Senior Management)	2	
Police Authority Chief Executive	1	
Police / Local Authority Members	3	

organize emergent themes into a broader explanatory framework (Gioia, Corley and Hamilton, 2013).

Analysing these interviews identified recurring themes and points of tension relating to organizational change: questions around devolution or centralism; the role of Business Managers; the role of partners; governance structures and processes; risk management; and the development of a corporate orientation on resource management. Some of these are common with reforms generally associated with NPM; others have particular resonance within policing – for instance the interplay between risk management and resource management. As our research progressed we began to understand these issues as the general terrain onto which more specific, and we think more fundamental, issues relating to character and radical change could be mapped.

Change at Sunnydale was dramatic and widespread, and its effects ongoing, even though the first stage of organizational restructure began seven years before our research. Radical change took place alongside an organizational imperative to provide basic continuity of service. People making sense of the change were continually reflecting on the relationship between change, their job requirements, and the need to provide a service to the public. However, not all interviewees were equally unsettled. This was not simply explained in terms of hierarchical level (or rank).

Instead, we identified a range of reactions amongst middle managers. At one end, some had to cope in isolation with changes that brought them into conflict with their character. At the other end, reform empowered some middle managers who experienced a synchronicity between changes in their job and organization and their character. In between were middle managers who experienced negative effects of change but were not experiencing conflict with character. These middle managers were not prospering because they were relating negative effects, but they were also not experiencing the sharpest, most negative effects of reform since they were not isolated and saw themselves as working on behalf of other colleagues, as part of collective endeavour.

We suggest this aspect of collective endeavour, and a sense of working on behalf of and in support of other colleagues is an important element in understanding the effects of reform on managerial work in policing. Police officers have all worked on the front line, and have common experiences of induction, socialization and training, as well as shared experience of risk. This is noteworthy, given that reforms to bring direct entrants into the police force, at middle level, and as officers, who have not carried out front-line work, as well as to recruit senior officers from other countries into leadership roles, change this model (Home Office, 2013).

Below we first substantiate our main idea: that there is a range of reactions to change. Then we identify in more detail additional factors that could explain how change relates to character.

A range of reactions to change

Three extracts show contrasting experiences of work and change. In these extracts, we only quote "cop-managers":

1. Chief Superintendent K

> we operate in this sort of vacuum of delegated authority ... there's a huge gap there, there's this vacuum that says our superintendents, our chief inspectors right, don't really know what authority they've actually got. They're not absolutely sure, unless it's written down, that says actually you can spend a thousand pounds ... Today was a classic. Today, I got asked for £130 today. Not for something really, you know, posh or whatever. They were asking for some fairly bog standard things that we need to do our job.

This Chief Superintendent was expressing their personal, ongoing struggle between needing budgetary oversight at the same time as working in a climate of devolved decision making. This supports a general finding – that middle managers bear the brunt of change (McKinley and Scherer, 2000; Redman et al., 1997). They felt the effects of a "vacuum of delegated authority" (having to implement the policy designed by top management), and were also in a difficult relationship with the front line who felt they had to ask, "for some fairly bog standard things". They could identify what was required, and at the same time were isolated from a shared sense of belonging, as a former front-line officer. They were frustrated at the thought of compromising effectiveness for officers at street level doing "our job". Character and change are out of synch.

Below is a second example, in the midpoint of our range:

2 Chief Superintendent C

> So there was lots and lots of things hitting the force ... We ended up being kicked around the park by anybody who had a microscope to come and look at us ... And some of these people ... we ended up [seeing] them as total charlatans; had no idea what you were talking about, had limited experience in the environment that we were working, yet they wanted to give us the advice.

Chief Superintendent C is relating challenges to do with changes that affected the force working under a regime of inspection. However, unlike Chief Superintendent K, Chief Superintendent C experienced solidarity with other colleagues undergoing the same kinds of change. They were also frustrated but more easily able to link their efforts to a broader category of belonging, since their job requirements meant they were coping with negative effects of change on behalf of others. They had widespread responsibilities as a divisional commander – for them, "we" was Sunnydale, rather than the police service as a whole. Because they could align the requirements of their job with the work of colleagues, they experienced change differently. They could see themselves as battling on behalf of others – the "we" being "kicked around". In relating having to work with, "total charlatans" who "wanted to give us the advice" they display, to use Van Maanen's phrase (1975: 220, also above), "an 'in the same boat' collective consciousness" and this shows their experiencing greater coherence in terms of the work they were asked to do as a middle manager and their character.

A third example illustrates the other end of the range:

3 Chief Superintendent J

> you've got much more of a kind of a team [Sunnydale] feel, you know, the kind of greater good thing, as opposed to the parochial it's my money and I'm keeping it sort of attitude that might have been there ... sometimes I have to remind myself and a couple have reminded me that, you know, as the chair of the group ... they are accountable to me and we should be just treating it as, you know, I've been given the kind of authority to actually chair the group.

This Chief Superintendent had a newly created, strategic post – leading partnership engagement. Initially, they relate new-found, common ethos at the force following change. Interestingly, they describe past failings in their own force as "parochial", with people believing "it's my money and I'm keeping it". They describe their role in institution-building – as chair of a partnership group "Making Sunnydale Safer", which comprised policing, local authority and other stakeholder organizations. Their job could be compared alongside Chief Superintendent K and Chief Superintendent C, in that all three were responsible for one NPM-like change (tighter budgetary constraints, audit and inspection, partnerships). However, developing partnerships did not bring Chief Superintendent J into conflict with other colleagues, or compromise solidarity or belonging. Their new role afforded possibilities to enact a new self at work where change, the content of their work, and their character were in synch. They were not surviving in isolation, nor battling as part of a collective. They were thriving.

Having outlined this range of reactions, the following sections offer more fine-grained detail on change and character, and substantiate our framework further. We do this with reference to three aspects of change which featured to some degree in all interviews: (1) structure, (2) cuts, (3) civilianization. The first two are common to other public sector reform, the third raises issues especially pertinent and sensitive in policing.

Structure

Many policing functions were devolved to the four Basic Command Units (BCUs); alongside this was some devolution of management. Business Managers and HR managers had a small staff devolved from central Finance or HR. This management structure was acknowledged by interviewees, and stakeholders, as complex because devolution had been partial (some functions remained force wide, others were owned by BCUs) and because reporting responsibilities crossed lines:

> they [Sunnydale] keep moving between centralization and devolved activity, and certainly communications drop into that, as does HR problems, personnel problems, those kind of things.
>
> *(Police Authority Member)*

The resulting pressures fell on both cop-managers and civilian-managers but this aspect of change caused greater distress to those who had been front-line police officers, who were used to working with norms of command and control. One officer, described how:

> I can only *invite* my business manager to my management meetings, I can only *invite* my HR manager, because they've got five other, four other masters actually it's more difficult because I can't hold them to account.
>
> *(Superintendent A, their emphasis)*

In terms of the broader literature on NPM and governance reform, Superintendent A relates a widely understood problem: if hierarchies are dissolved in favour of network forms, it can be harder to identify who is responsible. But, as is clear from their emphasis on "invite", there is more going on here. Police officers are accustomed to working with hierarchical modes of governance – appropriately given their powers and the need for control and accountability. They don't expect to "invite" subordinates to meetings but do expect to be able to "hold them to account". The effects of socialization into the force, and internalized norms in relation to chain of command would mean any "invitation" from a senior officer to a junior officer of theirs could be called an invitation, but it would have the same force as an order. Because this Superintendent had ingrained characterological expectations – about appropriate conduct in a command and control environment – they were experiencing incoherence and isolation following the restructure. This example supports our analysis in Chapter 1 of a shift away from hierarchical governance modes: network modes of governance can be harder to scrutinize (see Table 1.1), but over and above this, there is an additionally negative impact of change resulting from conflict with character.

This can be contrasted with the views of this civilian-manager:

> things have got missed … They've directed them in error to the wrong person. Missed out a couple of ranks in the process. So you're then talking about an inspector will come to me and say [anonymised] asked me to do this. I'll sit there and say, "oh where's that come from?", "I don't know" {laughs} And it just complicates the whole process and there isn't that clear understanding.
>
> *(Business Manager D)*

This civilian-manager also experienced the negative effects of the restructure. They are discontent for the same reasons as Superintendent A (restructuring has blurred lines of accountability and reporting), but express this differently. They also see issues relating to restructuring as frustrating, but their experience is not relating an incoherence in terms of a clash with character. The problem is experienced less personally and, in a sense, located outside or apart from who they are: it is about "things", a "process", lack of "clear understanding". They are describing something dysfunctional but this does not provoke conflict with ingrained norms. Recalling Holt's (2006: 1662) distinction between "being *something* (a *characteristic* possessed by oneself)", rather than "becoming *someone* (a *character* recognized by others); this kind of confusion might prevent them from having a desirable characteristic – being effective. But it is not the same as the characterological angst Superintendent A expresses about not being able to be recognized clearly as a person's "master", and instead having to "invite" them to meetings.

A third example illustrates someone prospering following change:

> I don't think anybody actually totally understands the full scope of the role. And that might be me thinking naively that they don't, but that is my personal

perception, that they probably don't understand how effective I actually think it is at the moment.

(HR Manager F)

This civilian-manager is not experiencing adverse effects as a result of change. They are enjoying a new role only made possible by change. They feel owing to their position they can see the benefits of devolution but this would take time to filter through to others. What is interesting about this extract is they understand distance from others in positive terms. Though separate, they see separation as privileged positioning, rather than isolation, "they probably don't understand how effective I actually think it is". Somewhat speculatively, one might expect this kind of confidence or comfort in believing one is ahead of everyone else could be easier for a civilian-manager to achieve, rather than a cop-manager. Police officers experience tight-knit solidarity, through training, socialization and common exposure to hazard. They could be arrogant of course, but believing one was so far apart because of change, to the extent no one else could empathize, "I don't think anybody actually totally understands", might be a source of anxiety, particularly if we acknowledge the importance of feelings of membership and belonging to professional identity (as discussed in the preceding chapter). For this civilian-manager though, this was a source of pride.

Cuts

National cuts were applied at Sunnydale in such a way that every BCU had to make the same percentage saving. This was recognized to have created confusion between (a) cost cutting in pursuit of mandatory efficiency gains within BCUs and (b) the more systemic, organizational goal of effective management of resources. A stakeholder described the confusion:

> If you've got a department that is required to find x percent savings, then that's what it'll do [but] there hasn't been a sense of well we need to actually target the savings, where operationally and strategically those savings are best found.

The consequences of change caused by cuts were multilevel and multilayered. They were multilevel because national priorities occurred alongside a planned programme of organizational change, and at the same time budgetary pressures were driving changes at departmental levels. They were multilayered because although each department had to make the same percentage of savings – the effects on departments varied. They were involved in different kinds of police activity, had different performance and expenditure cycles, and were associated with different areas of police work. Expenditure was sometimes impossible to predict. Superintendent C described an operation involving extensive search of woodland in pursuit of two murderers:

> could you ever have foreseen the likelihood of two separate murderers with no connection to each other, deciding to hide in the same piece of wood; in the same wood? ... Not only that, but one of them we'd actually got locals organizing themselves, arming themselves to go in and find this person and kill them ... You could have had virtually warfare. We had no choice [except] to mount that operation. Not with anybody's foresight, not with anybody's financial plans, not within even the bounds of reasonably being foreseeable, I spent [over a million pounds].

It is revealing to see how emphatically, in a short extract, this Superintendent describes not being able to predict: "could you ever have foreseen", "Not with anybody's foresight, not with anybody's financial plans, not within even the bounds of reasonably being foreseeable". They were experiencing incoherence in terms of the policing they judged necessary, and the pressure of cuts. They were aware of having to manage costs but also of having no choice, confronting possible "warfare".

Several interviewees talked about cuts in terms of the wider public interest:

> We can save money around overheads, but essentially that notion of value, you don't waste money do you. You have what you need to deliver the service to the best of your ability. End of ... we shouldn't have bottom drawers full of cash, because then we're not using them for the public good.
> *(Chief Superintendent B)*

This attempt to combat the negative effects of cuts indicates discontent but does not convey any sense of incoherence or conflict in terms of character. Instead there is a continuing imperative to provide service to the public consistent with one's character, "to the best of your ability". What is also interesting about this extract is that it shows that coping with change in the middle level of an organization is not just about struggling with restructure and associated problems. It is ongoing contestation over the terms used to describe change (Bisel and Barge, 2011). The way this officer does this is to connect "value" to "public good", rather than "cash". Their bottom line, which they underscore saying "End of", is the service provided.

As explained in Chapter 2, "public good" resists quantification. Partly because of this it makes an effective challenge to the terms in which change at Sunnydale was conveyed, where (senior) managerial discourse centred on "resource". "Public good" is also an effective way to contest the terms used to describe change because of ingrained, characterological expectations about public service. Again Holt's (2006) distinction is helpful: between "being *something* (a *characteristic* possessed by oneself)", – a resource manager – and "becoming *someone* (a *character* recognized by others)" – a police officer serving the public.

Superintendent W (in a newly created post as head of "corporate development") described how implementing efficiencies was a matter of engaging officers. On our spectrum, they were prospering:

> officers will say management are trying to make their job more effective you know, or make the job better ... and it's in that way that we'll start to engage frontline as it were ... that's the way I need to get the buy-in and to get them to understand what we're trying to achieve rather than just talk about high level numbers which they're not interested in, as I wasn't when I was a PC.

Superintendent W recognized their role was very different from front-line officers but saw this as maturation, describing a natural separation between managerial and front-line work, the front line are "not interested ... as I wasn't when I was a PC". Rather than incoherence or isolation they saw their work as necessarily different from the front line, and complementing it. Their experience as a front-line officer is not something they feel they lost on the way to becoming a manager. Instead, it lies at the roots of their present character, a source of confidence and empathy: a resource they feel will support implementation of change and secure commitment. (Speculatively, one might imagine they would not use management-speak like "buy in" with front-line officers.)

Civilianization

Civilian-managers had been managers in other organizations and were in posts historically only resourced from within the police. They often described working at Sunnydale in negative terms; indeed, their descriptions could be seen in terms of their own character. For example, several recounted confronting stereotypically negative aspects of public sector work:

> I see administration and bureaucracy somewhat swamping us. I've come from the private sector, so it's not a, you know, it's not a thing I'm used to at all.
> *(Head of Information Systems)*

> I have a private sector background and I'm, I suppose it's, I'm imbued with the idea of not spending money if you don't have to and trying to do as much as you can with the resources you have.
> *(Force Solicitor)*

The first extract relates expectations of conduct and a sense of being "used to" a way of working that one can readily connect to character. The second extract is an even nicer illustration, since it ties the habitual and learned effects of character (being "imbued") to a particular virtue, thrift.

Cop-managers – though generally acknowledging private-sector models could be useful – were cautious, if not suspicious, about civilianization:

> But fundamentally, don't confuse provision of state services with provision of business services. They're not the same.
>
> *(Chief Superintendent B)*

This way of describing civilianization reaffirms a core aspect to police character – as someone performing a public service. Other reactions to civilianization were frustrated:

> We've spent an inordinate amount of money on bringing in highly trained individuals, at fairly high pay rates as well within the organization and actually I can't see the benefit … they've all come in from different backgrounds. They've all got different qualifications … they all do it different.
>
> *(Chief Superintendent G)*

This expresses personal dissatisfaction "I can't see the benefit" with sweeping, significant change. Chief Superintendent G says "an inordinate amount of money" has gone on "bringing in" new entrants who are collectively, and repeatedly, described as "they". Unlike officers undergoing common training and socialization, and the extremely tight-knit culture of policing, "they" are "from different backgrounds [with] different qualifications" and "they all do it different".

To support our central claim that policing reforms have differential effects, here is one example of someone prospering owing to civilianization:

> when I go home at night, I'm going to the pub with my friends, you know, I can say oh I did this today, you know, and I'm proud to work for [Sunnydale], not you know, oh my goodness what's gone on in the press today.
>
> *(Head of Strategic Support)*

This civilian-manager was proud to align himself or herself with Sunnydale, but at the same time, they described this affiliation in a much more general way than we think police officers might. Cop-managers – particularly those who were negatively affected by change often feared there would be a negative impact on police work. Perhaps it is unkind to characterize the above quote in this way, but what one might call "bragging rights" of being associated with working for the police, of the kind that could be traded in at "the pub with friends", would apply no matter how well or badly change was being implemented. It would always be a special and different kind of organization for a civilian-manager to be associated with, even if managed poorly. However, for someone who was first a police officer, and later a manager, their feelings of belonging and membership could well be different.

A nontrivial point to make about this extract, again relevant to character, is that a high proportion of a police officers' friends whom they might meet "at the pub" would also be likely to be police. Policing has this in common with other occupations where there are strong socialization processes, common, prolonged and intense training, team-working, and shared exposure to risk (fire-fighting, mining, military service) – and we have discussed some of the reasons for this in the preceding chapter. The effects of change for a civilian-manager would change their relations with work colleagues, but for management-cops one might also expect ripples outside the workplace, and across the institution as a whole in terms of a wider community of fellow officers that they may have trained with or been deployed with. These institution-wide ripples could compound and intensify the negative experience of change across the service as a whole. This would happen in a way that is very unlike organizations in the same industry in the private sector.

Conclusion

Sunnydale allows us to make generalizable points about relations between change, and middle managers in policing. It shows that a division between "street cops" and "management cops" is insufficiently nuanced. The cop-managers we interviewed reacted to change differently under different circumstances. Their reactions differed from civilian-managers precisely because they (like all cops) had been street cops. An implication for understanding reforms is that not all of the middle layer will be squeezed, some will prosper even when change is dramatic, multilevel and multilayered but some middle managers will experience change negatively.

In policing we suggest there is an additional impact or dimension to widespread change which comes about because there can be conflicts with character. This is an important and distinctive aspect to policing because one would expect the roots of character (as police officers) to lie with experiences of front-line work. Virtue is a helpful way of thinking about this because it incorporates the idea that character is something that is developed over time. As we show in the following chapter, duty and other aspects of police work find expression in individual virtues because officers acquire character through training and by developing habits.

The ability of middle managers to cope with change, or even to prosper, depends partly on whether the content of managerial work and their character are in synch with change. As we suggest in Chapter 3 "good policing" is about exhibiting virtues consistent with legitimacy – discharging a duty to protect and serve the public, and a duty to apply the law equally without favour. For individual police officers who exhibit individual virtues that align with this institutional virtue, these kinds of principles will be learned and embodied. This principle-centred aspect to police work is intrinsically more consistent with hierarchical modes of governance than with markets and networks. Marketization and networks follow a different basic logic from duties. In addition, when it comes to managing cuts, the pressures from cuts do not fall evenly. Thinking about character allows us to scale up from individual level experiences to the service as a whole. The service-wide implications are that reforms and cuts may be more likely to bring cop-managers into conflict with their front-line character. This will harm the public good where it breaks a link between the public, the front line and the governance of police organizations.

6

TRAINING

This chapter discusses the development of character in policing in terms of the role of training. From the perspective of virtue ethics, this is particularly important to understand because virtues are practised and trained over time and an important element in cultivating virtues is habit. In our view, training is another under-examined aspect of police work (as well as the nature of managerial work in policing which we have just discussed). We return to the important theme of front-line work in the following chapter when considering why some describe policing as an "impossible job".

Training and virtue

Across a number of different disciplines there has been renewed interest in "virtue". Yet discussions are often at quite a general, theoretical level and they do not make reference to real-world settings like policing. One contribution of this book is to bring an explicitly normative perspective to bear on policing and so we pay close attention to context in this chapter. More widely though, the lack of detailed contextual analysis of virtues is a wider area for development in applied ethics. It is a problem that there are few empirical accounts of virtue in particular settings because virtues are not transcendent or universal principles. Instead, they take shape in particular settings and have meaning with respect to sets of social relations. They need to be understood in context, and looked at as things that develop over time. Unlike with the ethical systems of Kant and of utilitarianism, in virtue ethics to understand what is considered normatively "good" is behaviour over time, in relation to a particular social setting and in terms of a set of associated practices and customs. In other words, we think of good not in terms of an individual act but in the context of the good life.

One of the things that makes a virtue perspective especially relevant and helpful to understanding policing and the production of order is the role training plays in the life of police officers, in their induction and socialization into "the ranks". This is because one of the key aspects to looking at virtues in context is the concept of habit. There has been a great deal written about police culture and the socialization that occurs "on the job", but there has been less detailed examination of the habits associated with police training. This is significant because – notwithstanding the dilemmatic nature of police work – there is an important sense in which order is produced through police activities that are repetitive and practised.

The role of training is also significant because cultivating and encouraging certain habits is a common way to explain the development of character. Virtue and character are also often used to explain and understand what people do in moments of crisis, danger or risk. Policing is again an interesting setting here because it is when social order breaks down that questions relating to virtuous or vicious action by the public, the state and representatives of the state are especially pronounced. We return to some of these themes in studying disorder in the next chapter, but here to explore the development of character this chapter develops earlier work from a study of public order training (Morrell and Brammer, 2016). To locate our understanding of character in terms of the broader framework of virtue ethics as a whole we begin with discussion of the ideal of "the good life".

The good life

Virtue ethics is the oldest, most well-established approach to applied ethics that we have. Though it has ancient origins, it remains of contemporary interest (Alves and Moreira, 2013; Beadle, 2013a,b; Fontrodona, Sison and de Bruin, 2013; Hadreas, 2002; Koehn, 2013; Morrell, 2012a; Robinson, Stey and Alfano, 2013). It is of wider relevance than other normative ethical systems in the sense it can be compatible with both deontological (for instance Kantian ethics) and consequentialist approaches (for instance utilitarianism) (Dierksmeier, 2013; Morrell, 2004a), as well as with other approaches to ethics (Slote, 1995). In some ways this is because it asks a remarkably simple, central question: how can we live a good life? In other words, what does it mean as a member of the public, a parent, a friend, a police officer, or simply a human being – to act in the right way, over time?

As we discussed in Chapter 2, a number of problems nonetheless arise when working with virtue. There is no transcendental appeal or principle that we can invoke to evaluate what is virtuous in any given setting (MacIntyre, 1984a,b, 1988). This is in contrast to Kant's categorical imperative (which is very close to the "golden rule" of do unto others as you would have them do unto you), Mill and Bentham's recourse to a utility principle, or appeals to liberty (Nozick, 1974), or justice (Rawls, 1999). Virtue ethicists face the problem that when considering what constitutes virtuous action, context is crucially important. Virtue ethics is focused, "not so much on how to resolve problems as it is on how to live one's life" (McCracken, Martin and Shaw, 1998: 26). Even though some, including

Aristotle, have suggested there can be crowning virtues (his example is usually translated as magnanimity), the meaning and expression of these will vary with respect to context. In building up our account of institutional virtues we attempt to address this problem by rooting our account of policing and the public good in legitimacy (Chapter 3). We claim, that is, that to the extent it is founded on principles of procedural justice and the generation of a "deep" sense of security among the policed, good policing is that form, mode, style or way of practising police work which generates and reproduces legitimacy.

While research on virtue ethics has brought increasing sophistication in discussing the theoretical aspects of virtue, it is widely recognized that there is a need for more empirical research (Wright and Goodstein, 2007). A useful starting point then is to consider why virtues need to be understood in relation to a context. This is something we discussed in relation to policing as a whole in Chapter 2, and in relation to managerial work in the previous chapter, but it is also important to focus on the importance of context when it comes to front-line work and training.

Virtues in context

To recall the distinction between proximate and ultimate goals, questions about "virtue" in any sphere of practice – like policing – are always secondary to questions of what constitutes the good for human beings (Aristotle, 1094a7–8)[1]. This is partly why, when we consider virtues, there is no transcendent principle to which we can appeal. Instead what counts as virtue is always tied to particular sets of contingencies. What virtue means depends partly on the characteristics of a particular context, partly on how we understand the developing moral character of the responsible agent, and partly on the traditions and historical backdrop for their actions. From a virtue perspective, if we are to ask what is the right thing to do in any given situation, we need to try to account, somehow, for the contingencies of that particular situation and the wider socio-historical conditions for action in that setting, as well as consider the life-course and character of the agent taking that action. This does not mean we cannot rule out some actions as always vicious, or others as always virtuous, and we would not want to abandon the idea of what we called, in Chapter 2, a lowest common denominator of values, but it does make for a more complex picture.

One way to think of this is that with virtue ethics there are both social (Koehn, 2013), and temporal complexities (Beadle, 2013a) to consider. In terms of social complexities, we need to be sensitive to a place, institution(s), a set of beliefs and traditions, the practices and values of a community, and other diffuse, intangible expressions of norms and customs – for example what we might refer to in shorthand as "culture". In terms of temporal complexities, when we question whether someone did the right thing, we need to consider not just the action itself, but the overall life-course of the agent (Drake and Schlachter, 2008), the history for their actions and the kinds of things done in similar situations by people in similar roles.

These contextual complexities make it a challenge to speak sensibly in overly general terms about whether an action is virtuous. Popular writers do this, of course, and labels like heroic are often applied in policing – often with good reason. Running towards the sound of gunshots or explosions, or trying to disarm someone who is wielding a sword is brave – no matter how well one has been trained and no matter whether other colleagues would do this, or whether it is something expected of police officers. We can accept a common-sense and quite generalized idea about some actions that are virtuous (putting oneself at risk to save another) or vicious (causing needless suffering to another). These things are not really debated, but the issue of just *how* context-specific virtues are has been a question which people have struggled with for centuries. The classic example put forward is the contrast between the virtuous Spartan and the virtuous Athenian. They were very different from one another, but they were also products of very different circumstances. Sparta was a martial society prizing bravery, where death in battle or in childbirth were both honoured as kinds of service the state. Athens was a society built on commerce that prized wisdom, where the valued skills were those of business or statecraft.

It is not hard to bring this Sparta/Athens comparison up to date. We can connect it to the simple idea we expressed in Chapter 1 – that society is basically unfair. Access to different kinds of capital (social, cultural, financial) and life chances (Dahrendorf, 1979) differs according to various factors that are allocated to us at birth. The wealthy student who sets up an orphanage in Rwanda during their gap year may be no more virtuous than their counterpart who was born into poverty in the same postcode and who never makes it to university, but simply manages to avoid committing crime, despite all the temptation and lack of alternatives. This emphasis on context takes us to one of the benefits of the virtue perspective, because we look at situations in more depth and detail.

The idea that we must always attend to context seems very much in keeping with the perspective many contemporary criminologists have on crime and criminal justice (e.g. Sampson, 2013; Wikström et al., 2012). Also, as we described in Chapter 2, pursuing an understanding of "the public good" means addressing questions that are difficult to quantify and, ultimately, impossible to solve. Definitive conclusions are unrealistic. However, the challenges of understanding context are not fatal to any project working with virtue. Nor does it make attempts to work out what virtue means in a given setting futile (Beadle, 2013a), or mean we cannot seek principles that work alongside a virtue framework (Melé, 2009). It does, however, have important implications for considering how individual virtues in policing take shape.

Unless we acknowledge the idea that individual virtues in policing are different and tied to particular contexts in some way, we have to discuss virtue at a very high level of generalization and abstraction. We can quickly slip into the tabloid language of "heroic" cops, which then also perhaps sets up a sharper contrast with "crooked" cops. To give an example from a neighbouring public service, in nursing this kind of language ("angels") is incredibly unhelpful because it perpetuates gender stereotypes and it also legitimizes kinds of discourse about nursing being a vocation (undermining professionalism) and something people do as a calling (undermining the case for fair pay).

If we habitually talk about virtues (like heroism) or vices (crookedness) as though they are somehow free-standing – something an individual "has", or that make up a certain "kind" of person, or as if they are "traits" – this becomes similarly problematic. Put concretely, and in the language used in Chapters 3 and 4, this positions procedural justice as simply something "good cops" do, and not something that is (also) a core aspect of their practice that is shaped by the organizational and institutional context within which they are socialized and perform.

To understand the role of individual virtues in producing order, we need to recognize policing as a kind of work rather than just the expression of noble or base instincts. To call cops heroic or crooked, or attuned to community values or not, is a mistake in understanding policing governance because it relies on notions of individualized power and personal attributes. Or, to put it another way, it makes the person responsible for failings in a system as a whole. Criminologists and others have long held concerns about this question, for example in relation to the "bad apple" thesis used to explain police malfeasance. As Loader and Mulcahy (2003: 152) argue, this is a convenient explanatory device used to explain away, or at least minimize, examples of police inappropriateness, malpractice and violence, which wrenches such behaviours from their institutional contexts and relocates them in the personalities and preferences of individual officers. From a virtue ethics perspective, it is important to recognize the failure to account for context as an error in logic. Virtues are what we call in the previous chapter characterological (learned, embodied, relatively stable and enduring), but they are not character traits in the way we understand personality traits to be. This is because virtues are defined in relation to others and with reference to context.

Speaking of the kinds of virtues we want police officers to "have" does open the possibility of making virtues more easy to measure and test in the same way traits (such as openness or neuroticism) and states (such as organizational commitment or job satisfaction) are in applied psychology (e.g. Chun, 2005). And, it also can support the building of abstract, generalizable models or competency frameworks of the kind widely used in policing for performance appraisal and assessment. But we would caution against this because it is a form of reductionism. There is an important distinction to be made between models of virtue that emphasize highly generalized desirable qualities (perhaps "team working"), and much more nuanced considerations as to the workings of virtue in a given setting and the cultivation of virtue over time (Hartman, 2011; Sison, 2003). This is because, ultimately, virtue theorists are interested in questions of character in so far as these relate to the morality of agents in complex social worlds (Sison, 2008). Reducing this complexity to competency frameworks and checklists is dangerous and misunderstands virtue. Louden explains this well:

> Virtue theorists focus on good and bad agents rather than on right and wrong acts. In focusing on good and bad agents, virtue theorists are thus forced to deemphasize discrete acts in favour of long-term, characteristic patterns of behaviour.
>
> *(Louden, 1997: 205)*

Two quick examples will help to try to explain here. Very frequently we can see appeals made by regulators and those responsible for overseeing the police (as well as by individual officers) to the notions of "resilience" and particularly "leadership". At first glance these would seem unproblematically desirable qualities for individuals to have and worthy candidates for the tag of virtue (Morrell and Hartley, 2006b). Who would not want to be resilient, or a leader? Actually, if we consider the fuller context for these statements and the way they are being deployed in contemporary policing, something quite different is happening when these terms are used. They are becoming part of a language that is designed to make individuals responsible for overcoming failings and responsible for coping: what is sometimes called "responsibilization".

If we see failures as the result of a lack of resilience then this places the responsibility on individuals – or groups of individuals – rather than on seeing failings in the system as a whole. Like the view of power we introduced in Chapter 1, both these terms are building up a picture of power as something episodic and individualized. From a virtue ethics perspective, because it is crucial to understand virtues in their fullest context and in depth and detail, this leads us to a very different view of power, one that connects to our definition of governance as the production of order. Power from a virtue perspective is diffuse, expressed through the workings of an entire system and set of interrelations and traditions.

The appeal to "leadership" is perhaps particularly pernicious because, like "team" it implies consensus (Ford, Harding and Learmonth, 2008). Leaders implicitly have followers and this glosses over the possibility of conflict (Learmonth and Morrell, 2017). But against a backdrop of cuts and constraints there can be legitimate differences and even conflict as to how to prioritize resources. Terms like "resilience" and "leadership" could still be appropriate ways to describe virtuous action in some settings, and we do not want to close down the possibility of ordinary usage of terms to signal things that are worthy of praise or punishment. However, when used in a free-standing and overly generalized way they produce a particular picture of the police officer as a character. Rather than someone who is part of an interconnected web of relations between society (the public) and an activity (policing for the public good) we have a more atomized picture of how policing is done by powerful individuals – leaders who can deliver on targets, officers who are resilient and cope in the face of cuts and pressures and who are better than those who are less resilient. In contrast to "leadership" and "resilience", the concepts of procedural justice, legitimacy and shared values that we developed in Chapters 3 and 4 are much richer and more detailed, and they are also understood much more closely in relation to the public as the collective beneficiaries of "good policing".

There is also a problem in how academics typically carry out research on virtue. This exaggerates the problem of discussing virtues as though they are individual traits or in some way free-standing. Very often, discussion of virtue does not make reference to empirical data in any great depth. A great many discussions are theoretical, and many of those which describe themselves as empirical in some way often only use secondary data, or rely on reports in the media, or describe anecdotes. For instance, analysis of the 30 most cited articles titled on "virtue" in a leading business ethics journal suggests only 8 use primary data, and only 2 analyse secondary data using recognizably systematic methods (Morrell and Brammer, 2016). But to understand virtue in a setting requires a broader empirical base than this (McCracken et al., 1998). We need to take in various complexities, including attention to history, tradition, situated complexity and the development of character through habits. We build up a picture of how this happens in the rest of this chapter, examining the training of police for the policing of public disorder. This is an interesting setting because it sheds light on how order is produced.

Habits in public order training

The policing of "public order" is a very broad category that includes policing individuals, but (as is the focus here) it is also more typically associated with mass events – like demonstrations and protests, industrial action, and riots. These kinds of situations are particularly informative because they are where relations between the citizen and the state can be dramatically altered. In Chapter 1 we touched briefly on the idea that virtue ethics can be thought of in terms of stories and we revisit this in our concluding chapter. During periods of large-scale public disorder, there can be pivotal changes in the story of the development of the state, or in a political administration. There are also sometimes momentous and memorable changes in the development of individual people's life stories.

Considering the governance of the policing in such situations is also apposite because a significant body of work has demonstrated that when "done right" – that is, in a procedurally fair, communicative and respectful manner that demonstrates a sense of shared or at least common identity between police and demonstrator and even "rioter" – the policing of public order events can proceed in a way which minimizes the risk of *disorder* and thus contributes to the public goods of free expression and assembly (Reicher, Stott, Cronin and Adang, 2004; Reicher, Stott, Drury and Adang, 2007; Stott and Pearson, 2006). Whilst our discussion below revolves around what police can and should do once large-scale disorder has broken out, it is important to note that the work of Stott, Reicher and colleagues has shown that police can have a significant effect on whether order breaks down in the first place, as well of course as the speed with which it spreads. And, crucially, "doing it right" involves police officers engaging with protesters/demonstrators, using dialogue, and treating them as rights-bearing subjects able to make their own decisions within a democratically ordered environment. Overzealous action can actually be the trigger for more serious disorder.

In comparison to other ethical systems, a virtue perspective on disorder seems helpful because often there can be conflicts between different duties and imperatives in policing such circumstances. O'Kelly and Toole (2006: 402) (writing about a North American setting) identify policing as a paradigm case where there is an ongoing conflict between competing obligations that cannot be satisfied:

> the moral obligation to do no harm to other individuals comes into direct conflict with the obligation to carry out one's duty to protect the community – an obligation that may require the use of injurious force against another individual. In order to carry out one moral obligation, a law enforcement official may have to violate the other.

These tensions are heightened during mass disorder because this can give rise to impossibly dilemmatic choices. Disorder also throws into relief some of the differences between policing and other public services. As a consequence of their powers and the legal context for police work, there is a need for officers to be individually accountable even in scenes of comparative chaos. The continuing need for discretion and situated judgement make this a revealing setting in which to analyse virtue and also the "production of order".

To consider what effect this has on "policing and the public good", we identify three broad categories of governance problems likely to surface in the context of public order. Each of these is relevant to considering virtue, and each is also relevant to considering the development of individual character.

First, most basically, the breakdown of order in society presents individuals from the police and the public with an array of dilemmas and possibilities for action that are not present in their everyday life. These are extreme circumstances, often important in the individual story that makes up someone's life, as well as part of a broader story about social history or the legacy of an administration. During mass disorder, some of the public deliberately break with the rule of law. Sometimes, even though these are breaches of the law, mass uprisings could later be judged to be virtuous: for instance in railing against an oppressive tyranny, or resisting inequity, or bringing about the fall of an unjust government. Other members of the public may then be confronted with the dilemma of whether to participate in disorder, or to continue to behave lawfully. Mass public disorder also prompts stark dilemmas for individual police officers. They may be immediately confronted with their role in perpetuating the actions of the state, perhaps being well-paid and well-fed while policing an impoverished constituency. Or it may be many years later that they recognize that having done something that was "wrong" has become part of their life story. They may have to make split-second decisions that have dramatic consequences for others as they result in arrest or the use of force. They may have to exercise courage, or they may succumb to the corrupting influence of being comparatively powerful. As we discuss in the following chapter, these dilemmas extend from officers at the front line, all the way up the command chain.

Second, mass disorder and phenomena such as crowd dynamics (Stott, 2011) show how groups of people can act in very different ways from individuals. Demonstrations and strikes, and even riots, can also be understood as socially shared, cultural knowledge: "repertoires of contention" (Tilly, 1995). Repertoires of contention provide groups with scripts that guide action. These are kinds of template on which collective performances, or resistance to authority can be footprinted, "learned cultural creations [which] emerge from struggle" (Tilly, 1995: 26). Rioting is sometimes described as mindless, but the contrary is likely to be true. Mindfulness (shared purpose) is a necessary legal condition for a riot. To break with society's rules so flagrantly may be reckless and frenzied, but it is not mindless (or else we would not be justified in punishing participants after the event). A founding principle of virtue ethics is that to assign praise or blame, we have to infer that a person has exercised choice.

Third, a riot can tell us things about the relationship between the state and the public. In the classical perspective on virtue ethics, the good person and the good state are defined relationally. The good, law-abiding member of the public is only possible because of the conditions provided (for "flourishing") by the good state. In turn, the good state itself needs to be made up of good members of the public (as well as other things like good practices, just laws and well administered institutions). Interestingly, for Aristotle, to be truly human actually requires the presence of the state: this is why in the *Politics* (1253a19–30) he says the state (the *polis*) is prior to the individual. These connections between the state and the member of the public are important for the perspective of governance as the production of order; they are also important because underpinning any attributions of virtue are some foundational, primary considerations of what is "the good life" for human beings (MacIntyre, 1997). When we see mass disorder, there is a clear implication of this in terms of a failure in terms of this link between the state and the public. Any society experiencing mass disorder is experiencing a vicious situation. This means that governance is not just about the "how" of restoring order, it is a "why" question: the degree to which the state is culpable for having created the conditions under which rioting occurs (Morrell, 2012a).

The discussion and analysis below draws on data as part of a longitudinal project looking at public order policing in the UK. The principal data sources relevant to this chapter (interviews) are shown in the first three rows of Table 6.1. In Chapter 7 we broaden this out to include other sources of data from documents and observation. From July 2010 to September 2013, research combined interviews with police officers and retired officers. It also included observation of large-scale public order training, observations of a specialist public order training unit dealing with a variety of scenarios relating to "lock-ons" (arm tubes, padlocks, chains, obstructions), and some secondary data on the UK autumn 2011 riots (transcripts of debate in Parliament, written and oral evidence to a parliamentary Select

Committee and reports in Great Britain, 2012a,b,c; *The Guardian*, 2012; Lewis et al., 2011; Metropolitan Police, 2012; Ministry of Justice, 2011).

The main primary data source as shown was interviews, and a biographical method of interviewing informed by narratology. This is an approach to understanding the world through stories and story-telling (narrativization). It draws on different methods for analysing stories, and is rooted in techniques of literary analysis (Bal, 1985; Czarniawska, 2010). Here we use "story" and "narrative" interchangeably, which is not to deny that it can be helpful to differentiate between the two (see Gabriel and Griffiths, 2004). Simply speaking, we collected stories relating to police training over the course of our interviewees' careers.

In concert with, and consistent with, this emphasis on story-gathering, interviews also allowed for probing in relation to narration of particularly salient events (Chell, 2004): a common, anchoring question in interviews was "What was your most memorable public order incident?" The value of combining a biographical method with a narratological approach to analysis is that it allows insight into elements of chronology, sequence and learning. Taking a virtue perspective on policing and the public good this can tell us more about the formation and reinforcement of habits and the development of character (Beadle, 2013a). Though, strictly speaking, one-off interviews are a cross-sectional method, they were used to give insight into explicitly temporal aspects to personal stories (learning, and memories of pivotal incidents).

We also interviewed some officers more than once, subsequent meetings and interviews (including telephone, and skype interviews) were usually not recorded, but notes taken at the time or shortly afterwards – these later meetings ranged from the briefest of telephone calls to two-hours long. Interviews enabled access to observation of public order training in 2011. Later in 2011 the context of the empirical research unexpectedly changed because of "the riots" which we discuss in more detail the following chapter. Then, through 2012 and 2013 additional interviews were carried out with a wider group of officers, many of whom were public order specialists. This chapter focuses on the role of training and development of character and to so it concentrates on interviews with officers who had a particular specialism in public order, and who all had a minimum of ten years' service – with one exception as described below.

To provide analytical focus, in discussing findings, we concentrate on the first category of governance problems (as described above), which sees mass disorder as an extreme situation, presenting the citizenry and the police with an array of dilemmas and possibilities that are not usually present, and that can be pivotal for societies, administrations and the individuals involved. A number of qualifiers should be made explicit prior to introducing and discussing our findings.

First, we are not equating virtuous action with lawful action. Though there is overlap, at times illegal action can be virtuous, and at times to behave lawfully may not be virtuous – this is the dilemma at the heart of Sophocles' play *Antigone*, itself an instruction in virtue (Nussbaum, 2001). (When she is banned from burying her brother properly, Antigone has to choose between obeying the unjust laws of a

TABLE 6.1 Data Sources Relating to Public Order

Data Sources	Kind of Data	Data Sources	Analytical Approach	Main Role in Analysis	Role in the Book
Interviews, taped	Primary	Transcripts	Realist Story-gathering / Biographical analysis	Raw data eliciting stories	Chapter 6
Field interviews, combination of taped and un-taped	Primary	Transcripts or Notes (during or shortly after)			
Interviews via phone calls, Skype calls, emails	Primary	Notes (during), some later transcribed	Content analysis	Sense-checking (technical terms, procedures, legislation)	
Observation: Training Scenarios	Primary	Substantive field notes	First person, realist observation	Raw data critical incident	Chapter 7
Observation: Training Videos and live incidents	Secondary	YouTube footage from various sources, News broadcasts	Realist video observation	Triangulation and contrast or sense-checking with primary observation	
Documents: Select Committee Evidence, Reports	Secondary	Transcripts available on www.parliament.org.uk	Realist Story-gathering / Content analysis	Analysing accounts given by members of the public and other stakeholders	Chapter 7

tyrant or honouring traditions.) Social progress is often marked by protests and demonstrations that are unlawful, but which lead to changed legislation. This is worth emphasizing because most of the ancient accounts of virtue ethics were very conservative with regard to the institutions of the state. The importance of freedom and equality for individual members of the public is either underplayed or even absent in the ancient city-state or *polis* – governed by a minority, male elite with "a single moral perspective and … enough wealth to live at leisure and hold political office without pay" (Kraut, 2002: vii). A virtue of the *polis*, perhaps unsurprisingly given the ravages of war in ancient Greece, is it provides stability. Consequently, in terms of the relationship between the government and the public, Aristotle seems to have regarded a weak or vicious government as preferable to no government at all and so he is most sensibly understood as a traditionalist rather than as someone who will support mass disorder (although see Goldstein, 2001).

Second, we are not suggesting the police always act virtuously during disorder, whether they act lawfully or not. Nor are we suggesting that the police we interviewed always acted virtuously or are exceptionally virtuous either as police officers or members of the public themselves. Neither are we suggesting the police are a virtuous force within society, nor would we say that the appropriate default position in considering mass disorder is to see those attempting to restore order as acting virtuously or on the side of "the good". Instead, we suggest mass public disorder – and the preparation for how to police mass disorder – is a useful setting for considering how to develop a contextual account of virtue in policing replete as it is with questions of fairness, legitimacy and group relations. In turn this tells us more about the relationship between "policing and the public good". The next section draws attention to four such features of policing. All illustrate the importance of habit in the development of character, and all are based on empirical data and a methodology that allows access to social and temporal complexity.

Giving an account of actions

As the extracts below show, accounts of actions by officers are rehearsed, documented, indexical (tied to settings and times) and institutionalized. The reason this is significant in the context of virtue is it illustrates the two aspects of contingency and development of character.

> you think it through in your own mind … you think it through as you write in your pocketbook or a statement, "I did that because I was thinking that" … and all the time you justify, "I did that because of that." And there are [pause] I've stood in the witness box, I've stood in front of the gaffer and said, "I did this because of this, this and this." And you can feel under pressure thinking at times. "Did I make the right decision or didn't I?"
>
> *(Keith, Retired Officer, Public Order Specialist)*

the more you write down about your thinking as well the better. I mean we constantly face, you know, legal challenge whether it's through judicial reviews or other direct litigation, you know, through ... civil courts ... And we try and write, start writing as much down as possible ... what am I thinking about? What am I concerned about ... that can really help you afterwards ... helping understand the things that were going through your mind at the time.

("Ant", Public Order Commander)

Keith was discussing the way he would be called to account for use of force in mass disorder. "Ant" was describing dilemmatic choices in policing disorderly crowds, where some people are caught up in disorder. In both settings there is a need for action to be described in great detail because of the potential seriousness of the consequences of using force, or curtailing liberties. Whether activity is deemed lawful, necessary and appropriate depends not just on legislation, but on an assessment of the contingencies of each situation. Keith's personal – what could be called "storying" (Sims, 2003) – of events: "you think it through", "I was thinking", "you write in your pocketbook"; is a form of habituation or rehearsal for a public story that is instantiated and made concrete through particular actions, and kinds of professional being, "I've stood in the witness box, I've stood in front of the gaffer and said". The influence habituation and rehearsal of this kind has on the development of character is evident in the above extract in Keith's emphasis on personal identity, "you can feel under pressure thinking at times. 'Did I make the right decision or didn't I?'" and so this practice potentially encourages reflexivity (Wood and Williams, 2016). Similarly, Ant's description of a learned habit of documenting is not just for external scrutiny but to aid recall of decisions in complex environments. Police officers are also often called on to speak whilst being recorded, for instance when interviewing suspects.

These extracts show how accounts of work, actions and identity (discussed in Chapters 4 and 5) are bound together with consideration of the context. We are not saying being called to justify one's actions automatically results in the cultivation of virtue, but it may be we can link to the ancient (Socratic) idea that ethical behaviour involves being able to give an account of one's actions (something which, probably not coincidentally, is a core aspect of procedural justice). As a society, we ideally want those who are entitled to exercise force to be able to account for why they have done so after the event. Also, we would ideally want them to think about whether they would be able to justify the use of force before the event whatever the circumstances confronting them – i.e. to have the ability to anticipate the consequences of their actions. Habituation, repeatedly giving an account, and a set of institutional practices supporting this, may be the only way to cultivate this skill.

Normatively, police officers have to record critical decisions contemporaneously, or very shortly afterwards. These should be truthful and accurate and be records that are specific and indexical in different ways (with reference to time, place, other parties and their actions). The records are handed over shortly after the event, they belong to the institution not the individual, and they are potentially scrutinized in an open court. Failure to follow these practices is often a signal of vicious conduct, the most shocking example in British policing following the Hillsborough disaster (see Scraton, 2016). Normatively though, these practices are notable for how different this makes policing as an activity. All of these would contrast with what we might expect to know about a consequential political or business decision, for instance to introduce a tax, or to close a factory. Often these decisions would be made by an individual but attributed to a collective (the Cabinet, or a Board), there would be no publicly available minutes of the relevant meeting, and a rationale (if given) would be prepared by others than those who took the decision (such as "spin doctors", or a public relations department)

Remaining individually responsible

As we mention several times, a well-known characteristic of police work is that it is dilemmatic (Brown, 1988), but some suggest that a "crisis" can be associated with an authoritarian control structure, with the front line being given less discretion and instead subject to commands. This can compromise effective solutions because if we frame problems as crises then, "[n]ot only are we likely to be addicted to Command but we are also likely to be allergic to Leadership" (Grint, 2010: 313). In interviews, and also observation of training, it was noticeable that during what in everyday terms one would understand as "crisis", individual officers continued to experience this dilemmatic aspect to policing. They still had decisions to make, even when confronted with apparently monolithic phenomena such as a rioting crowd. Consequently, those at the front line should remain individually responsible even in situations where, from a distance, police presence and response could seem homogeneous and militaristic. This came through in explanations for use of force:

> the officer has to have in their own mind that honest held belief that that's going to be a lawful use of power, just as much as an officer in line with all his colleagues with a baton [.] every baton strike you do isn't under some kind of general order, hit them, it's "I'm making up my own mind that it is proportionate and necessary to hit this particular demonstrator because of the threat they pose."
>
> *(Arthur, Public Order Commander)*

> you can be told what to do and where to go, you can be told to draw your baton and use force but to actually make the decision to get hands-on with someone and to strike them is your responsibility and you are held solely accountable for that and each strike is in itself a separate use of force.
>
> *(Andrew, Front-line Specialist in Public Order with two years experience as a PC)*

Again, in both cases, each officer emphasizes the importance of being able to account for their decision, for which they are individually responsible. This does not devolve commanding officers of responsibility though. For instance, their framing of the situation in a briefing and their style and tone could affect the decision-making of an individual officer in relation to use of force (perhaps more so in pre-planned operations rather than spontaneous ones).

It is interesting to consider this theme of individual responsibility in relation to the members of the public who participate in rioting. As we discuss in Chapter 7, a contemporaneous phenomenon at one stage during the research was large-scale disorder in August 2011. Rather than in some way excuse people for being swept up by a phenomenon, the courts took a harsh approach to sentencing rioters, to provide a deterrent effect. This mood was reflected in comments by the Prime Minister and Members of Parliament in a day the House of Commons was recalled to debate the riots (which we discuss in more depth in Chapter 8):

> the Sentencing Council says that those people found guilty of violence on our streets should expect to have a custodial sentence.
> *(David Cameron, Prime Minister)*

> Can he [Prime Minister Cameron] assure my constituents that those who are found guilty of being caught up in this mayhem will feel the full force of the law, including prison sentences?
> *Angie Bray, MP for Ealing and Central Acton*

These extracts indicate that not only were individual rioters held responsible irrespective of others' actions, they were actually punished more severely for choosing to take part and joining in with the actions of rioters. There is a clear implication for both the police and the public here. Even when public order breaks down and it seems there is mass chaos, the question of individual virtue (and vice) is important.

This aspect of remaining individually responsible seems important if we reconsider one theme form Chapter 1 – which is the sense of labelling something as "governance failure". Vicious conduct in management, in terms of corporate scandals, or large-scale incompetence and failure, is usually explained in rather vague terms. For instance, U.S. Treasury Secretary Geithner's testimony before a congressional oversight panel explained the Global Financial Crisis in terms of "risk appetite", "systemic risk", "distress in money markets", "financial stress", and "deep-seated problems" (U.S. Treasury, 2009). There is almost a routine reference to "governance failure" in discussions of Enron, Worldcom et al. But in mass public disorder, notwithstanding the extreme and atypical climate for action, the speed with which situations unfold, and crowd-level phenomena, there is an obvious need for people on all sides to remain responsible as individuals.

Recognizing the role of emotion

As we have said, much of the literature on virtue is written at a theoretical and abstract level, so there is no in depth consideration of what happens in a particular context. As a result, discussions can underemphasize the role emotion plays in virtue, and in the development of character, because emotions are responses to particular sets of circumstances. Relatedly, there is a risk that discussions of virtues are over-generalized and that virtues become thought of as traits – rather than interdependent and resulting from the context. But emotions are temporary states.

One reason virtue appeals as a way of understanding policing is that policing involves a great deal of emotional labour. In virtue ethics, unlike models of rational choice, emotion is seen not as a distraction or as in some way compromising decision-making, but as an integral part of the process. For instance, Aristotle says being angry in and of itself is not problematic provided one is angry at the right things, with the right people, for the right length of time (Aristotle, 1125b32–3). Officers conveyed clearly to us the role emotions such as fear played in decision-making and in doing so underlined the benefits of habituation and reinforcement, of the kind associated with the development of character. Often "emotional labour" describes a burden or imposition, or something superficial and inauthentic (Noon, Blyton and Morrell, 2013). For some though, it may be that identifying oneself as skilled at performing emotional labour is actually part of the motivation for joining the police.

Several officers referred to "adrenaline", which we interpreted not as a literal description of a state, but as a metonym (shorthand) for one or more emotions like fear, anger, fight-or-flight, and also enjoyment and excitement. Others explained they were aware of the dangers of a "red mist" descending and explained that being in control of emotions was a very prevalent theme in their practice. Dan emphasized the need for training to "kick in" when describing having to clear a 300-metre street of hostile crowd:

> when we arrived it was a very, very tense situation and my heart was certainly racing and my blood was racing ... I was very conscious of losing my colleagues either side because [the risk of] being dragged into the crowd was very, very high. So that kind of awareness, when you're, the adrenaline is pumping your vision becomes very much restricted – tunnel vision ... hopefully in that situation your training kicks in because your ability to make decisions is considerably restricted.
>
> *(Dan, Public Order Commander)*

Keith referred to emotion to contrast the conditions under which decisions are evaluated, from the circumstances where they are taken:

> when its looked at and everyone's sat down with their cup of tea and their lunch ... it's a very different [situation] there's no adrenaline involved and I

sometimes question are we really fair on officers because you're sitting back, it's a nice time of day, there's no pressure on you, you're just purely looking at the instance, very different to three o'clock in the morning with somebody who appears aggressive and you think they're trying to kill me ... If you said to me, "Has it got better as you've got older?" I'd say yeah because you have all this experience to base it on, when you're young you don't have that experience do you?

(Keith, former Public Order Trainer)

Again, the emphasis of habituation, the need to be able to give an account, and development of character interlock here. Policing during such crisis situations offers an example where, ideally, there is an underpinning governance framework in terms of the law, and a set of institutional practices that try to document the way in which a particular event in its complexity is mapped onto a general infrastructure. Training should also enable officers to remain aware of the role emotion plays in informing, or potentially compromising, effective decisions. For instance, developing a pre-conscious competence in using the national decision-making model may support decision-making in high stress situations.

The importance of practice

A key part of habituation and the cultivation of virtue is practice. This is a central theme in the classical account of the virtues and yet the role of practice has not been described with reference to empirical data in literature to date. Unlike Kantian and utilitarian systems, which rely on the application of a universal principle, and are thus in a sense cross-sectional (though see Dierksmeier, 2013), virtue ethics emphasizes learned, characterological and socially interdependent qualities.

There is a paradox at the heart of training for mass disorder though. Large bureaucracies such as the police are tasked with preparing for and routinizing the unpredictable. There is a need for common procedures to ensure standardization, for health and safety reasons, to minimize exposures and also to deliver training within a certain budget. Each officer may have, say, two days training a year in public order, and this has to cover worst case scenarios. Often these are designed in terms of an escalating scale of disorder – meaning everyone arrives with a mental script as to what will happen in the day. At the same time, however, a recurring theme in interviews was that public order incidents are unique in some way. Mass public disorder, and events such as riots, are extremely rare, but the police nonetheless have to prepare for them. Richard, a Public Order Commander described this in terms of what would happen with the most specialist units who are often held back in reserve:

if they've had 100 deployments ... to actually get out of the van, to actually use a word of command that you've used in training ... is one out of a 100, one out of more than 100 because generally speaking you're there, you're doing crowd control so you're just locked in a cordon, you're not going to run in line and form a wedge and you know, show of strength and all of the tactics, you're just you know, in real life it's restrained to sitting in a van, standing and looking at people ... dynamically, fighting street to street like Northern Ireland, like a little bit of having the riots, it's very rare.

(Richard, Public Order Commander)

In attempts to reproduce fidelity in training scenarios, we found certain elements of public order training were more pronounced and potentially more violent or physically hazardous than the typical experience of actual public order scenarios. Richard went on to describe his force's approach to training:

[Force name withheld] has got a reputation within the region of being very robust in its training. When we do have the regional exercises, there's always little comments that we seem to be a bit more fierce or violent in the exercises than the other forces ... we train very, very hard and if I was to make an instantaneous reflection ... the reality is never anywhere near as difficult and as taxing as the training.

One interesting feature of watching officers prepare for a regional training day was to see how their day began with practising how to deal with petrol bombs. Sometimes called Molotov cocktails, these are large glass bottles, filled with petrol where the petrol is held in place by a piece of twisted cloth. The cloth soaked in petrol acts as a primitive fuse. Lighting the cloth, then throwing the bottle results in a burst of flame when the glass shatters and the petrol inside the bottle ignites and spreads. Before the large-scale training scenarios, ranks of officers lined up in small groups and in a very measured way (in protective clothing), practised walking through the flames caused by a petrol bomb. One trainer was ushering the officers through the flames, at times advising how to stamp them out, another trainer was repeatedly picking up and lighting petrol bombs before throwing them at the feet of the next rank of officers. It was thought-provoking to see people walking through flames to start work. Since this had become a practised routine, in context, it seemed normal. It was clearly not "brave" – instead it was a routine made possible by combining technique and equipment. Even so, one could imagine how identical behaviours in a different context – moving towards petrol bombs, or simply staying holding a line – in other circumstances could be "brave" irrespective of having been rehearsed. It was also thought-provoking to consider what situation would lead a member of the public to make and throw petrol bombs.

Conclusion

In using virtue ethics to inform our understanding of policing, it is important to acknowledge there are a number of things which are uncomfortable in early visions of how the *polis* should be governed. For example, Aristotle is sometimes –

simplistically – interpreted as believing that some people are naturally slaves and some naturally masters. He is also often taken to advocate the exclusion and subjugation of women, which again many say is too simplistic a reading (Dobbs, 1996; Nichols, 1992; Swanson, 1992). Even so, he certainly can be recruited in different ways: as a defender of the powerful, the rich and of elites. Nussbaum (2001: xx) describes his "first and most striking defect" as being "the absence … of any sense of universal human dignity, a fortiori of the idea that the worth and dignity of human beings is equal". Of course we reject such defects and these do not mean we cannot modify this framework.

One thing virtue ethics does offer is the ability to talk coherently about social and temporal complexities such as the role of habit, as well as the influence of emotion. Another key feature of this account of virtue is that the individual and the group are related to one another. The good person is possible because of the good society (*polis*), and vice versa. The setting of large-scale public disorder is a useful and illustrative one to consider the different aspects of his account and the value of considering virtue in the light of political arrangements and habituation. Individuals remain responsible for their choices even in such settings.

In Chapter 3 we developed an idea of legitimacy as a crowning institutional virtue in policing. The context of police training shows that, in a sense, we cannot get very far talking about virtues in the abstract. They need to be understood in terms of a way of doing things, a group, and a context in all its historicity. Virtues are learned over time and context-dependent, they only make sense in the context of the development of character (Arjoon, 2000). Rather than being assigned to individuals at any one moment in a cross-sectional way, or in some sense carried by, or within individual agents (like traits are), virtues are more complex. They need to be seen in the light of the development of someone's character over their entire life-course, or over the entire time that they inhabit a role. They also find expression in interactions with others.

The meaning of an action and its status in terms of virtue is socially complex and also stretches in time – both prospectively in terms of someone's development, and also retrospectively in terms of its historical context. Virtues are "tradition-constituted" (Fives, 2008: 169). This longitudinal aspect is not the only source of complexity because virtue is interdependent: defined relationally with reference to other people and groups; and also rooted in the values, and mores of a society or collective. The context of training is helpful because it connects habit and character. In the following chapter we move from the setting of training to consider the actual work of the police once more. Again we look at public disorder, but this time focusing on what happens in practice.

Note

1 Aristotle is conventionally cited using a page, column, and line format. For example, his phrase: "one swallow does not make a summer, nor does one day; and so too one day, or a short time, does not make a man blessed and happy" is on page 1098, column a, lines 17-19, or more succinctly: (1098a17–19).

7
DISORDER

This chapter anchors discussion of front-line policing in a theoretical framework that has been applied to a number of jobs in public management. This is the idea of an "impossible job". This is a phrase coined by Hargrove and Glidewell (1990), and it has a particular meaning. The chapter proceeds as follows. First, we review the literature on impossible jobs. We then introduce the context for our study. Drawing on extensive multi-site, multi-method data we analyse public disorder focusing on the 2011 riots. We conclude by outlining three theoretical extensions to the "impossible jobs" framework.

Impossible jobs

A number of related terms can describe the intractable problems public agencies sometimes face, among them "wicked problems" (Rittel and Webber, 1973), "adaptive problems" (Heifetz, 1994) or "messes" (van Bueren, Klijn and Koppenjan, 2003). When it comes to considering these in relation to a job, the principal framework public management scholars have in mind is Lipsky's (2010) street-level bureaucracy (discussed in Chapter 5) (Brodkin, 2011; Maynard-Moody and Musheno, 2012). For street-level bureaucrats, dilemmas arise because the complexities of the individual case have to mesh with the machinery of the state. Rather than being resolved at a policy level, such problems reside with, and are worked on by, individuals (the second half of Lipsky's title being *Dilemmas of the Individual in Public Services*). Though dilemmas are products of institutional arrangements and constraints, it is the individual public servant who grapples with them at street-level (Foldy and Buckley, 2010; Lipsky, 2010).

Erwin Hargrove and John Glidewell's (1990) edited book, *Impossible Jobs in Public Management*, suggested that in some street-level agencies (e.g. social work, mental health, policing), those running the agencies had impossible jobs (Dobel, 1992; Hult, 1992; Porter, 1991). Four criteria define impossible jobs:

> [1] unpopular client base; [2] intense conflict among the stakeholders; [3] low public confidence in manager's professional authority; [4] weak or negative agency myth.
>
> *(Moynihan 2005: 214)*

So, these jobs are not impossible because of dilemmas at the individual case-level, or the problems Lipsky identifies: the social construction of the client, the challenge of giving individualized consideration within a bureaucracy, the problem allocating benefits and sanctions, the struggle to translate and implement policy amid constraints and ambiguity (Lipsky, 2010). Instead, an impossible job is impossible because some public agencies can never make good on the service they promise to deliver to all constituencies. This framework is relevant to our understanding the relationship between policing and the public (Chapter 2) because it connects distinctive features of policing to the challenge of working with "the public good" in this setting. Table 7.1 below summarizes these connections.

The framework has attracted widespread use and remains popular, but it has become overgeneralized (Maranto and Wolf, 2012). As Table 7.1 shows, the extent to which police work meets the criteria of an "impossible job" varies according to which audience, stakeholder- or client-group one considers, and in what circumstances. Policing can be thought of as "more" or "less" "impossible" in relation to different problems in different times and places (for example being unable to deliver a solution in areas were crime is high; or disappointing when failing to live up to impossibly high expectations in areas of low crime). The role of this chapter is to propose three theoretical extensions to the framework:

1. We differentiate between jobs and tasks (jobs can combine possible and impossible tasks).
2. We give a clearer account of the relationship between street-level jobs and impossible jobs (some street-level bureaucrats face impossible tasks).
3. We give a richer account of the concept of a client base (sometimes "the" client base can fracture, or grow very rapidly, and can change very quickly from legitimate to illegitimate).

Our context is the study of how police officers in England train for, and confront, riots. (We use "riots", notwithstanding this has a particular meaning in law, partly because "public order" can describe an ongoing approach to control or exclusion e.g. Beckett and Herbert, 2008; rather than response to extreme events).

Each of the four impossible jobs criteria above signals a two-way relationship between: (i) the image, purpose and "character" of the agency discharging a service, and (ii) the wider public. This wider public includes users and recipients (the clients of the "street-level bureaucrat"), but – a difference from Lipsky's main

TABLE 7.1 "Impossible Jobs" Policing and the Public Good

Dimension	Explanation in the Context of Policing	Implications for Policing and the Public Good
Unpopular or illegitimate clients	Though the end beneficiary of effective policing is the public, the police often have more direct clients who are seen as unpopular or illegitimate in some way by wider society. For instance, the wider public often have very little sympathy for, indeed at times despise, suspects and arrestees. This can lead to the police being seen as too soft or ineffective, perhaps because they are not seen as dispensing justice (understood as some form of punishment), or perhaps because they are seen as more concerned with the rights of the illegitimate perpetrator than the victim. Police powers such as arrest or detention, or the use of force, are often used in public spaces and this can mean members of the public become classified as "illegitimate" in real time. Perceptions of crime are also socially constructed and often reflect prejudices or populism, rather than being a function of, say, harm.	Part of the wider task of "policing" could be a civic project. This could involve education of the public – not just about police procedures, penalties and the law – but also about the reasons for criminal behaviour and about the demands placed on the police. In terms of its contribution to the public good, policing needs to be seen not just in terms of positive accomplishments (solving crimes for instance) but in terms of limiting harm and preventing "bads" (Chapter 2).
Conflict among stakeholders	Rival traditions within the history of criminology show competing explanations of criminal behaviour, ranging from deterministic accounts (crime is largely a product environmental factors such as poverty) to voluntarist accounts (crime is always an individual choice and should be treated or punished accordingly). The extent to which criminals are to blame divides different stakeholders in criminal justice and members of the public. More generally, much police work is about providing contingent solutions to disputes, between parties at multiple levels that are therefore also stakeholders, which almost inevitably means disappointing at least one of those parties (and quite frequently both/all of them).	This suggests that the label "the public good" is something of a misnomer. Instead, there are multiple publics (Chapter 1). The different publics are not just those who have different views on crime and punishment, or victims, but also those who are subject to the criminal justice system. Allied to this is the importance of being seen to be procedurally just to different publics in terms of categories of ethnicity, gender, class and so on, since this underpins legitimacy (Chapter 3).

Dimension	Explanation in the Context of Policing	Implications for Policing and the Public Good
Low confidence in professional authority	While the police remain one of the more trusted institutions in society, police work is not often well understood. Much crime goes unsolved, and demand exceeds capacity, which can mean the police being seen as incompetent by those most affected by such issues. Conversely, many unpopular activities are not illegal and the police have to uphold the rights of some unpopular groups which can lead to their being seen as partial. Historical sources of unfairness and poor community relations, the legacy of injustice and the spatial concentration of crime make policing especially unpopular in hard-pressed, high crime areas, and the police can be detested within some communities.	Policing could be better understood if it were seen as a form of work (Chapters 5 and 6), like other occupations but with distinctive elements – such as a very strong sense of group identity – that can support virtuous action that we might associate with bravery or loyalty, or vicious conduct such as covering up for colleagues (this chapter).
Weak or negative agency myth	This final condition can be seen as a result of the interaction of the previous three factors. The declared mission and purpose of police forces tends to be to protect and serve the public. However, among some parts of the public, or after watershed events such as Orgreave or the Hillsborough inquiry, these words can seem hollow or bitterly ironic. The police may seem more like representatives of the state or oppressors. If different groups doubt the very mission of an agency it makes leading that agency impossible because some will never be satisfied.	Legitimacy is critical to policing (Chapter 3). Policing in a way that contributes to the public good involves giving consideration to different publics. These may doubt the espoused mission of the police as being to serve and protect (see Sharp and Atherton, 2007). Another complexity is some people appear to believe the police are potentially omnipotent. For some, all problems relating to crime could be solved if only there were "more police" – and their default response is to call for more police and greater police powers.

focus – it extends more broadly to other stakeholders. The image, purpose and character of a public agency also depend on public perceptions, a political context, stakeholders such as the media, and contextual features, that can change over time. The impossible jobs framework complements the idea of street-level bureaucracy, but suggests we need to consider the fuller social and historical context of a public agency, as well as consider the dilemmas of the individual public servant, and the client (in the impossible jobs framework "client" is used broadly to refer to the users of an agency's services, or the targets of its attention).

Using these criteria, impossible jobs could be characterized as common in public management (Dobel, 1992). Indeed, though their original focus was the heads of public agencies, the impossible jobs framework has since been applied widely to describe entire contexts and activities – drug counselling, mental healthcare provision, foster care, correction, administering welfare, social work, sexual health, and policing (Frederickson and LaPorte, 2002; Jobes, 2003; Rosenthal and Kousmin, 1997; Vinzant and Crothers, 1996). Partly because of its popularity, "impossible job" has become more a kind of shorthand and less of an analytical framework – applied so widely it has become overgeneralized (Maranto and Wolf, 2012). This is not just because "impossible" is a catchy tagline or slogan, it is because it may be an understatement to describe only some, agency-head level, jobs as impossible. "All public management jobs are in some sense impossible" (Dobel, 1992: 146). To test Hargrove and Glidewell's (1990) ideas, we applied their framework to consider a context we viewed as especially challenging – riot policing. Mindful of problems with single case analyses (Konisky and Reenock, 2012), which characterizes much of the literature on law-enforcement (Nicholson-Crotty and O'Toole, 2004), we use data gathered from multiple sources and sites.

Policing "riots"

In Chapter 6 we described how the main data sources used to look at the training of police for public disorder were interviews. As well as interview research we carried out:

- documentary analysis: videos and leaflets; conceptual models specific to the forces we observed, and from the Association of Chief Police Officers (ACPO) (models of conflict management, command structures, strategic principles and tactical considerations); national policies from ACPO; and scenario-specific materials such as scripts); televised, transcribed debate in Parliament when Members of Parliament (MPs) were called to debate the riots (approximately 70,000 words); Select Committee testimony from police officers, witnesses and stakeholders between September and November 2011 (approximately 160,000 words); the government's response (Great Britain, 2012), the report by the Metropolitan Police (2012) *4 Days in August*, and other relevant reports (*The Guardian*, 2012; Lewis et al., 2011; Ministry of Justice, 2011, 2012);

- observations: four, large-scale scenarios that simulated progressively more volatile situations, culminating in riot; publicly available footage of training at the relevant forces; senior officers' pre-scenario briefings and post-scenario debriefings (eight in total); observations of a specialist public order training unit dealing with a variety of scenarios relating to "lock-ons" (arm tubes, padlocks, chains, obstructions).

As discussed in Chapter 6, in all interviews we asked "What was your most memorable public order incident?" to tap into the salience and specificity of critical incidents (Flanagan, 1954). Interviewees referred to incidents in the August disorder and other memorable incidents. In analysis we looked across data sources for commonality and overlap to identify recurring themes and to support triangulation (Nesbit et al., 2011). We also looked within each data source for features of accounts or scenarios that were unique and different with a focus on "privileging the individual voice" (Borins, 2012: 168; see also Dodge, Ospina and Foldy, 2005; Maynard-Moody and Musheno, 2000; Ospina and Dodge, 2005). This was important since we found consistent support for a context-sensitive perspective on virtue – each public order incident had its own unique complexities.

The August riots

On 6 August, protest following the London Metropolitan police's fatal shooting of Mark Duggan, a black resident of Tottenham, led to a riot (see also Great Britain, 2012; Dodd and Davies, 2011; *The Guardian*, 2012; Hope, 2012). Mr David Lammy, MP for Tottenham, spoke movingly to Parliament about the origins of initial rioting:

> A grieving family and my constituents deserve to know the truth ... Why did the Duggan family first hear about the death of their son not from a police officer, but when the news was broadcast on national television? Why, when they arrived at Tottenham police station to ask questions and to stage a peaceful protest, were they made to wait for five hours before a senior police officer was made available to them? Why, when that peaceful protest was hijacked by violent elements, were a few skirmishes allowed to become a full-scale riot, with far-reaching consequences?

Events at Tottenham were a trigger for large-scale rioting across many English cities between 6 and 9 August (Waddington, 2012). The scale of this was remarkable – over the next year over 3,000 people were prosecuted for related offences (Ministry of Justice, 2012). Unlike the original protests about Mark Duggan, many rioters had no clear goal, and often operated in small, widely dispersed groups with varying motives and actions. Alongside organized criminal gangs, other groups and individuals carried out vandalism, arson, indiscriminate, opportunistic or targeted looting, or attacked police officers. In parliamentary debate on the 11th, Prime

Minister David Cameron asserted Mark Duggan's death had been "used as an excuse by opportunist thugs in gangs, first in Tottenham itself, then across London and in other cities". In response, the Opposition (minority) Leader Ed Milliband stated, "[w]e need a sustained effort to tackle the gangs in our cities – something we knew about before these riots". Politicians in badly affected areas described opportunist and gang-related criminality, "opportunistic looting" (Ms Cooper, MP for Normanton, Pontefract and Castleford), "deliberate, organized, violent criminality" (Ms Blears, MP for Salford), "mindless idiots who capitalized on an opportunity to nick [steal] some trainers [shoes] or a plasma TV" (Ms Alexander, MP for Lewisham East), "organized criminality that trashed the centre of Manchester" (Mr Lloyd, MP for Manchester Central).

During the riots, gangs suspended territorial postcode (zip code) rivalries, calling a temporary truce to exploit the chaos. However, later large-scale analysis concluded, gang involvement in disorder was "significantly overstated" (Lewis et al., 2011: 4). A special issue of the criminology journal, *Criminal Justice Matters* (Hope, 2012), explicitly challenged Prime Minister Cameron's account of the riots as "criminality, pure and simple". Instead, contributors pointed to comparable "flashpoint" dynamics in previous riots (Waddington, 2012), to "poverty and deprivation, chronic youth unemployment" (Jefferson, 2012), and a "carnivalesque" style of protest (Spalek, Isakjee and Davies, 2012). Hope (2012: 3) drew parallels with Johnson and Farrell's (1992) study of the L.A. riots:

> civil unrest in L.A. called for the deployment of a much greater number of emergency personnel and exacted a much heavier toll; a wider range of different ethnic and social groups participated, affecting many more communities and places than previously; the destruction and losses appeared to be more systematic and targeted; and the rioting spread out beyond the areas that had experienced it before.

Later work has reached equally discordant findings. Having described our focal case, we present our findings using Hargrove and Glidewell's framework, taking each dimension in turn and combining analysis of the August riots alongside other informative incidents.

The client base

A key theme in the August riots was that use of technology unexpectedly and radically altered the police's client base: spreading criminality in real time through "copycatting". One experienced public order commander described rapid transfer of information as a key characteristic of the riots: "the speed [it] flashed around the country into people's living rooms and on their handhelds". As well as being replicated across London, events spread north. A front-line specialist public order officer described his experience in Leicester (100 miles away):

we'd seen on television what was going on ... we expected that we would get similar, it started off just as pockets of small disorder with kids mainly running around on their bikes, balaclavas on, smashing windows, shops, and then it progressed into them looting shops and throwing bricks, bottles at police.

Justin, a front-line police officer in Birmingham during the disorder, said, "I know people were surprised at how quickly it spread around London and copycatted into Birmingham and up North." This matched Select Committee testimony. Acting Commissioner Tim Godwin, Metropolitan Police, stated, "[w]e were not expecting that level and spread, that replication, that copycatting of sheer criminality". A former gang member, Nathan Chin, testified, "Everyone was copycatting Tottenham".

Remote coordination and contemporary instant messaging technology amplified this copycatting. The client base mushroomed. Other aspects of the riots illustrated more familiar challenges for practice – when should the police intervene, and how should they intervene? These are not just problems for commanders. John described how judgement is necessary even in the chaos of riot, because it is difficult to assess client legitimacy: "when you wave your arm ... there are sometimes 10 people in that space doing different things ... you've got various options, you can use force to protect others [or] property, or you could arrest [or] retreat, or you could liaise with your colleague, [or] you can talk to them".

There is an additional complication for Hargrove and Glidewell's framework. Riot police, by their attributions and actions (such as decision to detain or arrest), can change the legitimacy of the client base – either individuals or groups – in real time. Individual arrests lead to members of the public being classified as illegitimate in some way and such actions can also influence the behaviour of others in a crowd if they are seen as provocation. Alternatively, crowd behaviour as a whole can change quite quickly so that an event itself becomes seen as one that is illegitimate – moving from protest to disorder. The Metropolitan Police had to defend themselves against criticisms for not intervening more forcefully in events at Tottenham, and many suggested this incited further disorder. Referring to subsequent riots, Ms James (MP for Stourbridge) described how "we heard a lot about the stand-and-observe order that was apparently given to the police in particular circumstances. We all agree that that was terrible". Although Acting Commissioner Tim Godwin conceded in Select Committee testimony that failure to intervene had been problematic, our interviewees indicated perceptions of "stand-and-observe" were sometimes mistaken. At times, police lines were cordons protecting strategically important facilities. Joe described his second night in Birmingham, "stood on a cordon for probably about six hours ... just protecting one road which led directly to ... the two main police control rooms":

it's frustrating to the police on the ground because you can hear on the radio everything that's going on and that certain areas are under attack, but those areas aren't really of that much strategic importance ... so a shop somewhere a couple of miles away isn't as important as protecting the central, like, controlling hub of the whole of the city ... if [the command center] went down, which was where everything was being controlled from, then obviously it would have been a lot worse.

While perceived inaction may be problematic, arrests and the use of force can have a dramatic effect on crowds; one finding was that even changes into protective clothing could change crowd behaviour. One commander commented, "as soon as we put on the NATO helmets, the bricks start flying" – suggesting additional protective clothing somehow gave permission to protesters to use greater force. Two front-line officers independently supported this point: "if we change into the helmets people will start, they'll raise their level of aggression to match us," and, "if people think that they can actually injure the police, maybe they'll be less likely to [throw bricks]."

Perhaps the distinctive aspect to the client base for police during mass disorder is that they are confronted with publics whose membership, goals, legitimacy and power, can all change rapidly. Jake, a former public order trainer, described how off-the-shelf approaches were inappropriate in August because one thing that took the police by surprise was the changed profile of offenders:

> if you look at the August riots, yes they would have fitted into our disorder model ... but the profile of the offenders changed. The NEET [Not in Employment Education or Training] label would fit a lot of them but not all of them, there was a student-teacher, there was a social worker or a youth worker.

More generally, any crowd may appear unitary and homogeneous, but contain considerable heterogeneity (Stott and Reicher, 1998), for instance in relation to pursuing different agendas. At Tottenham this seemed to be the case with the initial protest by the Duggan family being "hijacked" (Mr Lammy, MP for Tottenham). Another officer described his most memorable experience policing a UAF counter-demonstration (Unite Against Fascism, an anti-fascist pressure group) that was "hijacked" by more militant protesters: "we were walking round in a snake [a marching cordon], I was having quite a pleasant conversation [with] a group of professionals", when violence erupted unexpectedly: "it just changed within five minutes to the point that there was a horse charge" (mounted officers were called on and used to disperse the crowd).

Conflict among stakeholders

The job of riot policing becomes impossible not just because the client base of rioters is seen as unpopular or illegitimate among a wider public, but because more immediate stakeholders (residents, business owners, politicians, "community leaders") have conflicting views about the nature of the problem confronting police, about its causes, and about what would constitute a satisfactory solution. In his opening statement on the riots, the Prime Minister identified how stakeholder conflict made riot policing impossible, "the police are damned if they do and damned if they don't. Nowhere is that truer than in public order policing." He continued, "I want to be clear that, as long as officers act within reason and the law, this Home Secretary will never damn the police if they do." Of course though, at all levels, the problem is precisely that what constitutes "within reason" partly depends on judgement, partly on perspective, and partly on the context.

An MP from Prime Minister Cameron's own party, Nadine Dorries, criticized the lack of robust intervention: "[i]f these riots had broken out in any city or town in Australia or America, the police would have had at their instant disposal water cannon, plastic bullets and tear gas". These sentiments were not uncommon, but command officers rejected these tactical options at the time, and later discounted them in testimony as excessive or inappropriate. One reason was that in August they were dealing with small, highly mobile, remotely coordinated groups, rather than static crowd "stand-offs".

A public order trainer explained how expectations about a traditional British way of policing made interaction between crowds and use of force complex. This British model "places a high value on tolerance and winning the consent of the public" (Her Majesty's Chief Inspectorate of Constabulary, 2009: 5). He explained:

> you have this paradoxical situation where [we] aspire to be a tolerant society and everybody has their freedoms and the police must therefore have limited power, but that limited power does tend to lead to these quite static long drawn-out demonstrations or protests that become unlawful.

A Bronze commander echoed this when discussing concerns that had followed the policing of a G20 summit protest in London two years before the August riots: "the British model of policing still holds good, but in terms of public order it's creaking just a little bit and there were massive questions about our use of force". Effective policing under this "British model" requires cooperation from the public. This may be hardest to secure in the neighbourhoods that need it most, whether this is a result of contemporary poverty or historically poor relations between some communities and the police. In relation to poverty, when asked about the August riots, Chief Constable Fahy of Greater Manchester testified, "we deal with a very challenging area. There are very high levels of deprivation … you can only do the enforcement if you are getting the information and the support from local people through your long-term relationship and your long-term style of policing."

Fahy's comments underline the importance of understanding policing as an activity over time. If we consider the origins of the 2011 riots, Tottenham itself has a very troubled history of minority and police relations. But the riots following Mark Duggan's death were not characterized by race, either in Tottenham or elsewhere in the country. Gavin Barwell MP for Croydon Central – South London – identified, "a tiny minority" of "wreckers" who "came from a wide range of ethnic backgrounds" (his description was significant since on news media, the emblematic, recurring image of the riots was a burning furniture store in an iconic location of Croydon). Mr Umunna, MP for Streatham, another London borough with a history of police and minority tension, said, "to racialize this issue is gravely wrong and does our country a great misservice". Chief Constable Chris Sims of West Midlands Police described them as "more about greed than anger". Front-line officers we spoke to were sceptical the activity they personally policed was in any way linked to race: "people can say that it was because of Mark Duggan being shot in London, but realistically it wasn't, it was just burglary, large-scale burglary is all it was" and, "there was no political motivation … it was pure, simple looting … it wasn't for rioting, it was stealing stuff".

Focusing on stakeholder conflict helped us to identify another difference between police working in conditions of public disorder and "street-level bureaucrats". As well as working with crowds, the police often work in space that is ostensibly public, but that has become owned in some way – as tribal and territorial (Beaumont and Nicholls, 2007; Beckett and Herbert, 2010; Wahlström, 2010). Societies as a whole can also be divided (Ellison and Smyth, 2000; Weitzer, 1995). In discussions of other public order incidents, such as counter-demonstrations, officers described having to protect the rights of highly divisive groups in public spaces – the most frequent cases where this was an issue concerned the policing of football. While football hooliganism is no longer the problem it once was, fierce rivalries between some clubs remain. Jake described his most memorable experience at a football match between Leeds and Manchester United. Leeds fans knew that the away buses picked up fans from a particular point and waited there after the game. Some buses were late and Jake and his colleagues had to "escort the group of Man Utd fans through probably 10,000 Leeds fans, through a very narrow kind of passageway … it all got confused and actually turned into quite a lot of disorder". The intense rivalry and, for some, hatred between Manchester United and Leeds fans made this an impossible situation because there was no solution where all parties would leave satisfied. The best outcome was minimizing harm and of avoiding "bads". Unlike temporary disputes, supporting a team is a life-long expression of identity – rooted in love of one's own team and camaraderie with supporters but also understood in terms of past grievances, defeats and victories, legends and sagas (it is outside our scope but virtue ethics could offer a way of understanding the life of a fan, for instance the idea that a "real fan" would disavow violence). Being a fan means membership of this in-group will never end until death. Part of understanding in-group identity is defining oneself in contrast to out-groups. Though only a minority of fans are hooligans, conflict among stakeholders is almost hard-wired and – even though a moment's thought reveals this is a strange situation – it is seen as normal that we expect the police regularly to "referee" this. At times, policing tactics potentially contribute to disorder by being injudicious or heavy-handed and exaggerating sources of conflict (Stott, Adang, Livingstone and Schreiber, 2008).

Agency myth

Turning to August's "BlackBerry riots" (Halliday, 2011), the unusual and signal feature of these is they spread via closed network instant messaging. Assistant Chief Constable of West Midlands Police, Sharon Rowe, described the impact of this technology: "[w]e are into a totally new game now". Michael, who policed events in London, emphasized the effects of both mainstream media and information sharing through networks: "it's almost instant, and they've definitely had a feeder impact into why it erupted elsewhere". In Hargrove and Glidewell's terms, technology fuelled a remarkable and rapid weakening of the agency myth – the idea of the police as powerful and in control of the streets. Acting Commissioner Godwin, reflecting on a key lesson from August, concluded, "the most important thing is that people are not seen to get away with it".

But, in August 2011, tens of thousands of people across England did believe they could "get away with it" and that because police were powerless in the face of mass disorder, offences like looting, vandalism and arson would go unpunished. Remote coordination via instant messaging meant "rioters" were highly mobile and could disperse and regroup very quickly, switching targets in real time – completely unlike the static protests practised in the public order training we witnessed. The scale of the riots posed other problems for standard operating procedures (SOPs), rendering some conventional public order tactics useless. Asked whether the police should have deployed water cannon or rubber bullets, Chief Constable Fahy of Greater Manchester Police said:

> It was a very fluid situation, fast moving situation. Water cannon have a very short period of time that they can be used, but the fact is the mob would have just run away from them ... Rubber bullets, again the whole thing was too fast moving.

Our interviewees at command and front line confirmed this: "water cannon is really a dispersal tool" (Commander), "systems that we use aren't designed to cope with that scale of disorder" (front-line officer).

Another relevant agency myth is the police are impartial in important ways – they do not favour any race, they serve all the public, and are apolitical. But protest after Mark Duggan's shooting showed some believed police racial impartiality was a myth. Tottenham has experienced police and minority tension for many years, with one watershed moment in British policing coming in 1985, after the murder of Constable Keith Blakelock during a riot at Broadwater Farm – a high-density social housing complex. It was from Broadwater Farm that protesters at Duggan's death began their march, at the very origin of the riots (Waddington, 2012). This shaped the way officers policing in this environment thought about their job. One involved in policing the very earliest stages of the riots explained how travelling to events made him and his colleagues extremely anxious:

of course Tottenham's got history, you know, with Keith Blakelock, so we knew we were [being driven] to something that had got a historical context and a certain dynamic to it, we all knew about Duggan beforehand, and because it was still coming over the TV, the news channels on our iPhones, we knew the moment we got there, we were going to get committed.

Another officer, Martin, with four years' experience of policing in a Midlands city told us, "in my day-to-day job in the police … some people are still convinced, that the police is a racist organization [but] it goes to great strides, more than any other organization, to be as diverse as possible". We found it interesting Martin described the problem as some being "still convinced", which seemingly concedes this was partially true of police in the past. This is not something that we can speak to with our data, but it indirectly highlights a complexity in public order – that could not be replicated in training – which is police need to deal with the legacy of previous police practice, or perceptions of practice, and a collective memory of past grievances (Stott et al., 2015). As the officer quoted above indicated, referring to an event almost 30 years earlier, "Tottenham's got history" and "a certain dynamic." The recognition that situations can have "history" is at the heart of virtue ethics.

Several officers went further, and explained that the agency myth of the police as politically impartial was frequently undermined and that they were seen collectively as representatives of the state, rather than servants of the public. Sometimes police presence or practice transformed and united otherwise heterogeneous elements of the crowd, as Jason a commander explained: "people turn up to a protest with very different motives … forget their original protest and unite against the police … we become the embodiment of the government in the eyes of the protesters". Offering a much longer, historical view, Andrew recalled policing the intensely political miner's strike (1984/5). He experienced how some striking miners would "see me as the political engine of Maggie Thatcher … just a uniform, representative of [the state] – that was hard and nasty".

Protective riot clothing can especially weaken the agency myth of the police as public servants because it makes officers more anonymous. Over and above wearing uniforms, it can mean people perceive the police as state representatives rather than public servants. A commander acknowledged this; when wearing riot gear, "you're presenting yourself as a target, you are more anonymous, you're dehumanized". A consequence is that this also makes officers less mobile: one explained, "it's about a stone of extra kit once you've put it all on and then you carry the shield". This weakens the agency myth in another basic way: an officer in riot gear is less able and less likely to catch someone by chasing them.

Confidence in professional authority

Just one month before the riots, the Metropolitan Commissioner Sir Paul Stephenson, and an Assistant Commissioner, John Yates, resigned in the wake of the phone-hacking scandal at the *News of the World* newspaper (Longstaff, 2011). Stephenson's predecessor, Sir Ian Blair, had also resigned following the election of the London Mayor Boris Johnson, who publicly called for him to step down, and after what was called a "sustained period of media annihilation" (Greer and MacLaughlin, 2011: 23). The mayor was asked about this by the Chair of the Select Committee, Keith Vaz, MP:

> To paraphrase Oscar Wilde, to lose one Commissioner was a misfortune but to lose both looks like carelessness. What is this problem about retaining Commissioners at the Met [Metropolitan police]?

Though the Mayoral role is new, political and media pressure, and challenges to professional authority are not, certainly when it comes to policing London. Sir Robert Mark (1972–1977) resigned after publicly disagreeing with the Home Secretary Roy Jenkins, and criticizing legislation he felt made senior officers more responsible to political appointees (Hobbs, 2010). His successor Sir David McNee (1977–1982) faced similar challenges following large-scale rioting at Brixton (London), where a resulting inquiry criticized police tactics. He was later asked to resign by the Home Secretary when an intruder broke into Buckingham Palace and came into the Queen's room (he refused). McNee's successor, Commissioner Kenneth Newman (1982–1987), though widely acknowledged as a public order specialist, was heavily criticized for the way he handled the Broadwater Farm riot and was said by the founder of *Policing*, the magazine of the Police Federation to have been "fortunate not to face a public inquiry" (Judge, 2007: 29).

In the midst of the 2011 riots both the Home Secretary, Ms Teresa May, and Prime Minister Cameron publicly undermined police authority with comments that were rejected by Sir Hugh Orde, the Chair of the Association of Chief Police Officers (ACPO). Ms May announced she had ordered all Chief Constables to cancel police leave; Orde stated the Home Secretary "had no power whatsoever" to do so (Jones, 2012: 545). At one stage (before the parliamentary debate) Prime Minister Cameron suggested using water cannon and plastic baton rounds which Orde rejected as "the wrong tactic, in the wrong circumstances" cautioning, "excessive force will destroy our model of policing in the long term" (Hoggett and Stott, 2012: 174).

Public confidence in police authority vanished on the mainstream media as rioters were shown seemingly acting without sanction. Acting Commissioner Godwin explained: "we saw images of looting, which apparently was being untackled … that encouraged a few more to look at the opportunity for smash and grab activity". Joe, a comparatively inexperienced front-line officer, reported surprise at one instance where professional authority evaporated during the riots. He saw a crowd of young people in a Birmingham shopping centre [mall] ignore the instructions of a senior officer: "the inspector ordered them to clear the centre, no-one really moved, no-one cared, they just sat there watching". A commander, Andrew, told us how criminality resulted from a lack of police authority: "the next day wasn't about Mark Duggan in my view it was about, 'Blimey you know if we put the police at full stretch we can [run] round the corner and then nick everything from Currys'" (a consumer electronics retailer).

The scale and spread of the riots revealed the police were hopelessly outnumbered at times. A member of the public, Lynn Radose, told a Select Committee what happened when her neighbours reported a fire in an apartment building: "the fire service told them they can't get there because there's no police – there weren't any police anywhere, I cannot stress that enough for you". Inspector Bethel (in the Metropolitan Police report *4 Days in August*) identified an incident where "officers were not only the front line, they were the last line" (2012: 42). One commander we interviewed, described having to "save life" as the most basic of protocols, "preservation of life, prevention & detection of crime, preserving Queen's peace … your three core things".

One interesting aspect to police authority is that responsibility for decision-making applies from the front line up, even in the midst of the seeming chaos of a riot. An assumption we had prior to the research was that riot situations lead to pure command and control leadership, but there were several reasons pure command and control was not realized. One was that British police are generalists – in contrast to most European countries or more decentralized models of policing. One commander explained: "We don't have a standing army of public order trained police officers, we don't have a third force in this country like the French … Spanish." Another drew a contrast with the decentralization and variety of US police forces, "in one location in Virginia for example, if you're on the university campus, there are four Police services that might come to your assistance depending on the type of the offence".

Locating authority at the front line is necessary so that individual officers remain responsible for their actions. Charles, a public order trainer, explained:

> you can be ordered to … run down the road with a shield, but the decision whether you lock that individual up … rests with you … if you've got somebody stood in front of you with a brick and they're just about to throw it … I don't think there's much of a choice [but] it's you who has got to stand in the witness box and justify why you arrested, hit them, sprayed them [with gas], used any sort of force.

However, at the front line, chaos and noise compromises communication. Anthony, a Bronze commander, explained how the nature of leadership changed during riot situations:

> Leadership becomes very tactile, words of command aren't necessarily given it's more pushes and shoves, the noise, the helmets, you have to be very, very hands-on. You have to be quite autocratic [but] I'd hate to give an order and it be followed blindly. The opportunity to arrest is always there.

This is significant because the decision to arrest changes the legitimacy of a client and it can also be that an arrest will incite a crowd: a trigger (Adang, 2011) undermining authority and, in a public order situation, weakening the agency myth of the police as impartial. An added difficulty in terms of police practice and standard operating procedures (SOPs) (in England) is that arrests result in two officers being taken off the front line, so officers are conscious they may be putting colleagues at more risk. Conversely, as the events of August 2011 showed, not to arrest can be problematic if perpetrators ignore the authority of officers and are seen to be "getting away with it" (Tim Godwin, Acting Commissioner).

Front-line officers we interviewed were very conscious of how their individual practice could quickly change crowd perceptions of police authority. They were also very aware that police practice could affect wider public perceptions through other media. John, a public order trainer described a London embassy protest:

> At the very front of the crowd ... I was shocked at how many photographers, in quotes [sic], there were. An extremely high number ... who were not journalists were presumably instructed in the process. That was very hard to manage, to identify how to deal with them always, constantly making decisions about what you have to do next.

The Police Executive Research Forum has identified parallel issues in the US, in describing public perceptions of the use of force, complexities in crowd composition, the effects of arrest and role of the media, alongside individual officer discretion (Narr et al., 2006).

Implications

A limitation of the impossible job label, a "semantic trap" Hargrove and Glidewell themselves identify, is it lends itself to absolute categories. Static, overgeneralized frameworks represent a gap in theoretical understanding (Maranto and Wolf, 2012). We suggest riot policing tests the limits of Hargrove and Glidewell's framework, and this leads us to identify three theoretical extensions – (i) a differentiation between impossible jobs and impossible tasks, (ii) a link between street-level bureaucrats and impossible jobs, (iii) a need to revisit the assumption of a stable or unitary client base.

Impossible jobs and impossible tasks

Though Hargrove and Glidewell use the terms synonymously (1990: ix), a helpful distinction can be drawn between jobs and tasks. Any "job", such as police officer, provides a source of meaning and sense of self; as well as being an expression of traditions, history and kinds of jurisdiction (Glaeser, 2000). A job is something we understand within a common set of social categories and kinds of membership. Sennett traces the etymology of job to something carried around – indicating there is something to jobs that coheres and transcends particular situations (Sennett, 1998). Whereas jobs are in these senses holistic, tasks can be thought of as the component parts of a job.

Not all policing *tasks* are inherently impossible. At the senior management level, though, any street-level policing task, once aggregated, can translate into an "impossible job". This applies whether one considers how officers deal with burglary, drugs, criminal damage, dangerous driving or a host of other issues. Different stakeholders will always have competing ideas about how resources should be spent, about what the police should prioritize, about what the police are responsible for, and how the police should discharge that responsibility. An interesting feature of the 2011 riots was that it made "impossibility" readily apparent to street-level officers. Policing riots is only one of the tasks they perform, it is one seldom carried out, and it was, here, very serious: "the riots are unique in that the majority of public order isn't about the riots" (Albert, Public Order Commander); "[August was] as close to, you know, a fully blown riot shall we say as I've ever done in my 16 years in the job" (Michael, front-line officer). Even for the most highly trained public order police, their job rarely involves such tasks because riots are rare and extreme events. However, when they do occur, policing riots can be "impossible tasks" at the front line. The difference between impossible and possible tasks becomes clearer if we contrast the training with the reality.

During observation and interviews relating to public order training, officers drew sharp distinctions between training and real life or the field; "public order is so unpredictable that it's very rare that every incident or evolution of an incident, you are prepared for" (John, Bronze-level commander). Understandably, the challenge of recreating these scenarios was a concern for public order trainers. Jake had worked for seven years as a trainer and described the challenge as being to develop an "unrealistic capability to get reality into a training scenario". In other words, trainers were expected as a matter of routine to deliver training that reflected the fidelity of public order scenarios, but within the typical constraints of a large bureaucracy, as he described it, "in controlled environments that have to be safe".

As we saw during observation of training, there is an almost paradoxical need for the riot, as an event, to be repeatable – so officers respond consistently across different forces, interpret the law in the same way, and achieve comparable levels of expertise to inform deployment. Above and beyond shared knowledge of SOPs, they also need to be able to cope with danger and risk. Training enables officers to cope with recurrent features of riots that involve risk – "repertoires of contention" (Tilly, 2003), such as "brickwork" (defending oneself against a barrage of bricks), or coping with petrol bombs. We describe these features of their training as coping with a possible – albeit difficult – task. But certain aspects to riots, which did not seem to be reproducible in training, seemed to be impossible at the front line.

In the August riots there were some particularly striking problems, owing to the sheer scale of rioting, its dispersal, opportunism both in looting and in targeting of the police, real time remote coordination through instant messaging technology, and the role of the mainstream media and political class in creating pressures on police. Comparing notes on training exercises with observation of riot footage in August 2011, we could see the sheer scale of disorder meant many police tactics could not be deployed, for instance: formation of cordons, alignment of shields to protect against a barrage, crowd containment tactics, deployment of specialist arrest teams. These tactics were learned doing difficult, but possible tasks, but they did not work when confronted with the impossible – when the client base had grown exponentially, there was no confidence in professional authority, and the agency myth had evaporated.

The distinction between difficult and impossible tasks was well underlined in one comment from Arthur, a Bronze commander, describing specialist public order training:

> [it] is hard and … arduous, it's you know, two, three days long, very, very physical, very tiring, very demanding going into large disused hospitals, disused hotels where we have our trainers that would dress up … all padded … and, you know, they've got baseball bats and it's not uncommon to chuck a fridge down the stairs when you're on your way out.

Arthur was describing training at a higher intensity than he was ever likely to face, but explained, "The danger and the level of fear and anxiety in real life is greater because it's not training." A former trainer, Adam, described this saying:

> At the back of their mind everybody has still got that safety net that you can blow the whistle and stop it, you can't do that with reality … down an alleyway or outside a club or at a fight or what not, no-one can blow a whistle and say, "Checkmate" [shouted to indicate an exercise was finished].

A feature of some rioting, which cannot be recreated, is the collective will and force of a highly hostile crowd. It would not be correct to say such crowds do not play by any rules, because they can act in ways that are coordinated and purposeful, but they certainly have different rules. Andrew described a scene he was confronted with during the August riots, where, overnight, people had divided a street by dragging a huge plastic chute from a building site across it. They filled this with debris and set fire to it:

> To my amazement I then saw little teams of rioters coming round from the side street of Aldi [a supermarket] pushing shopping trolleys loaded with bricks and then you had people taking it in turns to lob [throw] bricks at us … and I thought "it doesn't take long does it." You know that people that have just been really aggressive and not coordinated a few hours ago, to actually … they are now organized and they have got a logistic train and are turning up and they've got people who can only throw bricks until exhausted and they were just taking it in turns.

As we observed, defending oneself from missiles is a common feature of public order training, and a routinizable task, which the police can train for, but they cannot recreate the kind of opposition that comes from a sustained, coordinated and organized force such as this. These "rioters" transformed this part of London, flagrantly defying an agency myth of the police as in control or as authority figures. They raided a building site to set up a supply chain of ammunition, worked in teams, and rested in shifts with no thought of health and safety, or budget, or an eye on when the exercise has to finish.

Impossible jobs and street-level bureaucrats

Riot policing provides an opportunity to clarify the relationship between the conceptual categories of impossible jobs and street-level bureaucrats. Hargrove and Glidewell's agency chief is, by definition, not at street-level. As we see it, part of the logic informing Hargrove and Glidewell's framework is that there is a kind of multiplier effect as you move up the chain of command. Street-level bureaucrats' jobs require discretion and the need to grapple with problems that are not solvable, so in the Lipskyian sense they are sometimes inexorably dilemmatic. This difficulty is amplified for the heads of agencies because they become responsible for the aggregation of these street-level dilemmas and need to try to manage public impressions of the agency myth, cope with stakeholders with conflicting goals and operate in a highly charged political context. However, in contemporary literature, impossible job is now used more widely and so we think there are fruitful connections to be made between impossible jobs and street-level bureaucracy.

A key finding here is that in the very rare context of riots the four dimensions of impossibility are considerations all the way through the command chain. It can be impossible at the front line to deal with a crowd that suddenly discovers itself to be powerful by virtue of numbers and common purpose (Reicher, 2011). This might have parallels in the impossible task a police commander faces trying to establish dialogue in an area with a history of poor police–community relations (Holgersson and Knutsson, 2011; Stott, 2011). Riot police deal with crowds whose behaviour can change their legitimacy in real time and who often have heterogeneous interests. This is unlike the dilemmas of the street-level bureaucrat, who grapples with the complexity of meshing the individual case onto bureaucratic policy and whose, "determinations are focused entirely on the individual" (Lipsky, 2010: 8).

Front-line police who confront riots may be part of a small sub-category of public servants who are *both* "street-level bureaucrats" and have to do the "impossible". This is partly because individual police officers have unique powers in comparison with other street-level bureaucrats – the powers to arrest and detain, and the right to use force (Waddington, 1999). It is partly because they deal with crowds. Also, and unlike most other "street-level" bureaucrats (Lipsky, 2010), riot police work outside, in public spaces, in full view of the media or (now) anyone with a mobile phone. For some, police officers also represent a common enemy in a way that other street-level bureaucrats do not. How effectively, or ineffectively, they carry out riot policing affects crowd behaviour in real time, intensifying conflict and potentially pushing people into actions that are illegitimate if protest escalates into disorder or worse. Accordingly, just as command-level decisions can, policing practice at the front line in a riot can directly affect each of – client legitimacy, the extent of conflict among stakeholders, and perceptions of the agency myth and of professional authority.

The client base can be volatile

Another important implication for the impossible jobs framework is that the client base of riot police can be highly volatile. Police action or inaction can cause elements within the crowd to change allegiances and switch focus, or to become violent; or it can influence a much wider public through the media and messaging. Sometimes inaction emboldens would be rioters, on other occasions, any kind of escalation or intervention such as containment or an arrest can be inflammatory.

Volatility in the client base is one reason front-line riot policing can be impossible, not only because the client base itself is not static, but because changes to it influence each of the other criteria (leader authority, agency myth, stakeholder conflict). The August riots demonstrated this strikingly and in ways that have implications for understanding contemporary society, as the latest technology facilitated "copycatting".

As well as volatility in the client base, in public order policing there can be highly organized and trenchant forms of opposition. This brings additional complexity, in that some groups use public order situations as a platform to continue a campaign against the police, whom they see as representative of the state, or because they have pre-existing grievances, or are seeking media exposure. Mark, a police officer for over 20 years, distinguished between spontaneous public order situations and those involving highly organized elements.

> It's fine in my mind where it is lawful protest, where it starts to go at the edges and the splinter groups and what have you join in and then the mark gets overstepped into what might be spontaneous disorder [but] you've got people who're almost trained in it like we are {laughs} and we have seen increasing evidence of people you know almost full-time anarchists who know quite a lot about our tactics and they've got their own ... professional anarchists eventually turn up and start anchoring themselves or chaining themselves to trees and going up you know doing all these fairly professional organized things in order to present obstacles to the police.

Mark accepts, pragmatically, that lawful protest can spill over – spontaneous disorder was "fine" as in to be expected. But his tone was one of bemusement when it came to those who were "professional" and apparently solely motivated by antagonizing the police. A further complexity is that some parts of these crowds continue to act lawfully, while others break the law. In these situations, what makes policing at the front-line impossible is that there is no one thing that is "the client base", because one cannot distinguish easily between lawful and unlawful, even though members of a crowd may be in extremely close spatial and temporal proximity to one another, and to police officers.

Conclusion

The "impossible jobs" framework (client illegitimacy, conflict among stakeholders, low confidence in authority, and weak agency) remains useful, but in some cases it can understate impossibility. More specifically, impossibility need not be restricted to the most senior level, because in policing mass disorder these criteria are intertwined and central to understanding decisions at the front line. This has implications for other settings where front-line decisions directly affect client legitimacy, such as in mental health (see Henderson, 2013 for an example relating to emergency medical services). It may be too, that without considering external clients or an end public, the job of middle-managers in policing becomes "impossible" where they have to reconcile conflicting stakeholders who are internal customers – senior management from above and the front line from below.

Second, analysis of training shows differences between tasks that are difficult but possible (defending against petrol bombs), and tasks that are impossible (dealing with a crowd with access to better, or at least more effective, technology than the police, or recreating the social dynamics of a riot). There is a practical implication here for police agencies as bureaucracies. Police agencies and trainers may be more effective if they have greater clarity about which tasks are possible (and routinizable) and which are impossible (and non-routinizable). With routinizable tasks, habit (as described in Chapter 6) may support the cultivation of virtue. However, if tasks cannot be routinized it may be a mistake to assume there are recipes for action. These are tasks where the discretion of offices, used in ways that based on values and appropriate norms, must be allowed to take precedence. Rather than a search for certainty or in looking elsewhere for "what works" (the model of the evidence-based approach we discuss in the following chapter), it may be helpful to emphasize and underline that officers retain discretion based on situated expertise. In other words, the kind of character they are encouraged to develop is one where they recognize they are dealing with uncertainty and have to find a local solution that fits their immediate context. This is a richer expression of individual craft and judgement than "what works".

A third contribution is to show that one challenge in public order policing is the client base can be highly volatile, and this often depends on the decisions commanders and front-line officers take. In riots this can change for entire groups in moments, and in some situations, client legitimacy is interdependent with the agency myth. One lesson from August was that rioting spread (the "illegitimate" client base of rioters grew) precisely because people perceived the police as powerless (when the agency myth that the police were in control vanished). Conversely, where conflict is almost hard-wired into a situation, tactics could incite disorder (see Stott et al., 2008). What might seem like virtues – demonstrating power and potential force, in the hope of heading off confrontation – could instead be interpreted as provocation.

Fourth, a practical implication is to consider how to manage real time interdependencies between client legitimacy, authority and agency myth. This prompts a basic question: what is the best way to deal with unfolding crises? A related, relevant practical implication is to consider the legacy of this 2011 crisis. While the police were confronted with apparently overwhelming odds, ultimately order was restored. This was done without water cannon, tear gas, firearms or deployment of the military – all things which some people called for. Although the police faced criticism for responding too slowly, and although the origins of the riots lay in protest following the killing of Mark Duggan, this may even represent an opportunity to reaffirm the agency myth and differentiating elements of British policing.

Calling a category of jobs impossible could seem like pessimism about the prospects for good governance (Maranto and Wolf, 2012). Alternatively it could lionize police officers since they somehow do "the impossible" (Dobel, 1992). This would be a very shallow and superficial labelling of virtue – just as crass as referring to all nurses as "angels" or all politicians as "liars". It is important to be careful on this issue because, as Nicholson-Crotty and O'Toole (2004) identify, much research in law-enforcement has been anecdotal, based on single cases or managers. This study addresses some of these limitations through fieldwork that combines methods and gathers and analyses different data sources over time. This offers scope to re-examine conceptual frameworks that are our collective theoretical currency in analysing the complexities of public management.

In terms of our wider discussion in this book, this chapter has shown that the character of police, the ways officers "think" and "do" policing, is indeed shaped by training and other formal processes of the organization – but only in part. The "impossible" nature of the job, and some of its constituent tasks, implies, first, that the inevitable space for contingency in policing means the responses of individual officers to the challenges they face must also draw from a wider, or perhaps deeper, perceptual and behavioural tool-kit. If it is to be ethical, this tool-kit must be based not on a formulaic understanding of what to do in particular situation but a more general set of norms and values – a sense of what is the "right thing to do" that is not limited by circumstance. This will be formed, of course, by the factors we discussed in Chapter 4: organizational justice, police cultures and so on.

Second, though, the external pressures placed on police organizations, by the multiple stakeholders concerned with policing operations, means that the character of police is inevitably affected by extra-organizational forces. It is not sufficient to claim that police officers are "made" in and by the police. Rather, their character is formed, at least partially, in the larger crucible of politics, press and public opinion. While we have been at pains in this book to underline that police organizations are in many ways alike to other organizations, this last point may indicate a crucial point of divergence. Police work is unlike many other forms of work precisely because of its social, cultural and political importance, and in particular the various forms of attention focused on police and engendered by their place in society. This may mean that, in contrast to the traditional view of police as a closed institution, the character of police officers, and of the agency as a whole, is particularly susceptible to external pressure.

8
EVIDENCE

To conclude, this chapter applies insights from virtue ethics to critique the concept of evidence-based policing. We identify tensions between virtues and this account of evidence, and also develop some useful directions for future research using stories. Our goal is to move the conversation about policing and "evidence" forward so it is not suffocated by an overly simplistic and reductionist picture of how we learn about the world, or how this learning can inform practice. In doing so, consistent with a virtue perspective, we underline the central role of ethics and situated expertise in policing.

Evidence-based policing

Evidence-based policing is a comparatively recent approach that relies on a familiar account of the status and purpose of social research: that we can learn about the world; and that this learning can and should inform practice. We do not wish to challenge this basic account because we are both sympathetic to it. Neither of us is "against evidence"; appeals to evidence can and should pay a part in influencing policy and practice, although the rhetorical aspects to this process are often overlooked (Greenhalgh and Russell, 2006; Majone, 1989). Instead, what we are interested in doing here is drawing out some tensions between "virtue" and evidence, and in drawing contrasts between "evidence-based" policing and other ways of relating research and practice that use stories or "narrative" (Learmonth, 2006; Learmonth and Harding, 2006; Morrell, 2008). This is important because there is an exclusionary quality to many conversations about research and practice in policing. These tend to assume that evidence-based policing is the one best way to relate research to policing as a practice. Evidence-based policing also involves an antipathy to stories – because the aggregation of knowledge depends on seeing things as the same, whereas what makes stories interesting is that they are different. A more fundamental, critical point we would make is that "evidence-based policing" is itself a story. It is just one way to understand how to generate knowledge and understanding about policing, and it is just one way to link knowledge to practice.

Drawing on the ideas we have developed in relation to virtue helps us to make a more striking departure from the principles associated with "evidence-based" policing because the essence of virtue ethics is that we pay attention to context. Whereas "evidence-based" policing is about "what works", and relies on the assumption that what works "here" is the same as what will work "there", virtue is about the particular complexities of a situation or case. The contribution we want to make by closing with a critique of evidence-based policing is to change the conversation about policing and research so it is not suffocated by an overly simplistic and reductionist vision of what policing "is". In doing so we underline the central role of ethics and judgement in policing.

What is "evidence-based" policing?

Over the past few years, "evidence-based" policing has become overwhelmingly the dominant way in which the relationship between research and practice is described in contemporary policing. The College of Policing provides the following definition of evidence-based policing (EBP), derived from Sherman's (1998) earlier work:

> **BOX 8.1 THE COLLEGE OF POLICING DEFINITION OF EVIDENCE-BASED POLICING**
>
> **In an evidence-based policing approach, police officers and staff create, review and use the best available evidence to inform and challenge policies, practices and decisions.**
>
> As a way of working, it can be supported by collaboration with academics and other partners.
>
> The "best available" evidence will use appropriate research methods and sources for the question being asked. Research should be carefully conducted, peer reviewed and transparent about its methods, limitations, and how its conclusions were reached. The theoretical basis and context of the research should also be made clear. Where there is little or no formal research, other evidence such as professional consensus and peer review, may be regarded as the "best available", if gathered and documented in a careful and transparent way.
>
> Research can be used to:
>
> - develop a better understanding of an issue – by describing the nature, extent and possible causes of a problem or looking at how a change was implemented; or

- assess the effect of a policing intervention – by testing the impact of a new initiative in a specific context or exploring the possible consequences of a change in policing.

Evidence-based policing does not provide definitive answers that officers and staff should apply uncritically. Officers and staff will reflect on their practice, consider how the "best available" evidence applies to their day to day work, and learn from their successes and failures. The approach should mean officers and staff can ask questions, challenge accepted practices and innovate in the public interest.

Available at: http://whatworks.college.police.uk/About/Pages/What-is-EBP.aspx, last accessed 15 November 2017.

There is little to disagree with here; indeed, who would not want to see policing that is "evidence-based" in this way? The definition provided above makes space for a variety of evidence to be utilized in a way intended not to provide "definitive answers" but for guidance – to be used critically by police officers and staff, who are envisioned as working reflexively to improve their practice. In many senses the College of Policing's account is sympathetic to some of the ideas put forward in earlier chapters, and it is certainly not antithetical to them. Notwithstanding the expansive definition provided above, though, a marked feature of EBP has been the way it has until recently been put into practice – experimental research, especially via the vehicle of the randomized controlled trial (RCT).

Initially associated with the evaluation of particular policies or tactics (e.g. hotspots policing, Weisburd et al., 2012), field experimental methods in policing, and in academic research on policing, now have a much wider range, often focusing on crime reduction/prevention but far from exclusively so (many of the recent studies of Body Worn Video have been experimental – e.g. Ariel et al., 2018). Experimental techniques are certainly a welcome addition to a research and policy evaluation environment previously dominated by observational studies, holding great promise in terms of identifying the effect of policing interventions on a range of different outcomes. RCTs and allied approaches also bring with them some practical benefits, such as enforcing the need to design and implement an "intervention", which can serve to focus both academics and practitioners on the question of what "new" or "good" police practice looks like, and direct their attention towards how a new programme or change in policy can actually be delivered (and perhaps the situations in which it cannot). Police organizations in the UK and beyond are increasingly committed to experimental evaluations of new policies and existing practices – to providing evidence, that is, on which to base their policing practice.

Yet experimental methods also bring into sharp relief some of the wider issues with EBP which we go on to discuss below. There has, indeed, been a long history within academic criminology, and more broadly in the social sciences, of resistance to or at least scepticism about the "promise" of experimental methods. This has stemmed from diverse sources:

- Epistemological concerns about the ability of experimental methods to generate truly "accurate" or even "useful" knowledge (Hope, 2009).
- Doubts about the "realism" of experiments, most notably in relation to the extent to which the method can require a simplification of or abstraction from the normal course of events so extreme as to make subsequent interventions based on the resulting evidence inapplicable in other locations, times or circumstances (Pawson and Tilley, 1997; cf. Cartwright, 2007).
- Ethical concerns about potential perverse outcomes arising from policy interventions founded on experimental studies (Carr, 2010).
- Worry that an overemphasis on the "gold standard" of experiments devalues the legacy of much seminal police research, and undermines ongoing attempts to use more diverse methods to help answer policing questions (Lumsden and Goode, 2016).
- Evidence that, for a variety of reasons, police officers can react negatively to being asked (or rather told) to implement experimental studies, resulting in passive or active undermining of the intervention (and consequently problems in maintaining treatment fidelity, MacQueen and Bradford, 2017), backfire effects (ibid.) and damage to professional integrity and the ability to use discretion (Wain et al., 2017).

To this list can be added some purely methodological factors (Shadish et al., 2002: 276) that at the very least limit the usefulness of experiments, but which also in many cases add further impetus to some of the issues outlined above. These include that:

- certain types of questions (e.g. those involving historical events) cannot be addressed experimentally.
- random assignment of treatments/interventions can be ethically (and indeed practically) challenging or impossible.
- experiments can often take a long time to produce answers.
- many important explanatory variables (e.g. age, gender) cannot be manipulated.
- experiments need to be built on extensive pre-existing bodies of work, and are thus often not well-suited to new and fast-changing situations.

It almost goes without saying that many of these issues would seem particularly salient in policing contexts, marked as they often are by ethical dilemmas, a fast-changing practice and policy environment and the frequent need to produce rapid answers to emerging questions, often with already stretched resources.

Similar concerns have been raised in other fields where the evidence-based approach has also established something of a foothold, such as management studies

(Morrell, 2008; Morrell et al., 2015; Morrell and Learmonth, 2017). Although, if the evidence-based approach really did provide corporations with "what works", one might have expected it to have been adopted more widely than has actually been the case – in many fields the "evidence-based" paradigm has simply not taken off.

In policing, however, it has become, arguably, dominant. There has been a powerful coalition of actors promoting "evidence-based" principles and language, and there are distinctive features about the conversation on evidence in policing. There are societies promoting evidence-based policing, regular conferences, transatlantic exchanges, clear career incentives, close collaborations between educational providers and police forces, virtual as well as bricks and mortar networks, officers who publicly proclaim to be "passionate" about evidence, and promotion of this approach as part of a broader project of professionalization by the College of Policing. What never seems to be explicitly acknowledged, however, is that the "evidence-based" agenda also fits well with the professional and career projects of academics who have trained to see the world in a particular way.

As with other areas of policy, the appeal to an evidence base seems to offer a solution to several problems: to capture and disseminate learning, to ensure consistency of standards and quality assurance, to diffuse successful innovations and to integrate practice with the best ideas from academic research. What we offer in this book is a very different way of thinking how policing itself should be framed, and in doing so we have chosen to call attention to things that inherently resist quantification – like virtue and "the public good". The fact these things resist quantification makes them less compatible with an evidence-based approach. There is no inherent contradiction between these different ways of thinking about policing and police work: a language of virtue and a language of evidence, but the whole-scale way in which evidence-based rhetoric has been adopted does give rise to tensions.

Although an evidence-based approach has some answers to some questions it does not, by any means, have all the answers, and should not, by any means, be used to approach all questions. For example, in common with others, we have argued that the identity and character of individual police officers can be seen as ongoing personal projects of sense-making, and as attempts to resolve or grapple with dilemmas that do not have any one solution. Moreover, the relationship between policing as an institution or practice and academic research should not simply be about academia acting as a service provider, or dispensing solutions like pills. Nor, more fundamentally, do academia or disciplines like law and criminology exist to "help" the police. They should not be "for" the police, they should be "for" the public, or at least the pursuit of knowledge. Many times in the book we have acknowledged that policing is dilemmatic, but then the research process is too:

> the research process is to be regarded not as a set of problems to be "solved", but rather as a set of dilemmas to be "lived with"; and the series of interlocking choices is to be regarded not as an attempt to find the "right" choices

but as an effort to keep from becoming impaled on one or another horn of one or more of these dilemmas.

(McGrath, 1982: 69)

One consequence of this is that not knowing the answer to something can actually be useful. Even if we have to act, if we are not sure of what the best course of action is, we will not have a false sense of confidence. Judgement is not simply implementing instructions – which is the implicit model of following "best available evidence". Instead it is about continual doubt and openness to the possibility of error.

At the heart of the evidence-based approach in policing, as in other fields, is a seemingly straightforward question – what does the best available evidence suggest is the right thing to do in this situation? But this apparently simple question can quickly unravel. Often policing is about exercising individual judgement, discretion, coping with uncertainties and complexity: it can be as much about what makes problems and settings different from one another as about what makes them the same. Moreover, being able to detect differences between similar situations can be as important – or more important – than understanding how similar situations can be compared. The evidence-based approach – across different fields – airbrushes out contextual complexities. As mentioned, it ultimately relies on saying that the answer to a problem "here" will also tell us what to in a situation "there". Yet at the heart of ethics, and virtue ethics in particular, is a recognition that situations differ – "what works", and more fundamentally what is "the good thing to do", can change as the context changes.

Advocates of an evidence-based approach would perhaps say that all we have done in this section is to mis-describe and unfairly caricature evidence-based policing, but let us look under the bonnet of the evidence-based approach.

Under the bonnet of the "evidence-based" approach

The most obvious, distinguishing feature of "evidence-based" policing is that it is derived from the model of evidence-based medicine (Sherman 1998), an approach that seeks to inform clinical judgements about the care of individual patients. Superior forms of evidence in medicine are results from randomized controlled trials, systematic reviews of the results of such trials, and meta-analysis, though clinicians are not restricted to considering these. What researchers aspire to is a way of evaluating the quality of "proven evidence" (McLaughlin, 2001: 352). In medicine, the recognized authorities (Sackett et al., 1996) set out ways of interrogating the available evidence together with comments on experimental design (evidence-based medicine uses a hierarchy of evidence with systematic reviews and randomized controlled trials at the top, comparable to what has become known in policing as the "Maryland Scale"). Here is the first part of Sackett et al.'s (1996) definition of evidence-based medicine:

(1) the conscientious, explicit, and judicious use of current best evidence in making decisions.

Anyone who has followed contemporary policing will have come across either this quote or some variant. It is more than likely they will also have been told by someone that this is "the definition" or the "origin" of the evidence-based approach. But it is not. It is part of the definition and part of the origin. This is because right at the heart of Sackett et al.'s (1996) definition is an emphasis on individual professional expertise and an emphasis on ethics. Here are the next two sentences of the same article, which emphasize individual expertise:

(2) The practice of evidence based medicine means integrating individual clinical expertise with the best available external clinical evidence from systematic research. By individual clinical expertise we mean the proficiency and judgment that individual clinicians acquire through clinical experience and clinical practice.

Then follows this sentence connecting expertise and ethics:

(3) Increased expertise is reflected in many ways, but especially in more effective and efficient diagnosis and in the more thoughtful identification and compassionate use of individual patients' predicaments, rights, and preferences in making clinical decisions about their care.

Please take a moment to consider this question – which elements of this model have spread like a virus taking over conversations about policing and research? Is it (1) a concern with aggregating, measuring, evaluating, ranking and quantifying "best evidence" (the "how" questions), or is it (2) recognition of the need for individual judgement based on experience (in our terms, character, habit and virtue), or is it (3) the importance of ethics (the "why" questions)? For us, the answer is obvious and also concerning – there has been an exclusive and almost fanatical focus on (1).

Aggregating, quantifying and ranking are techniques of commodification. They are consistent with market modes of governance because they make it easier to compare, price and cost things. In policing it seems rare to hear discussion of the importance of individual judgement and ethics in the same breath as appeals to evidence-based principles. It is much more common in our experience that when the evidence-based approach is being used (and it will often be the only approach ever considered) all the questions revolve around technique and methodology; for instance, can we use a randomized controlled trial here, what is our baseline, where on the Maryland scale would we rank existing evidence, and so on. To understand the appeal of evidence-based policing it is important to acknowledge that a key strand in the evidence-based approach is pragmatism: "what works" (Morrell, 2008).

"What works"

A key means by which advocates of evidence-based approaches achieve credibility is through appeals to a more pragmatic approach to policy and a concern with best value, or "what works" (Craig, 2003; Davies et al., 2000; Nutley et al., 2003). Appeals to evidence are useful because they imply an objectivity and independence. This means that those wanting to adopt changes to practice can be portrayed as delivering value-free assessment in line with particular outcomes, such as targets, rather than under the influence of any ideology. This made evidence-based rhetoric very much favoured by "New Labour" because they could pursue a programme of investment at the same time as being able to distance themselves from the historic negative associations between Labour and "overspending" on public services. Following austerity, appeals to "what works" are also politically helpful but for almost the opposite reasons. The "what works" mantra again sounds value-free, but it also disguises a prior question, which is about the levels of overall cuts. Logically, if you keep cutting investment you will get to the stage where things simply do not "work", or where you have to do fewer things. However, this possibility is written out of the language of evidence-based policing, because it reminds us relentlessly that the only questions of interest are the best available evidence and "what works".

As with the College of Policing definitions of EBP, there is, on one level, little to disagree with in the emphasis on "what works". What public servant would ever advocate a model of policing that did not "work"? More broadly who, anywhere, would promote doing something if they knew in advance it would not "work"? To say you are in favour of doing "what works" is similar to saying you like tea that is "not too hot": this is always true, because of what the words "too hot" mean. This is not to deny, of course, that in a very practical sense, initiatives like the What Works Centre have been able to provide much useful information to police and others dealing with particular problems of crime and disorder, including, notably, information on initiatives that are unlikely to work and which may even be harmful, such as the "Scared Straight" programme. Equally, none of this is to question the intentions or motives of those promoting an evidence-based approach. Without disagreeing with definitions of EBP, or the value of initiatives aimed at generating a clearer understanding of what does, indeed, work, our critique in this chapter is more fundamental. It stems from thinking there is a disconnect between these fairly generous "in theory" definitions, and initiatives such as the What Works Centre, and what "in practice" has all too often been a narrow and exclusionary focus on what "really counts" as evidence – randomized controlled trials.

Our critique also stems from a concern that recurs across history in the social sciences. This is that loud claims to being value-free or neutral actually involve smuggling in all sorts of values and being very partial. Saying that one is following a method that is free from any ideology is actually an intensely ideological thing to claim. To try to explain this, we can draw on this quote from Ghoshal (2005: 87):

> social scientists carry an even greater social and moral responsibility than those who work in the physical sciences because, if they hide ideology in the pretense of science, they can cause much more harm.

In other words, if a study involves the social world, we need to resist and question any claims that we can somehow simplify the moral playing field. There are also many features to life that utterly resist the language of "what works" because they rest on alternative principles. Using a distinction we introduced in the first chapter, the evidence-based approach and the language of "what works" is consequentialist; and there is a potential tension between a focus on consequences and a focus on principles or processes (Morrell, 2006a). As we argue in Chapter 3, perceptions of procedural justice are important in maintaining consent and underpin the crowning institutional virtue of legitimacy. Current empirical understanding supports this focus on procedural justice but a focus on procedural justice should also be a stance taken towards policing that is based on principles, or doing the right thing – even if we felt it did not "work" (according to whatever situation or measures, with whatever part of the public or over whatever timescale). Following "what works" can create tension with observing important principles.

To illustrate, we can briefly consider a private sector example – relating to what companies sometimes call "managing diversity". This involves hiring and promoting from within so a company reflects diversity in wider society (we are not drawing parallels with policing with this brief example, but in policing this is also a key concern, in terms of representativeness and legitimacy as discussed in Chapter 3). A key justification for why companies should manage diversity is the "business case" (Cornelius, 2002) – the corporate equivalent of "what works". The business case says companies should manage diversity not just because it is the right thing to do, but because it is profitable (lack of diversity compromises creativity and innovation, harms reputation, loses or fails to understand customers, etc.) A "business case" justification is problematic though (Noon et al., 2013). If we base the argument for managing diversity on consequences it leaves very unpalatable possibilities open. What happens if excluding some minorities has a pay-off – or in other words, "works" (for example, and only hypothetically, excluding some with disabilities or carer responsibilities)? And if diversity does not enhance profitability, should we drop it as a concern?

Policing on the basis of "what works" could also set up tensions with what is the right thing to do. At times we may be able to rule out clearly unethical implications of "what works" – based on the law or on clear principles. But one thing that virtue ethics emphasizes is that individual situations are problematic because of contextual factors. Indeed, choosing the very principles that should help us decide on what to do in grey areas is a fundamental problem. No "evidence-base" helps to choose between founding normative principles. Nor does an evidence base help with deciding complex trade-offs that depend on very particular sets of circumstances. For instance, in relation to public order, there may be a balance to be struck between someone's individual liberty to express themselves and more general common liberties such as a right to feel "safe". To take another example, policing hotspots may work in reducing criminality, but at a longer-term cost if it changes the nature of public space or the relationship between the police and local publics.

Another issue with this language is the implication that whatever is implemented under the "what works" banner can mistakenly be thought of as the best there is. Or, putting it slightly differently, if you are implementing "what works" it can be difficult to admit it is not working. Tim Hope's (2004) analysis of how an evidence-based approach was actually applied in trying to reduce burglaries concludes it was not so much a case of seeing "what works," but a case of "pretend it works" (the title of Hope's paper).

Implications

We would go as far as to say that the whole-scale adoption of the evidence-based approach by policy makers and senior police officers is a threat to understanding policing today. Though there is nothing wrong intrinsically with this way of understanding "evidence", nor with the idea of applying evidence to policing, the reason we make this provocative claim is that there certainly is a problem when the evidence-based approach becomes seen as "the only" way to understand "good policing". It is not, since it depends on the kind of problem you are addressing and also how you frame that problem. The evidence-based approach is a ready-made frame of reference, almost like putting on a pair of glasses that make the world monochrome. But choosing a lens to look through is incredibly important as the first step in approaching a problem. Indeed, part of our hoped-for contribution is to provide an alternative lens, and language, for understanding policing.

Having a ready-made way to think about practices like policing is dangerous. Policing is a complex, socially constructed activity that is also a means for the expression of state power. The ideal for a society, if we want many publics to "flourish", is that those with most power – i.e. in our case the police – will also have the most options open to them, the most discretion and the best judgement. In virtue ethics, the sources of good judgement are attention to context, good habits, practical experience and the development of character. These are nested within an overarching framework of institutions, customs and practices. Together these things can help build up a picture of policing as conducive to the public good. As we have shown, considerations of ethics and situated expertise are central to the model of evidence-based medicine but downplayed or even absent in evidence-based policing as it is practised – however generously it is defined.

Our emphasis on virtue is a helpful departure from this way of thinking because it emphasizes context in a way that is a fundamental challenge to the idea of an aggregated evidence base. Virtue is also a powerful critical lens through which to look at topics such as civilianization, direct entry, outsourcing and privatization. Since it is a well-established tradition of thought, there are a number of ways in which virtue has been studied empirically over time. This can lead to implications for future research in policing and potentially a restatement of the importance of narrative forms of knowledge. One exciting implication is that this can open up new possibilities for research. In closing, we offer a research agenda at the same time as setting out a clear departure from the prevailing way in which policing as a practice, and the practice of research are understood and related to one another.

Virtue and stories: a research agenda

One of the clearest contributions in terms of method, which takes us back to the very origins of virtue ethics, is the link between virtue, stories and story-telling. The evidence-based approach has an antipathy towards stories because it seeks aggregation of knowledge from multiple settings and in doing so it denigrates the things that are idiosyncratic, unique and different. But understanding what is unique and different about a situation is the very essence and lifeblood of stories. It is also central to understanding virtues – in terms of the need to pay close attention to context and the development of character (as we discussed in Chapters 5 and 6).

The narrative/story approach to understanding policing and the public good can allow for more flexibly employed theory and a greater opportunity to scale what Wright Mills (1959) referred to as the "ladder of abstraction". In other words it can help to examine both the big theoretical questions about the public good in terms of public services, society and the state (which we looked at in Chapters 1 and 2); and smaller-scale (no less important) theoretical questions about individual choices. The ability to move between these is important because virtue ethics allows us to understand the relationship between an individual or "agent" account of the good life and a shared or "structure" account of the good society and state. Stories are appropriate in examining how we understand this relationship because they are vehicles for interpreting change, making attributions, justifying and explaining behaviour, and summarizing complex scenarios (Barry and Elmes, 1997; Morrell, 2006a). They assist inferences and decision making processes as part of the process of sense-making which influences how we act in the world (Weick, 1995). This approach has several further advantages.

First, connecting virtue and stories is very much in keeping with our account of policing and the public good. Attributions of virtue (or vice) are retrospective and they involve studying the actions of an administration or service, or individual over time. In this sense they have important structural features in common with stories which can be defined as (i) "presentation" (or representation) of (ii) "a sequence of events" (Genette, 1982; Scholes, 1981; both in Rudrum, 2005). It is the combination of the events themselves and the way in which they are interpreted and relayed that make up a story. One thing that is illustrated in Chapter 6 is that the police are highly skilled and practised as story-tellers because they often have to account for their actions. Normatively, this skill should support the police in accurately telling factual, relevant and truthful stories that support good policing, and that enable wider society to interpret and understand police actions in ways that are conducive to good relations between the police and the public. As events at Hillsborough showed, vicious abuse of this skill in terms of altering statements and records after the event can result in the opposite (Hillsborough Independent Panel, 2012). Virtuous use of this skill is the basis for much of the criminal justice system, not simply in terms of giving accurate and truthful evidence, but in being able to identify (un)truth and (in)accuracy in other people's stories. Understanding more about how policing relies on and benefits from the skill of story-telling can be helpful to understanding practice. The ability to tell good stories about one's own competence and expertise is crucial in promotion for instance, and it could be that some are being unjustly rewarded – or held back – not because of their accomplishments or potential, but because of how well they are able to package and present this experience.

Second, stories offer a way to understand the relationship between the individual pursuit of *eudaimonia* (activity of the soul exhibiting virtue), and the common ideals of the good society and state (Kraut, 2002). For the public, part of whether they act virtuously is defined by their interaction with the state: whether they participate in deliberative decision making and respect societal constraints for instance – or more simply whether they help. This is relevant in considering the relations between the police and the public, for instance in the idea that the police can produce identity in others and act as a kind of social mirror (Bradford, Murphy and Jackson, 2014). Stories are even crucial in communicating the value and virtues of the evidence-based approach. Ironically, every presentation or lecture we have seen advocating the evidence-based approach relies most on individual cases of "what works" – in other words, stories of its successes – rather than an aggregated body of evidence. It is rare to hear about failures to replicate these successes – not because there is no evidence of these – but because these make for a less compelling story.

Third, as well as relying on shared norms, evaluating whether someone is acting virtuously depends on the particular context for their actions. In virtue ethics, "a concern for situated judgments supplants any simple belief in the unproblematic application of universal norms" (Emirbayer and Mische, 1998: 995). This attention to the particular features of a situation – with what makes it different from other similar situations – is crucial to determinations of virtue. The emphasis on sensitivity to context has made some contemporary academics more sympathetic to virtue ethics in preference to accounts that presuppose absolute standards of "the good". This is partly because universal assumptions can turn into dogma and mean that there is less potential for sophisticated dialogue about moral problems (MacIntyre, 1984a). Rather than understanding difference and idiosyncrasy, the evidence-based approach is oriented towards finding out what makes situations the same, because it tries to aggregate understanding to form an evidence base. This is the wrong approach to take with some problems.

Fourth and relatedly, we have said that a distinctive feature of virtue ethics is that it can show how individuals as agents and the group, or common structures and institutions, are related. When we consider the general form of the story we have a number of ways of making these connections between structure and agency. The study of stories provides a rich set of tools for analysing such accounts by examining the ways in which a sequence of events is interpreted and presented; studying what is valued or denigrated, what is downplayed or de-emphasized, what is omitted and what is included. This blurs the lines between fact and fiction because when we represent events in the form of a story it inevitably involves elements of construction – omission, emphasis, simplification. Often too, simply the way in which stories are relayed relies on conventions – the reliance on a beginning-middle-end format. Being aware of how these common sense-making structures are limitations to understanding is also important. For example, work by Ben Hart in *Police Professional* (Hart and Morrell, 2016) shows that officers who are highly experienced in investigating Threats to Life (TTL) could simultaneously acknowledge the potential value of an evidence-based approach and emphasize the importance of stories when assessing risk (please see Table 8.1).

All of these expert officers interviewed placed high importance on the value of understanding the narrative or story relating to a TTL. Moreover, there was a great deal of consensus (unprompted) on the value of stories in relation to the critical aspect of determining risk. In rare, complex and potentially lethal situations it could be that idiosyncratic details or particular nuances in the nature of the TTL, or in the accounts of witnesses or the person who has been threatened are crucial clues relating to risk. A broader point here is that it may be better to work with stories – which cannot be aggregated in the same way – and to acknowledge these as an alternative way of knowing rather than a necessarily inferior one. This may be more realistic and also more sensible than trying to erase or edit stories out.

Fifth, in terms of putting this into practice, one idea from social psychology can be brought in to consider this link between agent and structure. This is the idea of "social scripts" (Schank and Abelson, 1977). Scripts are shared knowledge structures that assist inference and allow us to navigate social complexity. They summarize cultural knowledge and reflect community norms that people are expected to fulfil (Morrell, 2004b). Although there are parallels with the theatrical sense of script these knowledge structures are not deterministic, and they are also shared across society. Even so scripts can be thought of as bundles of rules that influence choice. The basis for these rules is a basic set of shared cultural understandings, but scripts tell us what to expect or do in specific situations. In thinking about policing and the public good, scripts could play many roles. They could be helpful in following procedures (or detrimental), they could offer templates for communication to the public (or lead to poor communication), they could underpin attributions of public confidence (or make it harder to establish confidence). Scripts are conceptual inventories that are event or scenario-based, and their role is to assist choice (so they shape individual action). However, they concern well-known contexts and cultural knowledge (so they concern social structures and institutions). They may be particularly appropriate then in examining ideas of what is "good", because these kinds of appraisal are often based on shared norms. This means they may be one way to examine empirically the problem of how we can scale up from an individual account of the good, or an individual character, to a society or a public service that is based on the same principles.

TABLE 8.1 The Value of Stories in Understanding Threats to Life

	How important do you consider the narrative/story to be within an individual TTL?	What weight do you attach to the narrative that forms the context and background, when setting an investigative plan?	Which aspects of a TTL investigation would be most benefited by a narrative approach?	A. In what circumstances would you disregard the narrative of a TTL? B. In what circumstances would you disregard other knowledge in light of the narrative?
Officer A	Very significant.	This is the basis of all decision making in TTL and is hugely important.	The risk assessment.	A. I would possibly use a sound, data driven approach over the narrative one, but it would depend on the case. B. When I perceived the risk to be suitable to do so.
Officer B	For certain parts I'd say it's essential.	It's the critical part of a TTL.	Having a more structured narrative to the risk assessment and research that forms the initial assessment would be hugely helpful.	I don't think I ever would, even if there was a theory or piece of information that contradicted the narrative, I wouldn't ignore or play down that particular aspect of the story.
Officer C	Highly important. It's important to be able to judge reactions, motive and to be able to interpret situations based upon human judgements of people.	The risk assessment is critical, so a huge amount of significance.	I don't know, that may be a matter of personal choice or style.	I would look at the source and if the narrative and the origin was compelling then I would place more weight upon that than any data driven exercise. I would always lean towards a statistical or data driven resource because I think that would protect my decision making more.

	How important do you consider the narrative/story to be within an individual TTL?	*What weight do you attach to the narrative that forms the context and background, when setting an investigative plan?*	*Which aspects of a TTL investigation would be most benefited by a narrative approach?*	*A. In what circumstances would you disregard the narrative of a TTL?* *B. In what circumstances would you disregard other knowledge in light of the narrative?*
Officer D	It's the key part of any TTL.	It's the key component, so a significant amount of weight.	The risk assessment and opening aspects that set out what the issue is thought to be, i.e. is it a drugs debt, a respect issue or whatever.	I don't know really, that's hard to answer without seeing both options on paper and having it all set out in front of you.
Officer E	Very important in general but in certain places it's essential.	A lot – a significant amount.	The initial risk assessment.	I'm not sure.
Officer F	It can sometimes not make sense, but then we have so many holes at times in what we know, I think if we can establish the narrative from the people involved then that's crucial.	I think it helps set the risk level, but it doesn't necessarily affect the response as we do most things in most cases.	I'm not sure. I'd instinctively say the risk assessment and research, but it would also be useful for understanding what our interventions actually did.	A. If it was very limited or non-existent or there was clear contradictions within it. B. I think if it was complete, corroborated from other sources and compelling then it would be very strong.
Officer G	It's highly important. You can't quantify the strength of someone's feelings or motives nor extract future plans. These are complex criminals who are aware of police practice and procedure and have had these before in most cases. An evidence base can only be built around certain things – but not these things.	High value.	The risk assessment.	I would judge each case on its own merits and look at each issue/question to ask what basis is there for making that particular one. I would err towards a robust evidence base that had been subjected to a systematic review from a wider area. However, there are some things that no survey or data can assess – ultimately with no evidence to the contrary, it may be whether you believe one person or not.

	How important do you consider the narrative/story to be within an individual TTL?	What weight do you attach to the narrative that forms the context and background, when setting an investigative plan?	Which aspects of a TTL investigation would be most benefited by a narrative approach?	A. In what circumstances would you disregard the narrative of a TTL? B. In what circumstances would you disregard other knowledge in light of the narrative?
Officer H	I can't see any situations where this isn't the driving force behind understanding the TTL.	It's crucial so a lot of weight.	Knowing the links between groups to show who is who – the research of relationships and groups of people.	A. I'm not sure you ever could. Even if there were issues with it, it would still have some importance. B. Not sure.
Officer I	Very important.	It's very significant.	Risk assessing a case.	I think it's clear when there are either gaps in our knowledge or contradictions within a case and the narrative value would hinge on those. I don't know how that would play out by comparison to other information.
Officer J	It pivotal to establishing any form of response.	Yes, in conjunction with the people you're dealing with, it's very important.	The research, the people involved in a TTL and the risk they pose.	Not sure really.

When we try to understand virtue and the good through stories, there is an opportunity to look for themes, motifs and markers that resonate at these different levels of analysis. In terms of actual methods or techniques of data collection/construction, direct questions about what would be a good society might prompt the sort of active deliberation that is not typically in play when making scripted judgements. This is because scripts are largely pre-conscious. It could be more appropriate to explore their role indirectly, rather than through asking directly in an interview or focus group. One such method would be through less invasive techniques, for instance ethnography and observation (Rhodes, 2005). Another alternative would be to look for themes, motifs and markers in existing documents (relating to policy and procedure, memos) or even in artefacts (clothing, signs, furnishing, décor and the built environment) or in routines (procedures, rites and ritual).

Conclusion

Restating the importance of stories in policing is helpful in developing our ideas about virtue and taking them forward into research. It also helps to connect to some of the most seminal and influential literature in the field. Much of this relies on ethnography to provide us with a rich picture of police work (e.g. Skolnick, 1966, Van Maanen, 1979; see also Faull, 2017; Garriott, 2013). Histories offer comparably rich insights in terms of providing a sense of changes over time (Loader and Mulcahy, 2003; Petrow, 1994).

There is no inherent contradiction between pursuing the best available evidence and a virtue ethics approach. However, where there are potential tensions between virtue and evidence these are important to understand, because "evidence-based policing" is overwhelmingly the dominant way in which research and practice are related to one another by those with most power in the contemporary governance of policing. Consensus can be valuable, but monologue is dangerous. A perspective emphasizing virtue shows most clearly how "evidence-based" monologue is limited by skipping over fundamental questions to do with situated judgement and ethics. The powers the police have mean these questions should be ever-present and the complexities that they face also mean these should never be completely settled. Policing is dilemmatic and contested, and it is ongoing, imperfect and controversial. These things are also true of social research and as a result we caution against ready-to-hand solutions and self-justifying "what works" rhetoric. These things close down dialogue. In this book as a whole we have worked to provide a fresh basis for conversations about policing and to join together different literatures that do not often "talk" to each other. We hope in turn that this book will contribute usefully to conversations about policing and the public good.

REFERENCES

Ackroyd, S. and Kirkpatrick, I. (2003). Transforming the professional archetype: The new managerialism in the UK public services. *Public Management Review* 5(4): 509–529.

Adang, O. M. (2011). Initiation and Escalation of Collective Violence: An Observational Study, in T. D. Madensen and J. Knutsson (eds), *Preventing Crowd Violence*. Boulder, CO: Lynne Rienner, pp. 47–68.

Akbar, Z. and Venkatraman, N. (1995). Relational governance as an interorganizational strategy: An empirical test. *Strategic Management Journal* 16(5): 373–392.

Akers, R. L. (1999). *Criminological Theories: Introduction and Evaluation*. Abingdon: Routledge.

Albert, S. and Whetten, D. A. (1985). Organizational Identity, in L. L. Cummings and M. M. Staw (eds), *Research in Organizational Behavior*, Vol. 7. Greenwich, CT: JAI Press, pp. 263–295.

Albert, S., Ashforth, B. E. and Dutton, J. E. (2000). Organizational identity and identification: Charting new waters and building new bridges. *Academy of Management Review* 25(1): 13–17.

Alexander, C. E. (2008). *Rethinking "Gangs": Gangs, Youth Violence and Public Policy*. London: Runnymede Trust.

Alexander, M. (2012). *The New Jim Crow: Mass Incarceration in the Age of Color Blindness*. New York: The New Press.

Alink, F., Boin, A. and t'Hart, P. (2001). Institutional crises and reforms in policy sectors: The case of asylum policy in Europe. *Journal of European Public Policy* 8(2): 286–306.

Allen J., El Komy, M., Lovbakke, J. and Roy, H. (2005). *Policing and the Criminal Justice System: Public Confidence and Perceptions. Findings from the 2003/04 British Crime Survey Home Office Online Report 31/05*. London: Home Office.

Allen J., Edmonds, S., Patterson, A. and Smith, D. (2006). *Policing and the Criminal Justice System: Public Confidence and Perceptions. Findings from the 2004/05 British Crime Survey Home Office Online Report 07/06*. London: Home Office.

Allison, E. and Hattenstone, S. (2017). Now we know the shocking facts of deaths in custody, will Theresa May act? *The Guardian*, 2 November.

References

Alves, A. A. and Moreira, J. M. (2013). Virtue and commerce in Domingo de Soto's thought: Commercial practices, character, and the common good. *Journal of Business Ethics* 113(4): 627–638.

Anderson, B. (1983). *Imagined Communities: Reflections on the Origin and Spread of Nationalism*. London: Verso.

Anderson, B. (2013). *Us and Them?: The Dangerous Politics of Immigration Control*. Oxford: Oxford University Press.

Anderson, E. (1990). *Streetwise: Race, Class and Change in an Urban Community*. Chicago, IL: University of Chicago Press.

Antrobus, E., Bradford, B., Murphy, K. and Sargeant, E. (2015). Community norms, procedural justice and the public's perceptions of police legitimacy. *Journal of Contemporary Criminal Justice* 31(2): 151–170.

Ariel, B., Farrar, W. A. and Sutherland, A. (2015). The effect of police body-worn cameras on use of force and citizens' complaints against the police: A randomized controlled trial. *Journal of Quantitative Criminology* 31(3): 509–535.

Ariel, B., Sutherland, A., Henstock, D., Young, J., Drover, P., Sykes, J., … and Henderson, R. (2016a). Report: Increases in police use of force in the presence of body-worn cameras are driven by officer discretion: A protocol-based subgroup analysis of ten randomized experiments. *Journal of Experimental Criminology* 12(3): 453–463.

Ariel, B., Sutherland, A.*et al.* (2016b). Wearing body cameras increases assaults against officers and does not reduce police use of force: Results from a global multi-site experiment. *European Journal of Criminology* 13(6): 744–755.

Ariel, B., Sutherland, A., Henstock, D., Young, J., Drover, P., Sykes, J., … and Henderson, R. (2017). "Contagious accountability" a global multisite randomized controlled trial on the effect of police body-worn cameras on citizens' complaints against the police. *Criminal Justice and Behavior* 44(2): 293–316.

Ariel, B., Sutherland, A., Henstock, D., Young, J. and Sosinski, G. (2018). The deterrence spectrum: Explaining why police body-worn cameras "work" or "backfire" in aggressive police–public encounters. *Policing: A Journal of Policy and Practice* 12(1): 6–26.

Aristotle (1995). *The Complete Works of Aristotle*. The revised Oxford translation, 6th printing with corrections, ed. J. Barnes. Princeton, NJ: Princeton University Press.

Arjoon, S. (2000). Virtue theory as a dynamic theory of business. *Journal of Business Ethics* 28(2): 159–178.

Arnson, Cynthia J. (ed.) (1999). *Comparative Peace Processes in Latin America*. New York: Stanford University Press.

Ashforth, B. E. and Mael, F. (1989). Social identity theory and the organization. *Academy of Management Review* 14(1): 20–39.

Ashforth, B. E. and Mael, F. (1996). Organizational Identity and Strategy as a Context for the Individual, in J. A. C. Baum and J. E. Dutton (eds), *Advances in Strategic Management*. Greenwich, CT: JAI Press, pp. 19–64.

Ashmore, R. D., Deaux, K. and McLaughlin-Volpe, T. (2004). An organizing framework for collective identity: Articulation and significance of multidimensionality. *Psychological Bulletin* 130: 80–114.

Ashforth, B. E., Harrison, S. H. and Corley, K. G. (2008). Identification in organizations: An examination of four fundamental questions. *Journal of Management* 34(3): 325–374.

Ashforth, B. E., Rogers, K. M. and Corley, K. G. (2011). Identity in organizations: Exploring cross-level dynamics. *Organization Science* 22(5): 1144–1156.

Atkinson, R. and Flint, J. (2001). Accessing hidden and hard-to-reach populations: Snowball research strategies. *Social Research Update* 33(1): 1–4.

Auchter, Craig W. (1996). *The Democratic Problematic in Central America and the Surprising Case of Nicaragua*. Butler University Discussion Paper no. 89.

Augst, T. (1999). Composing the moral senses: Emerson and the politics of character in nineteenth-century America. *Political Theory* 27(1): 85–120.

Bache, I. (2003). Governing through governance: Education policy control under new labour. *Political Studies* 51: 300–314.

Bacon, M. (2013). The informal regulation of an illegal trade: The hidden politics of drugs detective work. *Etnografia e Ricera Qualitativa* 1: 61–80.

Bain, A. (2005). Constructing an artistic identity. *Work, Employment and Society* 19(1): 25–46.

Bal, M. G. (1985). *Narratology: Introduction to the Theory of Narrative*. Toronto: University of Toronto Press.

Ballas, A. A. and Tsoukas, H. (2004). Measuring nothing: The case of the Greek national health system. *Human Relations* 57(6): 661–690.

Balogun, J. and Johnson, G. (2004). Organizational restructuring and middle manager sensemaking. *Academy of Management Journal* 47: 523–549.

Banton, M. (1964). *The Policeman in the Community*. London: Tavistock Publications.

Barabashev, A. and Straussman, J. D. (2007). Public service reform in Russia, 1991–2006. *Public Administration Review* 67(3): 373–382.

Barry, D. and Elmes, M. (1997). Strategy retold: Toward a narrative view of strategic discourse. *Academy of Management Review* 22(2): 429–452.

Barton, A. (2011). *Illicit Drugs: Use and Control*, 2nd edition. London: Routledge.

Barton, H. and Beynon, M. J. (2015). Do the citizens of Europe trust their police? *International Journal of Emergency Services* 4(1): 1–21.

Bauman, Z. (1992). Life-World and Expertise: Social Production of Dependency, in N. Stehr and R. V. Ericson (eds), *The Culture and Power of Knowledge: Inquiries into Contemporary Societies*. Berlin: Walter de Gruyter.

Bayley, D. H. (2008). Police reform: Who done it? *Policing and Society* 18(1): 7–17.

Bayley, D. H. and Bittner, E. (1984). Learning the skills of policing. *Law and Contemporary Problems* 47(4): 35–59.

BBC (2015). Police cuts: G4S says private firms could save forces £1bn a year, BBC News, 19 November, available on www.bbc.co.uk/news/uk-34864781.

BBC (2016). QandA: Police and crime commissioners, BBC News, 21 April, available on www.bbc.co.uk/news/uk-politics-19504639, last accessed 1 November.

Beadle, R. (2013a). Managerial work in a practice-embodying institution: The role of calling, the virtue of constancy. *Journal of Business Ethics* 113(4): 679–690.

Beadle, R. (2013b). The misappropriation of MacIntyre. *Philosophy of Management* 2(2): 45–54.

Beadle, R. and Knight, K. (2012). Virtue and meaningful work. *Business Ethics Quarterly* 22(2): 433–450.

Beaumont, J. and Nicholls, W. (2007). Between relationality and territoriality: Investigating the geographies of justice movements in the Netherlands and the United States. *Environment and Planning A* 39(11): 2554–2574.

Beck, U. (1992). *Risk Society: Toward a New Modernity*. London: SAGE.

Becker, H. (1963). *Outsiders: Studies in the Sociology of Deviance*. New York: Free Press.

Beckett, K. and Herbert, S. (2008). Dealing with disorder: Social control in the post-industrial city. *Theoretical Criminology* 12(1): 5–30.

Beckett, K. and Herbert, S. (2010). *Banished: The New Social Control in Urban America*. Oxford: Oxford University Press.

Beetham, D. (1991). *The Legitimation of Power*. London: Macmillan.

Benesh, S. C. (2006). Understanding public confidence in American courts. *Journal of Politics* 68(3): 697–707.

Bentham, J. (1781 / 2006). *An Introduction to the Principles of Morals and Legislation*. Full text available on www.utilitarianism.com, last accessed 16 September 2017.

Berger, P. L. and Luckmann, T. (1966). *The Social Construction of Reality: A Treatise in the Sociology of Knowledge*. Garden City, NY: Anchor.

Berkman, M. B. and Plutzer, E. (2005). *Ten Thousand Democracies: Politics and Public Opinion in America's School Districts*. Washington: Georgetown University Press.

Bevir, M., Rhodes, R. A. W. and Weller, P. (2003). Traditions of governance: Interpreting the changing role of the public sector. *Public Administration* 81(1): 1–17.

Beyes, T. and Steyaert, C. (2012). Spacing organization: Non-representational theory and performing organizational space. *Organization* 19(1) 45–61.

Bhabha, H. K. (ed.) (1994). *The Location of Culture*. London and New York: Routledge.

Bisel, R. S. and Barge, J. K. (2011). Discursive positioning and planned change in organizations. *Human Relations* 64(2): 257–283.

Bittner, E. (1974). Florence Nightingale in Pursuit of Willie Sutton: A Theory of the Police, in H. Jacob (ed.), *The Potential for Reform of Criminal Justice*. Beverly Hills, CA: SAGE, pp. 17–40.

Blackwood, L. M. (2015). Policing airport spaces: The Muslim experience of scrutiny. *Policing (Oxford)* 9(3): 255–264.

Blackwood, L. M., Hopkins, N. and Reicher, S. D. (2013). "I know who I am, but who do they think I am?" Muslim perspectives on encounters with airport authorities. *Ethnic and Racial Studies* 36(6): 1090–1108.

Blackwood, L. M., Hopkins, N. and Reicher, S. D. (2015). "Flying while Muslim": Citizenship and misrecognition in the airport. *Journal of Social and Political Psychology* 3(2): 148–170.

Blader, S. L. and Tyler, T. R. (2003a). A four-component model of procedural justice: Defining the meaning of a "fair" process. *Personality and Social Psychology Bulletin* 29: 747–758.

Blader, S. L. and Tyler, T. R. (2003b). What constitutes fairness in work settings? A four-component model of procedural justice. *Human Resource Management Review* 13: 107–126.

Blader, S. L. and Tyler, T. R. (2009). Testing and expanding the group engagement model: Linkages between social identity, procedural justice, economic outcomes, and extrarole behavior. *Journal of Applied Psychology* 94: 445–464.

Boba, R. and Crank, J. P. (2008). Institutionalizing problem-oriented policing: Rethinking problem solving, analysis, and accountability. *Police Practice and Research* 9: 379–393.

Boin, A., t'Hart, P., McConnell, A. and Preston, T. (2010). Leadership style, crisis response and blame management: The case of Hurricane Katrina. *Public Administration* 88(3): 706–723.

Borins, S. F. (2012). Making narrative count: A narratological approach to public management innovation. *Journal of Public Administration Research and Theory* 22(1): 165–189.

Bottoms, A. and Tankebe, J. (2012). Beyond procedural justice: A dialogic approach to legitimacy in criminal justice. *Journal of Criminal and Law Criminology* 102(1): 101–150.

Bourdieu, P. (1991). *Language and Symbolic Power*. Cambridge: Polity.

Bovens, M. and Zouridis, S. (2002). From Street-level to system-level bureaucracies: How information and communication technology is transforming administrative discretion and constitutional control. *Public Administration Review* 62(2): 174–184.

Bowling, B. and Foster, J. (2002). Policing and the Police, in M. Maguire, R. Morgan and R. Reiner (eds), *The Oxford Handbook of Criminology*. Oxford: Oxford University Press.

Bozeman, B. (2007). *Public Values and Public Interest: Counterbalancing Economic Individualism.* Washington: Georgetown University Press.

Bradford, B. (2011). Convergence not divergence? Trends and trajectories in public contact and confidence in the police. *The British Journal of Criminology* 51: 179–200.

Bradford, B. (2014). Policing and social identity: Procedural justice, inclusion, and cooperation between police and public. *Policing and Society* 24(1): 22–43.

Bradford, B. (2015). Assessing the Impact of Stop and Search Powers on Individuals and Communities, in R. Delsol and M. Shiner (eds), *Stop and Search.* Basingstoke: Palgrave Macmillan, pp. 102–122.

Bradford, B. (2017a). *Stop and Search and Police Legitimacy.* Oxford: Routledge.

Bradford, B. (2017b). The Dog that Never Quite Barked: Social Identity and the Persistence of Police Legitimacy, in M. Bosworth, C. Hoyle and L. Zedner (eds), *Changing Contours of Criminal Justice: Research, Politics and Policy.* Oxford: Oxford University Press.

Bradford, B. and Jackson, J. (2016a). Cooperating with the police as an act of social control: Trust and neighbourhood concerns as predictors of public assistance. *Nordic Journal of Studies in Policing* 3(2): 109–129.

Bradford, B. and Jackson, J. (2016b). Enabling and Constraining Police Power: On the Moral Regulation of Policing, in J. Jacobs and J. Jackson (eds), *Routledge Handbook of Criminal Justice Ethics.* Oxford: Routledge.

Bradford, B. and Quinton, P. (2014). Self-legitimacy, police culture and support for democratic policing in an English constabulary. *British Journal of Criminology* 54(6): 1023–1046.

BradfordB., Hohl, K., JacksonJ. and MacQueen, S. (2015). Obeying the rules of the road. *Journal of Contemporary Criminal Justice* 31(2): 171–191.

Bradford, B., Huq, A., Jackson, J. and Roberts, B. (2014). What price fairness when security is at stake? Police legitimacy in South Africa. *Regulation and Governance* 8(2): 246–268.

Bradford, B., Jackson, J. and Stanko, E. A. (2009). Contact and confidence: Revisiting the impact of public encounters with the police. *Policing and Society* 19(1): 20–46.

Bradford, B., Jackson, J. and Hough, M. (in press). Trust in Justice, in E. Uslaner (ed.), *The Oxford Handbook of Social and Political Trust.* Oxford: Oxford University Press.

Bradford, B., Murphy, K. and Jackson, J. (2014). Officers as mirrors: Policing, procedural justice and the (re)production of social identity. *British Journal of Criminology* 54(4): 527–550.

Bradford, B., Sargeant, E., Murphy, T. and Jackson, J. (2017). A leap of faith? Trust in the police among immigrants in England and Wales. *British Journal of Criminology* 57(2): 381–401.

Brain, T. (2010). *A History of Policing in England and Wales from 1974: A Turbulent Journey.* Oxford: Oxford University Press.

Brain, T. (2013). *A Future for Policing in England and Wales.* Oxford: Oxford University Press.

Brewer, M. B. and Kramer, R. M. (1985). The psychology of intergroup attitudes and behavior. *Annual Review of Psychology* 36: 219–243.

Bridges, L. (2011). Localism and police reform: Improving or fragmenting accountability? *Criminal Justice Matters* 86(1): 34–35.

Bright, D. S., Winn, B. A. and Kanov, J. (2014). Reconsidering virtue: Differences of perspective in virtue ethics and the positive social sciences. *Journal of Business Ethics* 119(4): 445–460.

Brinkerhoff, D. W. and Brinkerhoff, J. M. (2002). Governance reforms and failed states: Challenges and implications, *International Review of Administrative Sciences* 68(4): 511–531.

Brodeur, J.-P. (2010). *The Policing Web.* Oxford: Oxford University Press.

Brodkin, E. Z. (2011). Policy work: Street-level organizations under new managerialism. *Journal of Public Administration Research and Theory* 21(2): 253–277.

Brogden, M. (1991). *On the Mersey Beat: Policing Liverpool between the Wars*. Oxford: Oxford University Press.
Brogden, M. and Nijhar, P. (2013). *Community Policing: National and International Models and Approaches*. Abingdon: Routledge.
Brooks, I. (1999). Managerialist professionalism: The destruction of a non-conforming subculture. *British Journal of Management* 10(1): 41–52.
Brown, A. D. and Starkey, K. (2000). Organizational identity and learning: A psychodynamic perspective. *Academy of Management Review* 25(1): 102–120.
Brown, J. M. (2013). *The Future of Policing*. London: Routledge.
Brown, J. M. and Heidensohn, F. (2000). *Gender and Policing*. Basingstoke: Macmillan.
Brown, M. K. (1988). *Working the Street: Police Discretion and the Dilemmas of Reform*. New York: SAGE.
Bryant, R., Bryant, S., Graca, S., O'Neill, M., Lawton-Barrett, K., Tong, S., Underwood, R. and Wood, D. (eds) (2012). *Blackstone's Handbook for Policing Students*, 7th edition. Oxford: Oxford University Press.
Burke, P. J. and Stets, J. (2009). *Social Identity Theory*. Oxford: Oxford University Press.
Burns, E. B. (1991). *Patriarch and Folk: The Emergence of Nicaragua, 1798–1858*. Cambridge, MA: Harvard University Press.
Butler, J. (1993). *Bodies that Matter: On the Discursive Limits of "Sex"*. London: Routledge.
Cai, Y., Jo, H. and Pan, C. (2011). Vice or virtue? The impact of corporate social responsibility on executive compensation. *Journal of Business Ethics* 104(2): 159–173.
Caldeira, G. A. (1986). Neither the purse nor the sword: Dynamics of public confidence in the Supreme Court. *American Political Science Review* 80(4): 1209–1226.
Caless, B. (2011). *Policing at the Top: The Roles, Values and Attitudes of Chief Police Officers*. London: Policy Press.
Caless, B. and Tong, S. (2015). *Leading Policing in Europe: An Empirical Study of Strategic Police Leadership*. London: Policy Press.
Campbell, J., Hollingsworth, R. and Lindberg, L. (1991). *Governance of the American Economy*. Cambridge: Cambridge University Press.
Candler, G. G., Azevedo, A. and Albernaz, R. O. (2010). Towards global scholarship in public affairs. *Public Administration* 88(3): 836–850.
Carcello, Joseph V. (2009). Governance and the common good. *Journal of Business Ethics* 89(1): 11–18.
Cardoso, E. and Helwege, A. (1992). *Latin America's Economy: Diversity, trends, and Conflicts*. Cambridge, MA: MIT Press.
Carr, P. J. (2010). The problem with experimental criminology: A response to Sherman's "Evidence and Liberty". *Criminology and Criminal Justice* 10(1): 3–10.
Carter Center (1995). Nicaraguan property disputes. Available on www.cartercenter.org/news/publications/peace/americas_reports.html, last accessed 16 September 2017.
Cartwright, N. (2007). Are RCTs the gold standard? *Biosocieties* 2(1): 11–20.
Centrex (2006). *Practice Advice on Professionalising the Business of Neighbourhood Policing*. London: ACPO/Centrex.
Chainey, S. and Macdonald, I. (2012). *Stop and Search, the Use of Intelligence and Geographic Targeting: Findings from Case Study Research*. London: NPIA.
Chakraborti, N. (forthcoming). Responding to hate crime: Escalating problems, continued failings. *Criminology and Criminal Justice*.
Chan, J. B. L. (1996). Changing police culture. *British Journal of Criminology* 36(1): 109–134.
Chan, J. B. L. (1997). *Changing Police Culture: Policing in a Multicultural Society*. Cambridge: Cambridge University Press.

Chattopadhyay, P., Tluchowska, M. and George, E. (2004). Identifying the ingroup: A closer look at the influence of demographic dissimilarity on employee social identity. *Academy of Management Review* 29(2): 180–202.

Chaudhuri, A., Graziano, S. and Maitra, P. (2006). Social learning and norms in a public goods experiment with inter-generational advice. *The Review of Economic Studies* 73: 357–380.

Chell, E. (2004). Critical Incident Technique, in C. Cassell and G. Symon (eds), *Essential Guide to Qualitative Methods in Organisational Research*. Thousand Oaks, CA: SAGE, pp. 45–60.

Choongh, S. (1997). *Policing as Social Discipline*. Oxford: Clarendon Press.

Chun, R. (2005). Ethical character and virtue of organizations: An empirical assessment and strategic implications. *Journal of Business Ethics* 57(3): 269–284.

Civitas (2015). The nine principles of policing, available on www.civitas.org.uk/pubs/policeNine.php, last accessed 3 November 2015.

Cockcroft, T. (2013). *Police Culture: Themes and Concepts*. Abingdon: Routledge.

Coicaud, J. M. (2002). *Legitimacy and Politics: A Contribution to the Study of Political Right and Political Responsibility*. Cambridge: Cambridge University Press.

Cole, G. F. and Smith, C. E. (2006). *The American System of Criminal Justice*, 10th edition. Belmont, CA: Wadsworth/Thomson Learning.

Cole, M. S. and Bruch, H. (2006). Organizational identity strength, identification, and commitment and their relationships to turnover intention: Does organizational hierarchy matter? *Journal of Organizational Behavior* 27(5): 585–605.

Cole, G., Smith, C. and DeJong, C. (2012). *The American System of Criminal Justice*. Belmont, CA: Wadsworth.

Coleman, R. (2004). Watching the degenerate: Street camera surveillance and urban regeneration. *Local Economy* 19(3): 199–211.

Collinson, J. A. (2006). Just "non-academics"? Research administrators and contested occupational identity. *Work, Employment and Society* 20(2): 267–288.

Colquitt, J. (2001). On the dimensionality of organizational justice: A construct validation of a measure. *Journal of Applied Psychology* 86(3): 386–400.

Colquitt, J. (2008). Two Decades of Organizational Justice: Findings, Controversies, and Future Directions, in C. Cooper and J. Barling (eds), *The SAGE Handbook of Organizational Behavior*. Newbury Park, CA: SAGE, pp. 73–88.

Cooper, C. and Taylor, P. (2005). Independently verified reductionism: Prison privatization in Scotland. *Human Relations* 58(4): 497–522.

Cooper, D. and Thatcher, S. M. (2010). Identification in organizations: The role of self-concept orientations and identification motives. *Academy of Management Review* 35(4): 516–538.

Cordner, G. (2000). Community Policing: Elements and Effects, in G. Alpert and A. Piquero (eds), *Community Policing: Contemporary Readings*. Prospect Heights, IL: Waveland Press.

Cordone, C. (1999). Police reform and human rights investigations: The experience of the UN Mission in Bosnia and Herzegovina. *International Peacekeeping* 6(4): 191–209.

Cornelius, N. (2002). *Building Workplace Equality: Ethics, Diversity and Inclusion*. London: Cengage Learning.

Craig, G. (2003). *What Works in Community Development with Children? Summary*. London: Barnardos.

Crawford, A. (2006). Networked governance and the post-regulatory state? Steering, rowing and anchoring the provision of policing and security. *Theoretical Criminology* 10(4): 449–479.

Crawford, A. (2009). Criminalising sociability through anti-social behaviour legislation: Dispersal powers, young people and the police. *Youth Justice* 9(1): 5–26.

References

Crenshaw, K. (1991). Mapping the margins: Intersectionality, identity politics, and violence against women of color. *Stanford Law Review* 43(6): 1241–1299.
Crisp, R. and Slote, M. A. (eds) (1997). *Virtue Ethics*. Oxford: Oxford University Press.
Crossan, M., Mazutis, D. and Seijts, G. (2013) In search of virtue: The role of virtues, values and character strengths in ethical decision making. *Journal of Business Ethics* 113(4): 567–581.
Crouch, C. (2006). *Capitalist Diversity and Change: Recombinant Governance and Institutional Entrepreneurs*. Oxford: Oxford University Press.
Currie, G. and Procter, S. J. (2005). The antecedents of middle managers' strategic contribution: The case of a professional bureaucracy. *Journal of Management Studies* 42(7): 1325–1356.
Currie, G., Finn, R. and Martin, G. (2009). Professional competition and modernizing the clinical workforce in the NHS. *Work, Employment and Society* 23(2): 267–284.
Currie, G., Tuck, P. and Morrell, K. (2015). Contesting, accepting, or escaping normative governance? The narration of tax inspectors' "Professional" identity. *Accounting Auditing and Accountability Journal* 28(8): 1291–1309.
Czarniawska, B. (2010). The uses of narratology in social and policy studies. *Critical Policy Studies* 4(1): 58–76.
Dahrendorf, R. (1979). *Life Chances*. Chicago, IL: Chicago University Press.
Daily, C. M., Dalton, D. R. and Cannella, A. A. (2003). Introduction to special topic forum corporate governance: Decades of dialogue and data. *Academy of Management Review* 28(3): 371–382.
Daly, M. (2003). Governance and social policy. *Journal of Social Policy* 32(1): 113–128.
Davies, A. and Thomas, R. (2003). Talking cop: Discourses of change and policing identities. *Public Administration* 81(4): 681–699.
Davies, H. T. O., Nutley, S. M. and Smith, P. C. (2000). *What Works? Evidence Based Policy and Practice in Public Services*. Bristol: The Policy Press.
Davies, J. S. (2007). The limits of partnership: An exit-action strategy for local democratic inclusion. *Political Studies* 55: 779–800.
Davis, E. (2005). *Memories of State: Politics, History, and Collective Identity in Modern Iraq*. Berkeley and Los Angeles: University of California Press.
Dawson, S., Mole, V., Winstanley, D. and Sherval, J. (1995). Management, competition and professional practice: Medicine and the marketplace. *British Journal of Management* 6(3): 169–181.
Department for Communities and Local Government (DCLG) (2006). *Together We Can: Improving Community Involvement in Community Safety*. London: Central Office of Information.
DCLG (2007). *An Action for Community Empowerment: Building on Success*. London: Department for Communities and Local Government.
DCLG (2011). *Citizenship Survey 2009/10*. London: Department of Communities and Local Government.
De Cremer, D. and Tyler, T. R. (2005). Am I respected or not?: Inclusion and reputation as issues in group membership. *Social Justice Research* 18(2): 121–153.
Delsol, R. and Shiner, M. (eds) (2015). *Stop and Search*. Basingstoke: Palgrave Macmillan.
Den Boer, M. (2002). Towards an accountability regime for an emerging European policing governance. *Policing and Society* 12(4): 275–289.
Denhardt, J. V. and Denhardt, R. B. (2007). *The New Public Service: Serving, Not Steering*. New York: M. E. Sharpe.
Dewey, J. (2007). *Human Nature and Conduct: An Introduction to Social Psychology*. London and New York: Cosimo Classics.

Dick, G. P. M. (2011). The influence of managerial and job variables on organizational commitment in the police. *Public Administration* 89: 557–576.

Dick, P. (2005). Dirty work designations: How police officers account for their use of coercive force. *Human Relations* 58(11): 1363–1390.

Dick, P. (2010). The transition to motherhood and part-time working: Mutuality and incongruence in the psychological contracts existing between managers and employees. *Work, Employment and Society* 24(3): 508–525.

Dick, P. and Cassell, C. (2002). Barriers to managing diversity in a UK constabulary: The role of discourse. *Journal of Management Studies* 39(7): 953–976.

Diefenbach, T. (2009). New public management in public sector organizations: The dark sides of managerialistic "enlightenment". *Public Administration* 87(4): 892–909.

Dierksmeier, C. (2013). Kant on virtue. *Journal of Business Ethics* 113(4): 597–609.

Dillman, D. L. (2008). Whither the common good? *Public Administration Review* 68(1): 184–187.

Dobbs, D. (1996). Family matters: Aristotle's appreciation of women and the plural structure of society. *The American Political Science Review* 90(1): 74–89.

Dobel, P. (1992). Review of impossible jobs in public management. *Journal of Policy Analysis and Management* 11(1): 144–147.

Dodd, V. and Davies, C. (2011). London riots escalate as police battle for control. *The Guardian*, 9 August.

Dodge, J., Ospina, S. M. and Foldy, E. G. (2005). Integrating rigor and relevance in public administration scholarship: The contribution of narrative inquiry. *Public Administration Review* 65(3): 286–300.

Doherty, M. (2009). When the working day is through: The end of work as identity? *Work, Employment and Society* 23(1): 84–101.

Dorrien, Gary (ed.) (2008). *Social Ethics in the Making: Interpreting an American Tradition*. New York: Wiley-Blackwell.

Drake, M. J. and Schlachter, J. T. (2008). A virtue-ethics analysis of supply chain collaboration. *Journal of Business Ethics* 82(4): 851–864.

Drew, J. and Prenzler, T. (2015). *Contemporary Police Practice*. Oxford: Oxford University Press.

Du Gay, P. (2000). *In Praise of Bureaucracy: Weber, Organization, Ethics*. London: SAGE.

Dubber, M. (2005). *The Police Power: Patriarchy and the Foundations of American Government*. New York: Columbia University Press.

Elliott, I., Thomas, S. and Ogloff, J. (2012). Procedural justice in contacts with the police: The perspective of victims of crime. *Police Practice and Research* 13(5): 437–449.

Elliott, I., Thomas, S. and Ogloff, J. (2013). Procedural justice in victim-police interactions and victims' recovery from victimisation experiences. *Policing and Society* (May): 1–14.

Ellison, G. and O'Rawe, M. (2010). Security governance in transition: The compartmentalizing, crowding out and corralling of policing and security in Northern Ireland. *Theoretical Criminology* 14(1): 31–57.

Ellison, G. and Smyth, J. (2000). *The Crowned Harp: Policing Northern Ireland*. London: Pluto Press.

Ellison, G., Pino, N. W. and Shirlow, P. (2012). Assessing the determinants of public confidence in the police: A case study of a post-conflict community in Northern Ireland. *Criminology and Criminal Justice* 13: 552–576.

Emejulu, A. (2008). The Intersection of Ethnicity, Poverty and Wealth, in T. Ridge and S. Wright (eds), *Understanding Inequality, Poverty and Wealth: Policies and Prospects*. Bristol: The Policy Press, pp. 155–180.

Emerson, R. W. (2002). *Character and Heroism*. Amsterdam: Fredonia.

Emirbayer, M. and Mische, A. (1998). What is agency? *American Journal of Sociology* 103(4): 962–1023.

Emsley, C. (1999). *Gendarmes and the State in Nineteenth Century Europe*. Oxford: Oxford University Press.

Ericson, R. (1975). *Criminal Reactions: The Labelling Perspective*. London: Ashgate.

Ericson, R. V. and Haggerty, K. (1997). *Policing the Risk Society*. Toronto: University of Toronto Press.

Evans, R. and Lewis, P. (2013). *Undercover: The True Story of Britain's Secret Police*. London: Faber & Faber.

Everingham, M. (2001). Agricultural property rights and political change in Nicaragua. *Latin American Politics and Society* 43(3): 61–93.

Exworthy, M. and Halford, S. (eds) (1999). *Professionals and the New Managerialism in the Public Sector*. Milton Keynes: Open University Press.

Ezzamel, M. and Burns, J. (2005). Professional competition, economic value added and management control strategies. *Organization Studies* 26(5): 755–777.

Ezzamel, M. (2001). A difficult act to balance: Political costs and economic costs in the public sector. *Accounting, Accountability and Performance* 7(1): 31–49.

Faull, A. (2017). *Police Work and Identity: A South African Ethnography*. London: Routledge.

Fassin, D. (2015). Maintaining Order: The Moral Justification of Police Practices, in D. Fassin *et al.* (eds), *At the Heart of the State*. London: Pluto Press, pp. 93–116.

Fielding, N. (1988). *Joining Forces: Police Training, Socialization, and Occupational Competence*. London: Routledge.

Fielding, N. (1989). Police Culture and Police Practice, in M. Weatheritt (ed), *Police Research: Some Future Prospects*. Aldershot: Avebury.

Fielding, N. (1994). Cop Canteen Culture, in T. Newburn and E. Stanko (eds), *Just Boys Doing the Business: Men, Masculinity and Crime*. London: Routledge: 46–63.

Fitzgerald, L. and Ferlie, E. (2000). Professionals: Back to the future? *Human Relations* 53(5): 713–739.

Fives, A. J. (2008). Human flourishing: The grounds of moral judgment. *The Journal of Value Inquiry* 42(2): 167–185.

Flanagan, J. C. (1954). The critical incident technique. *Psychological Bulletin* 51(4):327–358.

Fleming, J. (2008). Managing the diary: What does a police commissioner do? *Public Administration* 86(3): 679–698.

Fleming, J. (ed.) (2015). *Police Leadership*. Oxford: Oxford University Press.

Fleming, J. and McLaughlin, E. (2012). Researching the confidence gap: Theory, method, policy. *Policing and Society* 22(3): 261–269.

Floyd, S. W. and Lane, P. J. (2000). Strategizing throughout the organization: Managing role conflict in strategic renewal. *Academy of Management Review* 25(1): 154–177.

Floyd, S. W. and Wooldridge, B. (1992). Middle management involvement in strategy and its association with strategic type: A research note. *Strategic Management Journal* 13(S1): 153–167.

Foldy, E. G. and Buckley, T. R. (2010). Re-creating street-level practice: The role of routines, work groups, and team learning. *Journal of Public Administration Research and Theory* 20(1): 23–52.

Folger, R. (ed.) (1984). *The Sense of Injustice: Social Psychological Perspectives*. New York: Plenum Press.

Fontrodona, J., Sison, A. J. G. and de Bruin, B. (2013). Editorial introduction: Putting virtues into practice: A challenge for business and organizations. *Journal of Business Ethics* 113 (4): 563–565.

Forbes, T. and Prime, N. (1999). Changing domains in the management process: Radiographers as managers in the NHS. *Journal of Management in Medicine* 13(2): 105–113.

Ford, J. Harding, N. and Learmonth, M. (2008). *Leadership as Identity: Constructions and Deconstructions*. Houndmills: Palgrave Macmillan.

Foster, J. (2003). Cop Cultures, in T. Newburn, (ed.), *The Handbook of Policing*. Cullompton: Willan.

Frampton, W. (2015). Dorset Police and Crime Commissioner Martyn Underhill and Dorset County Council leader Robert Gould give their view on government funding, *Dorset Echo*, 21 December, available on www.dorsetecho.co.uk/news/14157876.Mixed_views_on_budgets_for_police_and_council_in_Dorset/?ref=twtrec, last accessed 1 November 2017.

Frederickson, H. G. and LaPorte, T. R. (2002). Airport security, high reliability, and the problem of rationality. *Public Administration Review* 62(s1): 33–43.

Frederickson, H. G. (1991). Toward a theory of the public for public administration. *Administration and Society* 22(4): 395–417.

Frederickson, H. G. (1994). Can public officials correctly be said to have obligation to future generations? *Public Administration Review* 54: 457–464.

Fuller, C. (2013). Urban politics and the social practices of critique and justification: Conceptual insights from French pragmatism. *Progress in Human Geography* 37(5): 639–657.

Gabriel, Y. and Griffiths, D. S. (2004). Stories in Organizational Research, in C. Cassell and G. Symon (eds), *Essential Guide to Qualitative Methods in Organizational Research*. London: SAGE, pp. 114–126.

Garriott, W. C. (2013). *Policing and Contemporary Governance: The Anthropology of Police in Practice*. New York: Palgrave Macmillan.

Gau, J. M. and Brunson, R. K. (2010). Procedural justice and order maintenance policing: A study of inner city young men's perceptions of police legitimacy. *Justice Quarterly* 27(2): 255–279.

Gau, J. M. and Gaines, D. C. (2012). Top-down management and patrol officers' attitudes about the importance of public order maintenance: A research note. *Police Quarterly* 15(1): 45–61.

Geller, A., Fagan, J., Tyler, T. and Link, B. G. (2014). Aggressive policing and the mental health of young urban men. *American Journal of Public Health* 104(12): 2321–2327.

Genette, G. (1982). Frontiers of Narrative, in *Figures of Literary Discourse*, translated by A. Sheridan, introduced by Marie-Rose Logan. New York: Columbia University Press, pp. 127–144.

Gerber, M. M. and Jackson, J. (2017). Justifying violence: Legitimacy, ideology and public support for police use of force. *Psychology, Crime and Law* 23(1): 97–95.

Ghoshal, S. (2005). Bad management theories are destroying good management practices. *Academy of Management Learning and Education* 4: 75–91.

Gibbons, M., Limoges, C., Nowotny, H., Schwartsman, S., Scott, P. and Trow, M. (1994). *The New Production of Knowledge*. London: SAGE.

Giddens, A. (1990). *The Consequences of Modernity*. Cambridge: Polity.

Gioia, D. A. Corley, K. G. and Hamilton, A. L. (2013). Seeking qualitative rigor in inductive research notes on the Gioia methodology. *Organizational Research Methods* 16(1): 15–31.

Girling, E., Loader, I. and Sparks, R. (2000). *Crime and Social Control in Middle England: Questions of Order in an English Town*. London: Routledge.

Glaeser, A. (2000). *Divided in Unity: Identity, Germany and the Berlin Police*. Chicago, IL: University of Chicago Press.

Glaser, J. (2015). *Suspect Race*. New York: Oxford University Press.

Goffman, E. (2002). *The Presentation of Self in Everyday Life*. Garden City, NY: Doubleday.

Goldsmith, A. J. (2010). Policing's new visibility. *British Journal of Criminology* 50(5): 914–934.

Goldsmith, A. J. and Lewis, C. (eds) (2000). *Civilian Oversight of Policing: Governance, Democracy, and Human Rights*. Oxford: Hart Publishing.

Goldstein, L. F. (2001). Aristotle's theory of revolution: Looking at the Lockean side. *Political Research Quarterly* 54(2): 311–331.

Goodsell, C. T. (1985). *The Case for Bureaucracy*, 2nd edition. Chatham, NJ: Chatham House.

Goodsell, C. T. (1990). Public Administration and the Public Interest, in G. L. Wamsley and J. F. Wolf (eds), *Refounding Public Administration: Modern Paradoxes, Postmodern Challenges*. London: SAGE, pp. 96–113.

Grandy, C. (2009). The "efficient" public administrator: Pareto and a well-rounded approach to public administration. *Public Administration Review* 69(6): 1115–1123.

Great Britain (2012a). *Policing Large Scale Disorder: Lessons from the Disturbances of August 2011. Sixteenth Report of Session 2010–2012*, Vol. 1: *Report Together with Formal Minutes*. London: The Stationery Office.

Great Britain (2012b). *Policing Large Scale Disorder: Lessons from the Disturbances of August 2011. Sixteenth Report of Session 2010–2012*, Vol 2: *Oral and Written Evidence*. London: The Stationery Office.

Great Britain (2012c). *Policing Large Scale Disorder: Lessons from the Disturbances of August 2011. The Government Response to the Sixteenth Report of the Home Affairs Committee Session 2010–2012 HC 1456*. London: The Stationery Office.

Green, A. I., Follert, M., Osterlund, K. and Paquin, J. (2010). Space, place and sexual sociality: Towards an "atmospheric analysis". *Gender, Work and Organization* 17(1) 7–27.

Greenberg, J. (2011). Organizational Justice: The Dynamics of Fairness in the Workplace, in Z. Sheldon (ed.), *APA Handbook of Industrial and Organizational Psychology*, Vol. 3: *Maintaining, Expanding, and Contracting the Organization*. Washington, DC: American Psychological Association, pp. 271–327.

Greenhalgh, T. and Russell, J. (2006). Reframing evidence synthesis as rhetorical action in the policy making drama. *Healthcare Policy* 1(2): 31–39.

Greer, C. and McLaughlin, E. (2011). "Trial by media": Policing, the 24–27 news mediasphere and the "politics of outrage". *Theoretical Criminology* 15(1): 23–46.

Gremler, D. D. (2004). The critical incident technique in service research. *Journal of Service Research* 7(1): 65–89.

Grindle, M. S. (2000). *Audacious Reforms: Institutional Invention and Democracy in Latin America*. Baltimore, MD: The Johns Hopkins University Press.

Grindle, M. S. (2007). *Going Local: Decentralization, Democratization and the Promise of Good Governance*. Princeton, NJ: Princeton University Press.

Grint, K. (2007). Learning to lead: Can Aristotle help us find the road to wisdom? *Leadership* 3(2): 231–246.

Grint, K. (2010). The cuckoo clock syndrome: Addicted to command, allergic to leadership. *European Management Journal* 28(4): 306–313.

Gurses, K. and Ozcan, P. (2015). Entrepreneurship in regulated markets: Framing contests and collective action to introduce pay TV. *The U.S. Academy of Management Journal* 58(6): 1709–1739.

Haas, N. E., VanCraen, M., Skogan, W. G. and Fleitas, D. M. (2015). Explaining officer compliance: The importance of procedural justice and trust inside a police organization. *Criminology and Criminal Justice* 15(4): 442–463.

Hadfield, P. (2006). *Bar Wars: Contesting the Night in Contemporary British Cities*. Oxford: Oxford University Press.

Hadreas, P. (2002). Aristotle on the vices and virtue of wealth. *Journal of Business Ethics* 39(4): 361–376.

Hales, G., May, T., Belur, J. and Hough, M. (2015). *Chief Officer Misconduct in Policing: An Exploratory Study*. Ryton-on-Dunsmore: College of Policing.

Hall, S., Critcher, C., Jefferson, T., Clarke, J. and Roberts, B. (1978). *Policing the Crisis*. London: Macmillan.

Halliday, J. (2011). London riots: BlackBerry to help police probe Messenger looting "role". *Guardian* Online, available on www.guardian.co.uk/uk/2011/aug/08/london-riots-blackberry-messenger-looting.

Hamm, J. A., Trinkner, R. and Carr, J. D. (in press). Fair process, trust, and cooperation: Moving toward an integrated framework of police legitimacy. *Criminal Justice and Behavior*.

Hardin, R. (2006). *Trust*. Cambridge: Polity Press.

Harding, N. and Learmonth, M. (2000). Thinking critically: The case of health policy research. *Technology Analysis & Strategic Management* 12(3): 335–341.

Hargrove, E. C. and Glidewell, J. C. (eds) (1990). *Impossible Jobs in Public Management*. Lawrence, KS: University Press of Kansas.

Harris, R. N. (1973). *The Police Academy: An Inside View*. New York: Wiley.

Harrison, S. and Wood, B. (1999). Designing health service organization in the UK, 1968 to 1998: From blueprint to bright idea and "manipulated emergence". *Public Administration* 77(4): 751–768.

Hart, B. and Morrell, K. (2016). Threatening judgement? *Police Professional*, 2 June.

Hart, P. T. (2011). Reading the signs of the times: Regime dynamics and leadership possibilities. *Journal of Political Philosophy* 19(4): 419–439.

Hartman, E. M. (2011). Virtue, profit, and the separation thesis: An Aristotelian view. *Journal of Business Ethics* 99(1): 5–17.

Harvey, D. (2012). *Rebel Cities: From the Right to the City to the Urban Revolution*. New York: Verso.

Haslam, S. A. and Ellemers, N. (2005). Social identity in industrial and organizational psychology: Concepts, controversies and contributions. *International Review of Industrial and Organizational Psychology* 20: 39–118.

Hawdon, J. (2008). Legitimacy, trust, social capital, and policing styles: A theoretical statement. *Police Quarterly* 11(2): 182–201.

Heifetz, R. A. (1994). *Leadership without Easy Answers*. Cambridge, MA: Harvard University Press.

Henderson, A. C. (2013). Examining policy implementation in health care: Rule abidance and deviation in emergency medical services. *Public Administration Review* 73: 799–809.

Hendrix, S. (1996/1997). Pride of ownership: Land tenure and conflict resolution. *Harvard International Review* 19(1): 40–43.

Heuer, L. amd Stroessner, S. J. (2011). The multi-value basis of procedural justice. *Journal of Experimental Social Psychology* 47(3): 541–553.

Hewison, A., and Morrell, K. (2013). Leadership development in the English National Health Service: A counter narrative to inform policy. *International Journal of Nursing Studies* 51(4): 677–688.

Hillsborough Independent Panel (2012). *The Report of the Hillsborough Independent Panel*. London: The Stationery Office.

Hinsch, W. (2008). Legitimacy and Justice, in J. Kuhnelt (ed.), *Political Legitimation without Morality?* London: Springer, pp. 39–52.

Hinsch, W. (2010). Justice, legitimacy, and constitutional rights. *Critical Review of International Social and Political Philosophy* 13(1): 39–54.

HMIC (Her Majesty's Inspectorate of Constabulary). (2009). *Adapting to Protest: Nurturing the British Model of Policing*. London: Central Office for Information.

HMIC (2013). *Stop and Search Powers: Are the Police Using Them Effectively and Fairly?* London: Her Majesty's Inspectorate of Constabulary.

HMIC (2015a). *Online and on the Edge: Real Risks in a Virtual World. An Inspection into How Forces Deal with the Online Sexual Exploitation of Children*. London: Her Majesty's Inspectorate of Constabulary.

HMIC (2015b). *PEEL: Police Effectiveness 2015 (vulnerability)*. London: Her Majesty's Inspectorate of Constabulary.

HMIC (2017). *State of Policing: The Annual Assessment of Policing in England and Wales*. London: Her Majesty's Inspectorate of Constabulary.

HMSO (2003). *Health and Social Care Community Health and Standards Act 2003: Explanatory Notes*. London: HMSO.

Hobbs, D. (1995). *Bad Business: Professional Crime in Modern Britain*. Oxford: Oxford University Press.

Hobbs, D. (2010). Obituary of Sir Robert Mark. *The Independent*, 5 October.

Hogan, J., Bennell, C. and Taylor, A. (2011). The challenges of moving into middle management: Responses from police officers. *Journal of Police and Criminal Psychology* 26(2): 100–111.

Hogg, M. A. and Abrams, D. (1990). Social Motivation, Self-esteem, and Social Identity, in D. Abrams and M. A. Hogg (eds), *Social Identity Theory: Constructive and Critical Advances*. London: Harvester Wheatsheaf, pp. 44–70.

Hogg, M. A. and Terry, D. J. (2000). Social identity and self-categorization processes in organizational contexts. *Academy of Management Review* 25(1): 121–140.

Hoggett, J. and Stott, C. (2012). Post G20: The challenge of change, implementing evidence-based public order policing. *Journal of Investigative Psychology and Offender Profiling* 9: 174–183.

Holdaway, S. (1977). Changes in urban policing. *British Journal of Sociology* 28(2): 119–137.

Holdaway, S. (2010). *Black Police Associations: An Analysis of Race and Ethnicity within Constabularies*. Oxford: Oxford University Press.

Holdaway, S. (in press) The re-professionalization of the police in England and Wales. *Criminology and Criminal Justice*.

Holgersson, S., and Knutsson, J. (2011). Dialogue Policing: A Means for Less Crowd Violence?, in T.D. Madensen, and J. Knutsson (eds), *Preventing Crowd Violence*. Boulder, CO: Lynne Rienner, pp. 191–216.

Hollenbach, David S. J. (2002). *The Common Good and Christian Ethics*. New York: Cambridge University Press.

Hollingsworth, J. R., Schmitter, P, and Streeck, W. (eds) (1994). *Governing Capitalist Economies: Performance and Control of Economic Sectors*. Oxford: Oxford University Press.

Hollingsworth, J. R. and Boyer, R. (eds) (1997). *Contemporary Capitalism: The Embeddedness of Institutions*. Cambridge: Cambridge University Press.

Holt, R. (2006). Principals and practice: Rhetoric and the moral character of managers. *Human Relations* 59(12): 1659–1680.

Home Office (2013). *Direct Entry in the Police: Government Response*. London: Home Office.

Home Office (2015). *Police Powers and Procedures England and Wales, Year Ending 31 March 2015*. London: Home Office.

Honneth, A. (2007). *Disrespect: The Normative Foundations of Critical Theory*. Cambridge: Polity Press.

Hope, T. (2004). Pretend it works: Evidence and governance in the evaluation of the Reducing Burglary Initiative. *Criminal Justice* 4: 287–308.

Hope, T. (2009). The illusion of control: A response to Professor Sherman. *Criminology and Criminal Justice* 9(2): 125–134.

Hope, T. (2012). Riots, pure and simple? *Criminal Justice Matters* 87(1): 2–4.

Huby, G., Harris, F. M., Powell, A. E., Kielman, T., Sheikh, A., Williams, S. and Pinnock, H. (2014). Beyond professional boundaries: Relationships and resources in health services' modernisation in England and Wales. *Sociology of Health and Illness* 36(3): 400–415.

Hudson, B. (1997). Michael Lipsky and Street Level Bureaucracy: A Neglected Perspective, in M. Hill (ed.), *The Policy Process: A Reader*. London: Prentice Hall, pp. 25–32.

Hudson, J. and Jones, P. (2005). "Public goods": An exercise in calibration. *Public Choice* 124: 267–282.

Hult, K. M. (1992). Review of "Impossible Jobs in Public Management" by Edwin C. Hargrove; John C. Glidewell. *The American Political Science Review* 86(2): 539–540.

Huq, A., Jackson, J. and Trinkner, R. (2017). Legitimating practices: Revisiting the predicates of police legitimacy. *British Journal of Criminology* 57(5): 1101–1122.

Hyde, P. and Davies, H. T. O. (2004). Service design, culture and performance: Collusion and co-production in health care. *Human Relations* 57(11): 1407–1426.

Hyden, G. and Bratton, M. (eds) (1992). *Governance and Politics in Africa*. Boulder, CO: Lynne Rienner.

Jackson, J. (2015). On the Dual Motivational Force of Legitimate Authority, in B. H. Bornstein and A. J. Tomkins (eds), *Cooperation and Compliance with Authority: The Role of Institutional Trust. 62nd Nebraska Symposium on Motivation*. New York: Springer, pp. 145–166.

Jackson, J. and Bradford, B. (2009). Crime, policing and the moral order: On the expressive nature of public confidence in policing. *The British Journal of Sociology* 60: 493–521.

Jackson, J. and Gau, J. (2015). Carving up Concepts?, in E. Shockley, T. M. S. Neal, L. PytlikZillig and B. Bornstein (eds), *Interdisciplinary Perspectives on Trust: Towards Theoretical and Methodological Integration*. New York: Springer, pp. 49–69.

Jackson, J., Bradford, B., Stanko, E. A. and Hohl, K. (2012a). *Just Authority? Public Trust and Police Legitimacy*. Oxford: Routledge.

Jackson, J., Bradford, B., Hough, M., Quinton, P., Myhill, A. and Tyler, T. R. (2012b). Why do people comply with the law? Legitimacy and the influence of legal institutions. *British Journal of Criminology* 52(6): 1051–1071.

Jackson, J., Bradford, B., Kuha, J. and Hough, M. (2014). Empirical Legitimacy as Two Connected Psychological States, in G. Mesko and J. Tankebe (eds), *Trust and Legitimacy in Criminal Justice: European Perspectives*. Heidelberg: Springer.

Jackson, N. and Carter, P. (1995). Organizational chiaroscuro: Throwing light on the concept of corporate governance. *Human Relations* 48(8): 875–889.

James, W. (1890/2007). *Principles of Psychology*, Vol. 1. New York: Cosimo Classics.

Jann, W. (2003). State, administration and governance in Germany: Competing traditions and dominant narratives. *Public Administration* 81(1): 95–118.

Jefferson, T. (2012). Policing the riots: From Bristol and Brixton to Tottenham, via Toxteth, Handsworth, etc. *Criminal Justice Matters* 87(1): 8–9.

Jennings, W. G., Lorie, A. F. and Lynch, M. D. (2014). Cops and cameras: Officers' perceptions of the use of body-worn cameras in law enforcement. *Journal of Criminal Justice* 42(6): 549–556.

Jessop, B. (1998). The rise of governance and the risks of failure: The case of economic development. *International Social Science Journal* 50(1): 29–45.

Jobes, P. C. (2002). Effective officer and good neighbour: Problems and perceptions among police in rural Australia. *Policing: An International Journal of Police Strategies and Management* 25(2): 256–273.

Jobes, P. C. (2003). Human ecology and rural policing: A grounded theoretical analysis of how personal constraints and community characteristics influence strategies of law enforcement in rural New South Wales, Australia. *Police Practice and Research* 4(1): 3–19.

Johnson, J. and Farrell, W. (1992). The fire this time: The genesis of the Los Angeles rebellion of 1992. *North Carolina Law Review* 71: 1403–1420.

Jonathan-Zamir, T., Mastrofski, S. D. and Moyal, S. (2013). Measuring procedural justice in police-citizen encounters. *Justice Quarterly* 32(5): 845–871.

Jones, C., Hesterly, W. S. and Borgatti, S. P. (1997). A general theory of network governance: Exchange conditions and social mechanisms. *Academy of Management Review* 22(4): 911–945.

Jones, M. (2008). Democratic governance and the role of the police. *Public Administration Review* 68(3): 581–584.

Jones, M. (2009). Governance, integrity, and the police organization. *Policing: An International Journal of Police Strategies and Management* 32(2): 338–350.

Jones, T. (2012). Review: "The politics of the police", R. Reiner (ed.), 4th edition. *Policing and Society* 22(4): 545–547.

Jones, T., Newburn, T. and Smith, D. J. (2012). Democracy and Police and Crime Commissioners, in T. Newburn and J. Peay (eds), *Policing: Politics, Culture and Control*. Oxford: Hart, pp. 219–245.

Jones, T. and Van Sluis, A. (2009). National standards, local delivery: Police reform in England and Wales. *German Policy Studies* 5(2): 117–144.

Jones, T. M. and Goldberg, L. D. (1982). Governing the large corporation: More arguments for public directors. *Academy of Management Review* 7: 603–611.

Jordan, J. (2008). Perfect victims, perfect policing? Improving rape complaints' experiences of police investigations. *Public Administration* 86: 699–719.

Judge, T. (2007). To go or not to go. *Police: The Magazine of the Police Federation of England and Wales*, December, p. 29.

Justice, B. and Meares, T. L. (2014). How the criminal justice system educates its citizens. *The Annals of the American Academy* 651 (January): 159–177.

Karllson, S. (2000). *Multilayered Governance: Pesticides in the South – Environmental Concerns in a Globalised World*. Linköping: Linköping University.

Kazancigil, A. (1998). Governance and science: Market-like modes of managing society and producing knowledge. *International Social Science Journal* 155: 69–79.

Keith, M. (1993). *Race, Riots and Policing: Lore and Disorder in a Multi-racist Society*. London: UCL Press.

Kelleher, C. A. and Wolak, J. (2007). Explaining public confidence in the branches of state government. *Political Research Quarterly* 60(4): 707–721.

Kelman, H. C. and Hamilton, V. L. (1989). *Crimes of Obedience*. New Haven, CT: Yale University Press.

Kelman, S. (2005). Public management needs help! *Academy of Management Journal* 48(6): 967–969.

Kiel, L. D. and Watson, D. J. (2009). Affective leadership and emotional labor: A view from the local level. *Public Administration Review* 69(1): 21–24.

Kim, P. S., Halligan, J., Cho, N., Oh, C. H. and Eikenberry, A. M. (2005). Toward participatory and transparent governance: Report on the Sixth Global Forum on Reinventing Government. *Public Administration Review* 65(6): 646–654.

Kincaid, J. (1997). Review of "Creating Public Value: Strategic Management in Government" by M. H. Moore. *Journal of Politics* 59(1): 257–258.

Klingner, D. E. (2006). Building global public management governance capacity: The road not taken. *Public Administration Review* 66(5): 775–779.

Klockars, C. B. (1985). *The Idea of Police*. Beverly Hills, CA: SAGE.

Kocher, C., Kumar, K. and Subramanian, R. (1998). Physician-hospital integration strategies: Impact on physician involvement in hospital governance. *Health Care Management Review* 23(3): 38–47.

Koehn, D. (2013). East meets West: Toward a universal ethic of virtue for global business. *Journal of Business Ethics* 116(4): 703–715.

Kohli, A. (2004). *State-Directed Development: Political Power and Industrialization in the Global Periphery*. Cambridge: Cambridge University Press.

Kohn, A. (1999). *Punished by Reward*. Boston, MA: Houghton Mifflin.

Kohn, M. (2000). Language, power, and persuasion: Toward a critique of deliberative democracy. *Constellations* 7(3): 408–429.

Konisky, D. M. and Reenock, C. (2012). Case selection in public management research: Problems and solutions. *Journal of Public Administration Research and Theory* 23(2): 361–393.

Konzelmann, S., Conway, N., Trenberth, L. and Wilkinson, F. 2006. Corporate governance and human resource management. *British Journal of Industrial Relations* 44(3): 541–567.

Kooiman, J. (ed.) (1993). *Modern Governance: New Government-Society Interactions*. London: SAGE.

Kraut, R. (2002). *Aristotle: Political Philosophy*. Oxford: Oxford University Press.

Kuipers, B. S., Higgs, M. J., Kickert, W. J. M., Tummers, L. G., Grandia, J. and Van der Voet, J. (2014). The management of change in public organisations: A literature review. *Public Administration* 92(1): 1–20.

Kwak, H. and McNeeley, S. (in press). Neighbourhood characteristics and confidence in the police in the context of South Korea. *Policing and Society*.

Learmonth, M. (2003). U.K. Hospital Chief Executives, Basically "a bunch of administrators"? The NHS Management Inquiry Reviewed, in M. N. Smyth (ed.), *Health Care in Transition*, Vol. 2. New York: Nova Science, pp. 61–80.

Learmonth, M. (2005). Doing things with words: The case of "management" and "administration". *Public Administration* 83(3): 617–637.

Learmonth, M. (2006). Is there such a thing as "evidence-based management"?: A commentary on Rousseau's 2005 presidential address. *Academy of Management Review* 31(4): 1089–1091.

Learmonth, M. (2017). Making history critical: Recasting a history of the "management" of the British National Health Service. *Journal of Health Organization & Management* 31(5): 542–555.

Learmonth, M. and Harding, N. (2006). Evidence-based management: The very idea. *Public Administration* 84(2): 245–266.

Learmonth, M. and Morrell, K. (2017). Is critical leadership studies "critical"? *Leadership* 13(3): 257–271.

Leftwich, A. (1994). Governance, the state and the politics of development. *Development and Change* 25(2): 363–386.

Lentz, S. A. and Chaires, R. H. (2007). The invention of Peel's principles: A study of policing "textbook" history. *Journal of Criminal Justice* 35(1): 69–79.

Leventhal, G. S. (1980). What Should Be Done with Equity Theory? New Approaches to the Study of Fairness in Social Relationships, in K. Gergen, M. Greenberg, and R. Willis (eds), *Social Exchange*. New York: Plenum, pp. 27–55.

Lewis, C. (2006). In pursuit of the public interest. *Public Administration Review* 66(5): 694–701.

Lewis, P. G., Newburn, T., Taylor, M., Mcgillivray, C., Greenhill, A., Frayman, H. and Proctor, R. (2011). *Reading the Riots: Investigating England's Summer of Disorder*. London: LSE and The Guardian.

Lewis, P. G., Provine, D. M., Varsanyi, M. W. and Decker, S. H. (2013). Why do (some) city police departments enforce federal immigration law? Political, demographic, and organizational influences on local choices. *Journal of Public Administration Research and Theory* 23(1): 1–25.

Libby, T. and Thorne, L. (2007). The development of a measure of auditors' virtue. *Journal of Business Ethics* 71(1): 89–99.

Liebling, A. (2004). *Prisons and Their Moral Performance*. Oxford: Oxford University Press.

Limbs, E. C. and Fort, T. L. (2000). Nigerian business practices and their interface with virtue ethics. *Journal of Business Ethics* 26(2): 169–179.

Lipsky, M. (2010). *Street-level Bureaucracy: Dilemmas of the Individual in Public Services*. 30th anniversary expanded edition. New York: Russell SAGE Foundation.

Lister, E. D. and Herzog, A. (2000). From advocacy to ambassadorship: Physician participation in healthcare governance. *Journal of Healthcare Management* 45(2): 108–116.

Lister, S. (2013). The new politics of the police: Police and crime commissioners and the "operational independence" of the police. *Policing* 7(3): 239–247.

Lister, S. (2014). Scrutinising the role of the police and crime panel in the new era of police governance in England and Wales. *Safer Communities* 13(1): 22–31.

Loader, I. (2000). Plural policing and democratic governance. *Social and Legal Studies* 9(3): 323–345.

Loader, I. and Mulcahy, A. (2003). *Policing and the Condition of England: Memory, Politics and Culture*. Oxford: Oxford University Press.

Loader, I. and Sparks, R. (2013). *Public Criminology?* Oxford: Routledge.

Loader, I. and Walker, N. (2007). *Civilising Security*. Cambridge: Cambridge University Press.

Loftus, B. (2010). Police occupational culture: Classic themes, altered times. *Policing and Society* 20(1): 1–20.

Longstaff, A. (2011). A question of confidence. *Police: The Magazine of the Police Federation of England and Wales*, August, pp. 13–15.

Louden, R. B. (1997). On Some Vices of Virtue Ethics, in R. Crisp and M. Slote (eds), *Virtue Ethics*. Oxford: Oxford University Press, pp. 201–216.

Loveday, B. (2006). Policing performance: The impact of performance measures and targets on police forces in England and Wales. *International Journal of Police Science and Management* 8(4): 282–293.

Lumsden, K. and Goode, J. (forthcoming). Policing research and the rise of the "evidence-base": Police office and staff understandings of research, its implantation and "what works". *Sociology*.

Lüscher, L. S. and Lewis, M. W. (2008). Organizational change and managerial sensemaking: Working through paradox. *Academy of Management Journal* 51(2): 221–240.

Lynn, L. E., Heinrich, C. J. and Hill, C. J. (2001). *Improving Governance: A New Logic for Empirical Research*. Washington, DC: Georgetown University Press.

McAra, L. and McVie, S. (2005). The usual suspects? Street-life, young people and the police. *Criminology and Criminal Justice* 5(1): 5–36.

McAra, L. and McVie, S. (2007). Youth Justice? The impact of system contact on patterns of resistance from offending. *European Journal of Criminology* 4(3): 315–345.

McAra, L. and McVie, S. (2012). Negotiated order: Towards a theory of pathways into and out of offending. *Criminology and Criminal Justice* 12(4): 347–376.

MacCoun, R. (2005). Voice, control, and belonging: The double-edged sword of procedural fairness. *Annual Review of Law and Social Science* 1:171–201.
McCracken, J., Martin, W. and Shaw, B. (1998). Virtue ethics and the parable of the Sadhu. *Journal of Business Ethics* 17(1): 25–38.
McGrath, J. E. (1982). Dilemmatics: The Study of Research Choices and Dilemmas, in J. E. McGrath, J. Martin, and R. Kulka (eds), *Judgement Calls in Research*. London: SAGE, pp. 69–102.
MacIntyre, A. (1984a). *After Virtue*, 2nd edition.London: Duckworth.
MacIntyre, A. (1984b). Does applied ethics rest on a mistake? *The Monist* 67(4): 498–513.
MacIntyre, A. (1988). *Whose Justice? Which Rationality?*London: Duckworth.
MacIntyre, A. (1997). The Nature of Virtues, in R. CrispandM. Slote (eds), *Virtue Ethics*. Oxford: Oxford University Press, pp.118–140.
MacIntyre, A. (1999). Social structures and their threats to moral agency. *Philosophy* 74(3): 311–329.
McKinley, W. and Scherer, A. G. (2000). Organizational restructuring: Unanticipated consequences. *Academy of Management Review* 25(4): 735–752.
McLaughlin, J. (2001). EBM and risk-Rhetorical resources in the articulation of professional identity. *Journal of Management in Medicine* 15(5): 352–363.
MacQueen, S. and Bradford, B. (2015). Enhancing public trust and police legitimacy during road traffic encounters: Results from a randomized controlled trial in Scotland. *Journal of Experimental Criminology* 11(3): 419–433.
MacQueen, S. and Bradford, B. (2017). Where did it all go wrong? Implementation failure – and more – in a field experiment of procedural justice policing. *Journal of Experimental Criminology* 13(3): 321–345.
Mael, F. and Ashforth, B. E. (1992). Alumni and their alma mater: A partial test of the reformulated model of organizational identification. *Journal of Organizational Behavior* 13(2): 102–123.
Maheshwari, S. R. (2005). *Public Administration in India: The Higher Civil Service*. New Delhi: Oxford University Press.
Majone, G. (1989). *Evidence, Argument, and Persuasion in the Policy Process*. New Haven, CT: Yale University Press.
Manning, P. K. (1977). *Police Work: The Social Organization of Policing*. Cambridge, MA: MIT Press.
Manning, P. K. (2010). *Democratic Policing in a Changing World*. Boulder, CO: Paradigm Publishers.
Maranto, R. and Wolf, P. J. (2012). Cops, teachers, and the art of the impossible: Explaining the lack of diffusion of innovations that make impossible jobs possible. *Public Administration Review* 73(2): 230–240.
Marks, A. and Thompson, P. (2010). Beyond the Blank Slate: Identities and Interests at Work, in P. Thompson and C. Smith (eds), *Working Life: Renewing Labour Process Analysis*. London: Palgrave, pp. 316–338.
Marquand, D. (2004). *Decline of the Public*. Cambridge: Polity Press.
Marr, A. (2007). *A History of Modern Britain*. London: Macmillan.
Mastrofski, S. D. (2004). Controlling street-level police discretion. *Annals of the American Academy of Political and Social Science* 593: 100–118.
Matza, D. (1964). *Drift*. New York: J. Wiley.
Mawby, R. (2002). *Policing Images: Policing, Communication and Legitimacy*. Cullompton: Willan.

May, J. (2015). Cutting police budgets would be a "disaster" – ex-Met chief. PoliticsHome, 16 November, available on www.politicshome.com/news/uk/home-affairs/news/60073/cutting-police-budgets-would-be-disaster-ex-met-chief/.

May, T., Gyateng, T. and Hough, M. (2010). *Differential Treatment in the Youth Justice System.* London: Equalities and Human Rights Commission.

Mayers, D., Shivdasani, A. and. Smith, C. W. (1997). Board composition in the life insurance industry. *Journal of Business* 70(1): 33–63.

Maynard-Moody, S. and Musheno, M. (2000). State agent or citizen agent: Two narratives of discretion. *Journal of Public Administration Research and Theory* 10(2): 329–358.

Maynard-Moody, S. and Musheno, M. (2012). Social equities and inequities in practice: Street-level workers as agents and pragmatists. *Public Administration Review* 72(s1): 16–23.

Mazerolle, L., Antrobus, E., Bennett, S. and Tyler, T. R. (2013). Shaping citizen perceptions of police legitimacy: A randomized field trial of procedural justice. *Criminology* 51(1): 33–64.

Mazerolle, L., Bennett, S., Antrobus, E. and Eggins, L. (2011). Key Findings from the Queensland Community Engagement Trial. CEPS Briefing Paper, June 2011.

Mazerolle, L., Bennett, S., Antrobus, E. and Eggins, E. (2012). Procedural justice, routine encounters and citizen perceptions of the police: Main findings from the Queensland Community Engagement Trial (QCET). *Journal of Experimental Criminology* 8(4): 343–366.

Mehozay, Y. and Factor, R. (2017). Deeply embedded core normative values and legitimacy of law enforcement authorities. *Journal of Research in Crime and Delinquency* 54(2): 151–180.

Melé, D. (2009). Integrating personalism into virtue-based business ethics: The personalist and the common good principles. *Journal of Business Ethics* 88(1): 227–244.

MellahiK., Morrell, K. and Wood, G. (2010). *The Ethical Business*, 2nd edition. London: Macmillan.

Mengistu, B. and Vogel, E. (2006). Bureaucratic neutrality among competing bureaucratic values in an ethnic federalism: The case of Ethiopia. *Public Administration Review* 66(2): 205–216.

Metropolitan Police Service (2012). *4 Days in August.* London: Metropolitan Police.

Meyer, J. P., Becker, T. E. and van Dick, R. (2006). Social identities and commitments at work: Toward an integrative model. *Journal of Organizational Behavior* 27: 665–683.

Meyer, R. E., Egger-Peitler, I., Höllerer, M. A. and Hammerschmid, G. (in press). Of bureaucrats and passionate public managers: Institutional logics, executive identities, and public service motivation. *Public Administration.*

Millie, A. (2013). What are the Police For? Re-thinking Policing Post-Austerity, in J. M. Brown (ed.), *The Future of Policing.* London: Routledge, pp. 52–63.

Millings, M. (2013). Policing British Asian identities: The enduring role of the police in young British Asian men's situated negotiation of identity and belonging. *British Journal of Criminology* 53(6): 1075–1092.

Ministry of Justice (2011). *Statistical Bulletin on the Public Disorder of 6th to 9th August 2011.* London: Ministry of Justice.

Ministry of Justice (2012). *Statistical Bulletin on the Public Disorder of 6th to 9 August 2011: September 2012 Update.* London: Ministry of Justice.

Mintzberg, H. (1979). *The Structuring of Organizations.* Englewood Cliffs, NJ: Prentice Hall.

Mintzberg, H. (1995). The Professional Organisation, in H. Mintzberg, J. B. Quinn and S. Ghoshal (eds), *The Strategy Process.* London: Prentice Hall.

Mo, T. O. (2008). Doctors as managers: Moving towards general management?: The case of unitary management reform in Norwegian hospitals. *Journal of Health Organization and Management* 22(4): 400–415.

Mok, K. (2002). Policy of decentralization and changing governance of higher education in post-Mao China. *Public Administration and Development* 22(3): 261–273.

Moore, G. (2012). Virtue in business: Alliance boots and an empirical exploration of MacIntyre's conceptual framework. *Organization Studies* 33(3): 363–387.

Moore, M. H. (1990). Police Leadership, in E. Hargrove and J. Glidewell (eds), *Impossible Jobs in Public Management*. Lawrence, KS: University Press of Kansas, pp. 72–102.

Moore, M. H. (1995). *Creating Public Value: Strategic Management in Government*. Cambridge, MA: Harvard Business School Press.

Morgan, R. and Newburn, T. (1997). *The Future of Policing*. Oxford: Oxford University Press.

Morgan, J. and Zedner, L. (1992). *Child Victims: Crime, Impact, and Criminal Justice*. Oxford: Oxford University Press.

Morrell, K. (2004a). Decision making and business ethics: The implications of using image theory in preference to rational choice. *Journal of Business Ethics* 50(3): 239–252.

Morrell, K. (2004b). Enhancing effective careers thinking: Scripts and Socrates. *British Journal of Guidance and Counselling* 32: 547–558.

Morrell, K. (2006a). Policy as narrative: New Labour's reform of the National Health Service. *Public Administration* 84(2): 367–385.

Morrell, K. (2006b). Governance, ethics and the NHS. *Public Money and Management* 26(1): 55–62.

Morrell, K. (2007). Aesthetics and learning in Aristotle. *Leadership* 3(4): 497–500.

Morrell, K. (2008). The narrative of "evidence based" management: A polemic. *Journal of Management Studies* 45(3): 613–635.

Morrell, K. (2009). Governance and the public good. *Public Administration* 87(3): 538–556.

Morrell, K. (2012a). *Organization, Society and Politics: An Aristotelian Perspective*. London: Palgrave.

Morrell, K. (2012b). Evidence-based dialectics. *Organization* 19(4): 461–479.

Morrell, K. (2015). The likely consequences of further cuts to police funding. *Policing Insight*, 23 November.

Morrell, K. and Brammer, S. (2016). Governance and virtue: The case of public order police. *Journal of Business Ethics* 136(2): 385–398.

Morrell, K. and Clark, I. (2010). Private equity and the public good. *Journal of Business Ethics* 96(2): 249–263.

Morrell, K. and Harrington-Buhay, N. (2012). What is governance in the "public interest"? *Public Administration* 90(2): 412–428.

Morrell, K. and Hartley, J. (2006a). A model of political leadership. *Human Relations* 59(4): 483–504.

Morrell, K. and Hartley J. (2006b). Ethics in leadership: The case of local politicians. *Local Government Studies* 32(1): 55–70.

Morrell, K. and Hewison, A. (2013). Rhetoric in Policy Texts: The role of enthymeme in Darzi's review of the NHS. *Policy and Politics* 41(1): 59–79.

Morrell, K. and Learmonth, M. (2017). Evidence Based Management, in A. Wilkinson, S. Armstrong and R. Lounsbury (eds), *The Oxford Handbook of Management*. Oxford: Oxford University Press, pp. 419–436.

Morrell, K. and Tuck, P. (2014). Governance, tax and folk tales. *Accounting Organizations and Society* 39(2): 134–147.

Morrell, K., Learmonth, M. and Heracleous, L. (2015). An archaeological critique of "evidence-based management". *British Journal of Management* 26(3): 529–543.

Moynihan, D. P. (2005). Managing for results in an impossible job: Solution or symbol? *International Journal of Public Administration* 28(3–4): 213–231.

Moynihan, D. P. and Pandey, S. K. (2007). The role of organizations in fostering public service motivation. *Public Administration review* 67(1): 40–53.

Mrotek, D. D. (2001). The drama of dysfunction: Value conflict in US managed care. *Human Relations* 54(2): 147–172.
Murphy, K., Bradford, B. and Jackson, J. (2016). Motivating compliance behaviour among offenders: Procedural justice or deterrence? *Criminal Justice & Behavior* 43(1): 102–118.
Murphy, K., Hinds, L. and Fleming, J. (2008). Encouraging public cooperation and support for police. *Policing and Society* 6(1): 136–155.
Myhill, A. and Bradford, B. (2012). Can police enhance public confidence by improving quality of service? Results from two surveys in England and Wales. *Policing and Society* 22(4): 397–425.
Myhill, A. and Bradford, B. (2013). Overcoming cop culture? Organizational justice and police officers' attitudes toward the public. *Policing: An International Journal of Police Strategies and Management* 36: 338–356.
Nagin, D. S. (1998). Criminal deterrence research at the outset of the twenty-first century. *Crime and Justice* 23: 1–42.
Nardelli, A. (2015). How the UK civil service has changed in 10 charts. *The Guardian*, 19 November.
Narr, T., Toliver, J., Murphy, J., McFarland, M. and Ederheimer, J. (2006). *Police Management of Mass Demonstrations: Identifying Issues and Successful Approaches*. Police Executive Research Forum, available on www.policeforum.org/assets/docs/Critical_Issues_Series/p olice%20management%20of%20mass%20demonstrations%20-%20identifying%20issues% 20and%20successful%20approaches%202006.pdf.
Neocleous, M. (2000). *The Fabrication of Social Order: A Critical Theory of Police Power*. London: Pluto Press.
Nesbit, R., Moulton, S., Robinson, S., Smith, C., DeHart-Davis, L., Feeney, M. K., Gazley, B. and Hou, Y. (2011). Wrestling with intellectual diversity in public administration: Avoiding disconnectedness and fragmentation while seeking rigor, depth, and relevance. *Journal of Public Administration Research and Theory* 21(S1): 13–28.
Newburn, T. (2017). Response to Professor Ben Bradford. Talk given at the launch of the Global City Policing Institute, 15 November, City Hall, London.
Nicholls, A. (2010). Fair trade: Towards an economics of virtue. *Journal of Business Ethics* 92(2): 241–255.
Nichols, M. P. (1992). *Citizens and Statesmen: A Study of Aristotle's Politics*. Lanham, MD: Rowman and Littlefield.
Nicholson-Crotty, S. and O'Toole, L. J. (2004). Public management and organizational performance: The case of law enforcement agencies. *Journal of Public Administration Research and Theory* 14(1): 1–18.
Noon, M., Blyton, P. and Morrell, K. (2013). *The Realities of Work*, 4th edition. London: Macmillan.
Nozick, R. (1974). *Anarchy, State, and Utopia*. New York: Basic Books.
Nussbaum, M. C. (2001). *The Fragility of Goodness*, revised edition. Cambridge: Cambridge University Press.
Nutley, S. M., Walter, I. and Davies, H. T. O. (2003). From knowing to doing: A framework for understanding the evidence-into-practice agenda. *Evaluation* 9: 124–148.
O'Brien, Thomas W. (2009). Reconsidering the common good in a business context. *Journal of Business Ethics* 85(1): 25–37.
O'Kelly, C. and Dubnick, M. J. (2006). Taking tough choices seriously: Public administration and individual moral agency. *Journal of Public Administration Research and Theory* 16(3): 393–415.

O'Malley, P. and Hutchinson, S. (2007). Converging corporatization? Police management, police unionism, and the transfer of business principles. *Police Practice and Research* 8(2): 159–174.

O'Reilly, J., Lain, D., Sheehan, M., Smale, B. and Stuart, M. (2012). Managing uncertainty: The crisis, its consequences and the global workforce. *Work, Employment and Society* 25(4): 581–595.

Oliveira, A. and Murphy, K. (2015). Explaining negative attitudes toward police: Does race or social identity matter more? *Race and Justice* 5(3): 259–277.

Ooi, E. and Lajbcygier, P. (2013). Virtue remains after removing sin: Finding skill amongst socially responsible investment managers. *Journal of Business Ethics* 113(2): 199–224.

Ospina, S. M. and Dodge, J. (2005). It's about time: catching method up to meaning–the usefulness of narrative inquiry in public administration research. *Public Administration Review* 65(2): 143–157.

Pardo, I. (2000). *Morals of Legitimacy: Between Agency and System*. New York: Berghahn Books.

Parker, M. (2002). *Against Management: Organization in the Age of Managerialism*. London: Polity Press.

Parlett, M. and Hamilton, D. (1976). Evaluation as Illumination: A New Approach to the Study of Innovative Programmes, in G. Glass (ed.), *Evaluation Studies Review Annual*, Vol. 1. Beverly Hills, CA: SAGE, pp. 140–157.

Parmar, A. (2011). Stop and search in London: Counter terrorist or counter-productive? *Policing and Society* 21(4): 369–382.

Patashnik, E. (2003). After the public interest prevails: The political sustainability of policy reform. *Governance* 16(2): 203–234.

Paternoster, R., Brame, R., Bachman, R. and Sherman, L. W. (1997). Do fair procedures matter? The effect of procedural justice on spouse assault. *Law and Society Review* 31(1): 163–204.

Pawson, R. and Tilley, N. (1997). *Realistic Evaluation*. Thousand Oaks, CA: SAGE.

Perry, J. L. (2012). How can we improve our science to generate more usable knowledge for public professionals? *Public Administration Review* 72(4): 479–482.

Petrow, S. (1994). *Policing Morals: The Metropolitan Police and the Home Office 1870–1914*. Oxford: Oxford University Press.

Pettigrew, A. M. and McNulty, T. (1995). Power and influence in and around the boardroom. *Human Relations* 48: 845–873.

Pettigrew, A. M. (2005). The character and significance of management research on the public services. *Academy of Management Journal* 48(6): 973–977.

Pickhardt, M. (2005). Some remarks on self-interest, the historical schools and the evolution of the theory of public goods. *Journal of Economic Studies* 32(3): 275–293.

Pierre, J. and Peters, B. G. (2000). *Governance, Politics and the State*. London: Macmillan.

Plant, M. and Plant, M. (2006). *Binge Britain: Alcohol and the National Response*. Oxford: Oxford University Press.

PNUD (Programa de las Naciones Unidas para el Desarollo) (2006). *La Democracia en America Latina*. Buenos Aires: Aguilar.

Pockrass, R. M. (1986). The police response to terrorism: The Royal Ulster Constabulary. *Police Journal* 59(2): 143–157.

Police Professional (2016a). IPCC and PCCs gain decision-making powers in shake up of complaints and discipline system, 6 February, available on www.policeprofessional.com/news.aspx?id=25383.

Police Professional (2016b).Only six PCCs plan to recruit new deputies, 7 June, available on www.policeprofessional.com/news.aspx?id=26337.

Pollitt, C. and Bouckaert, G. (2004). *Public Management Reform: A Comparative Analysis*. Oxford: Oxford University Press.

Poppo, L. and Zenger, T. (2002). Do formal contracts and relational governance function as substitutes or complements? *Strategic Management Journal* 23(8): 707–725.

Porter, E. A. (1991). Modern knights and public dragons. *Journal of Public Administration Research and Theory: J-PART* 1(2): 244–248.

Porter, H. (2006). Blair laid bare: The article that may get you arrested, *The Independent*, 29 June 2006, available on http://news.independent.co.uk/uk/politics/article1129827.ece, last accessed on 8 June 2007.

Potter, R. H. and Rosky, J. W. (2013). The iron fist in the latex glove: The intersection of public health and criminal justice. *American Journal of Criminal Justice* 38(2): 276–288.

Pryce, K. (1979). *Endless Pressure: A Study of West Indian Life-Styles in Bristol*. Harmondsworth: Penguin.

Purnima, K. (2005). *Deepening Democracy: Challenges of Governance and Globalization in India/ Madhu*. New Delhi: Oxford University Press.

PytlikZillig, L. M. and Kimbrough, C. D. (2016). Consensus on Conceptualizations and Definitions of Trust: Are We There Yet?, in E. Shockley, T. Neal, L. PytlikZillig and B. Bornstein (eds), *Interdisciplinary Perspectives on Trust*. New York: Springer, Cham, pp. 17–47.

Quinton, P. (2011). The formation of suspicions: Police stop and search practices in England and Wales. *Policing and Society* 21(4): 357–368.

Quinton, P. (2015). Race Disproportionality and Officer Decision-making, in R. Delsol and M. Shiner (eds), *Stop and Search*. Basingstoke: Palgrave Macmillan.

Radburn, M., Stott, C., Bradford, B. and Robinson, M. (in press). When is policing fair? Groups, identity and judgments of the procedural justice of coercive policing. *Policing and Society*.

Rawls, J. (1999). *A Theory of Justice*, revised edition. Cambridge, MA: Harvard University Press.

Redman, T., Wilkinson, A. and Snape, E. (1997). Stuck in the middle? Managers in building societies. *Work, Employment and Society* 11(1): 101–114.

Reed, M. (2010). The Post-Bureaucratic Organization and the Control Revolution, in S. R. Clegg, M. Harris and H. Höpfl (eds), *Managing Modernity: Beyond Bureaucracy?* Oxford: Oxford University Press, pp. 230–256.

Reed, M. (2011). The Post-Bureaucratic Organization and the Control Revolution, in S. R. Clegg, M. Harris, and H. Höpfl (eds), *Managing Modernity: Beyond Bureaucracy?* Oxford: Oxford University Press, pp. 230–256.

Reed, M. and Anthony, P. (1992). Professionalizing management and managing professionalization: British management in the 1980s. *Journal of Management Studies* 29(5): 591–613.

Reed, M. and Anthony, P. (1993). Between an Ideological Rock and an Organizational Hard Place: NHS Management in the 1980s and 1990s, in T. Clarke and C. Pitelis (eds), *The Political Economy of Privatization*. London: Routledge, pp. 106–114.

Reicher, S. (2011). Mass action and mundane reality: An argument for putting crowd analysis at the centre of the social sciences. *Contemporary Social Science* 6(3): 433–449.

Reicher, S., Stott, C., Cronin, P. and Adang, O. (2004). An integrated approach to crowd psychology and public order policing. *Policing: An International Journal of Police Strategies & Management* 27(4): 558–572.

Reicher, S., Stott, C., Drury, J., Adang, O., Cronin, P. and Livingstone, A. (2007). Knowledge-based public order policing: Principles and practice. *Policing: A Journal of Policy and Practice* 1(4): 403–415.

Reiman, J. (1998). *The Rich Get Richer and the Poor Get Prison: Ideology, Class and Criminal Justice*. Boston, MA: Allyn & Bacon.

Reiner, R. (2010). *The Politics of the Police*, 4th edition. Oxford: Oxford University Press.
Reisig, M. D. and Kane, R. J. (eds) (2014). *The Oxford Handbook of Police and Policing*. New York: Oxford University Press.
Reisig, M. D., Bratton, J., and Gertz, M. G. (2007). The construct validity and refinement of process-based policing measures. *Criminal Justice and Behavior* 34(8): 1005–1028.
Reith, C. (1952). *The Blind Eye of History*. London: Faber & Faber.
Release (2013). *The Numbers in Black and White: Ethnic Disparities in the Policing and Prosecution of Drug Offences in England and Wales*. London: Release.
Reuss-Ianni, E. (1983). *Two Cultures of Policing: Street Cops and Management Cops*. New Brunswick, NJ: Transaction Books.
Rhodes, R. A. W. (1997). *Understanding Governance: Policy Networks, Governance, Reflexivity and Accountability*. Milton Keynes: Open University Press.
Rhodes, R. A. W. (2000). The governance narrative: Key findings and lessons from the ERC's Whitehall programme. *Public Administration* 78(2): 345–363.
Rhodes, R. A. W. (2005). Everyday life in a ministry: Public administration as anthropology. *American Review of Public Administration* 20(1): 1–23.
Rhodes, R. A. W. and Wanna, J. (2009). Bringing the politics back in: Public value in Westminster parliamentary government. *Public Administration* 87(2): 161–183.
Richards, P. (2004). *Pobladoras, Indígenas, and the State: Conflicts over Women's Rights in Chile*. New Brunswick, NJ: Rutgers University Press.
Rittel, H. and Webber, M. (1973). Dilemmas in a general theory of planning. *Policy Sciences* 4: 155–169.
Rix, B. (2015). Are PCCs still breaking the law? A statutory transparency update. *Policing Insight*, 21 May, available on https://policinginsight.com/analysis/are-pccs-still-breaking-the-law-a-statutory-transparency-update/.
Roberg, R., Novak, K., Cordner, G. and Smith, B. (2014). *Police and Society*. Oxford: Oxford University Press.
Roberts, J. (2001). Trust and control in Anglo-American systems of corporate governance: The individualizing and socializing effects of processes of accountability. *Human Relations* 54(12): 1547–1572.
Robinson, P. H. and Darley, J. M. (1997). The utility of desert. *Northwestern University Law Review* 91: 453–499.
Robinson, G. and McNeill, F. (2008). Exploring the dynamics of compliance with community penalties. *Theoretical Criminology* 12(4): 431–449.
Robinson, B., Stey, P. and Alfano, M. (2013). Virtue and vice attributions in the business context: An experimental investigation. *Journal of Business Ethics* 113(4): 649–661.
Rogers, C. (2014). Opinion: Police accountability in the age of austerity. *The Police Journal: Theory, Practice and Principles* 87(1): 1–2.
Rogers, C. and Thomas, G. (2013). Applying the Peelian vision in the age of commissioners. *Police Professional* 349: 16–17.
Rogers, R. (2016). 20 questions to ask your PCC candidates, *Policing Insight*, 23 March, available on https://policinginsight.com/opinion/20-questions-ask-pcc-candidates/.
Rosenthal, U. and Kouzmin, A. (1997). Crises and crisis management: Toward comprehensive government decision making. *Journal of Public Administration Research and Theory* 7(2): 277–304.
Ross, D. (trans.) (1980). *Aristotle, The Nichomachean Ethics*. Aylesbury: Hazell Books.
Roxbee Cox, J. W. (1973). The appeal to the public interest. *British Journal of Political Science* 3(2): 229–241.

Roycroft, M. (2013). A Blended Model for the Public–Private Provision of Policing for England and Wales, in J. M. Brown (ed.), *The Future of Policing*. London: Routledge, pp. 191–202.

Rudrum, D. (2005). From narrative representation to narrative use: Towards the limits of definition. *Narrative* 13(2): 195–204.

Ryan, B. J. (2011). *Statebuilding and Police Reform: The Freedom of Security*. London: Routledge.

Ryan, Jeffrey J., (2004). Decentralization and democratic instability: The case of Costa Rica. *Public Administration Review* 64(1): 81–91.

Ryan, R. M. and Deci, E. L. (2000). Intrinsic and extrinsic motivations: Classic definitions and new directions. *Contemporary Educational Psychology* 25: 54–67.

Sackett, D. L., Rosenberg, W. M., Gray, J. M., Haynes, R. B. and Richardson, W. S. (1996). Evidence based medicine: What it is and what it isn't. *BMJ* 312(7023): 71–72.

Said, E. W. (1978). *Orientalism*. London: Routledge & Kegan Paul.

Saleh, S. S., Vaughn, T., Rohrer, J. E. and Linden, T. (2002). The effect of governing board composition on rural hospitals' involvement in provider-sponsored managed care organizations. *Journal of Healthcare Management* 47(5): 321–333.

Sampson, F. (2012). Hail to the chief?: How far does the introduction of elected police commissioners herald a U.S.-style politicization of policing for the U.K.? *Policing* 6(1): 4–15.

Sampson, R. (2013). The place of context: A theory and strategy for criminology's hard problems. *Criminology* 51(1): 1–31.

Sargeant, E., Antrobus, E., Murphy, K., Bennett, S. and Mazerolle, L. (2016). Social identity and procedural justice in police encounters with the public: Results from a randomised controlled trial. *Policing and Society* 26(7): 789–803.

Savage, S. (2007). *Police Reform: Forces for Change*. Oxford: Oxford University Press.

Sbragia, A. M. (2000). Governance, the state, and the market: What is going on? *Governance* 13(2): 243–250.

Schank, R. C. and Abelson, R. P. (1977). *Scripts, Plans, Goals, and Understanding*. Hillsdale, NJ: Erlbaum.

Scherer, A. G. and Palazzo, G. (2008). *Handbook of Research on Global Corporate Citizenship*. Northampton, MA: Edward Elgar Publishing.

Scholes, R. (1981). Language, Narrative, and Anti-Narrative, in W. J. T. Mitchell (ed.), *On Narrative*. Chicago: University of Chicago Press, pp. 200–208.

Schön, D. A. (1983). *The Reflective Practitioner: How Professionals Think in Action*. New York: Basic Books.

Schubert, G. (1962). *The Public Interest*. Glencoe, IL: Free Press.

Schwarz, C. (ed.) (1994). *The Chambers Dictionary*. Cambridge: Cambridge University Press.

Scraton, P. (2016). *Hillsborough: The Truth*. London: Random House.

Sen, A. (2005). Human rights and capabilities. *Journal of Human Development* 6(2): 151–166.

Senarclens, P. (1998). Governance and the crisis in the international mechanisms of regulation. *International Social Science Journal* 50(1): 91–104.

Sennett, R. (1998). *The Corrosion of Character: The Personal Consequences of Work in the New Capitalism*. New York: Norton.

Sentas, V. (2014). *Traces of Terror: Counter-Terrorism Law, Policing, and Race*. Oxford: Oxford University Press.

Seymour, R. (2012). A short history of privatisation in the UK: 1979–2012. *The Guardian*, 29 March.

Shadish, W. R., Cook, T. D. and Campbell, D. T. (2002). *Experimental and Quasi-Experimental Designs for Generalized Causal Inference*. Belmont, CA: Wadsworth, Cengage Learning.

Shapiro, D. L. and Rynes, S. L. (2005). The role of management scholarship in the public sector. *Academy of Management Journal* 48(6): 989–997.

Sharp, D. and Atherton, S. (2007). To serve and protect? The experiences of policing in the community of young people from black and other ethnic minority groups. *British Journal of Criminology* 47(5): 746–763.

Shaw, E. (2008). *Losing Labour's Soul? New Labour and the Blair Government 1997–2007*. London: Routledge.

Sheaff, R. and West, M. (1997). Marketization, managers and moral strain: Chairmen, directors and public service ethos in the National Health Service. *Public Administration* 75(2): 189–206.

Shergold, P. (1997). The colour purple: Perceptions of accountability across the Tasman. *Public Administration and Development* 17(3): 293–306.

Sherman, L. (1998). *Evidence-Based Policing*. Ideas in American Policing Series. Washington, DC: Police Foundation.

Shotter, J. and Tsoukas, H. (2014). In search of phronesis: Leadership and the art of coming to judgement. *Academy of Management Learning and Education* 13(2): 224–243.

Silvestri, M., Tong, S., and Brown, J. M. (2013). Gender and police leadership: Time for a paradigm shift. *International Journal of Police Science and Management* 15(1): 61–73.

Simo, G. and Bies, A. L. (2007). The role of nonprofits in disaster response: An expanded model of cross-sector collaboration. *Public Administration Review* 67(2): 125–142.

Sims, D. (2003). Between the millstones: A narrative account of the vulnerability of middle managers' storying. *Human Relations* 56(10): 1195–1211.

Sindall, K. and Sturgis, P. (2013). Austerity policing: Is visibility more important than absolute numbers in determining public confidence in the police? *European Journal of Criminology* 10(2): 137–153.

Sison, A. J. G. (2003). *The Moral Capital of Leaders: Why Virtue Matters*. Cheltenham: Edward Elgar.

Sison, A. J. G. (2008). *Corporate Governance and Ethics: An Aristotelian Perspective*. Cheltenham: Edward Elgar.

Sison, A. J. G. and Fontrodona, J. (2013). Participating in the common good of the firm. *Journal of Business Ethics* 113(4): 611–625.

Sklansky, D. A. (2008). Work and Authority in Policing, in M. D. Dubber and M. Valverde (eds), *Police and the Liberal State*. Stanford, CA: Stanford University Press, pp. 110–135.

Skogan, W. G. (2006). Asymmetry in the impact of encounters with police. *Policing and Society* 16: 99–126.

Skogan, W. G. (2008). Why reforms fail. *Policing and Society* 18(1): 23–34.

Skolnick, J. H. (1966). *Justice without Trial: Law Enforcement in Democratic Society*. New York: Macmillan.

Slote, M. (1995). Agent-based virtue ethics. *Midwest Studies in Philosophy* 20(1): 83–101.

Snyder, R. and Mahoney, J. (1999). The missing variable: Institutions and the study of regime change. *Comparative Politics* 32(1): 103–122.

Spalek, B., Isakjee, A. and Davies, T. (2012). Panic on the streets of Birmingham? Struggles over space and belonging in the revanchist city. *Criminal Justice Matters* 87(1): 14–15.

Spivak, G. C. (1999). *A Critique of Postcolonial Reason: Toward a History of the Vanishing Present*. Cambridge, MA: Harvard University Press.

Stake, R. E. (2010). *Qualitative Research: Studying How Things Work*. New York: The Guildford Press.

Starbuck, W. H. (2003). Shouldn't organization theory emerge from adolescence? *Organization* 10(3): 439–452.

Starkey, K. (1995). Opening up corporate governance. *Human Relations* 48(8): 837–844.

Stenson, K. and Silverstone, D. (2013). Making Police Accountable: Governance and Legitimacy, in J. M. Brown (ed.), *The Future of Policing*. London:Routledge, pp. 429–445.

Stoker, G. (2006). Public value management: A new narrative for networked governance? *The American Review of Public Administration* 36(1): 41–57.

Stott, C. (2011). Crowd Dynamics and Public Order Policing, in T. D. Madensen and J. Knutsson (eds), *Preventing Crowd Violence*. Boulder, CO: Lynne Rienner, pp. 25–46.

Stott, C. and Pearson, G. (2006). Football banning orders, proportionality, and public order policing. *The Howard Journal of Crime and Justice* 45(3): 241–254.

Stott, C. and Reicher, S. (1998). Crowd action as intergroup process: Introducing the police perspective. *European Journal of Social Psychology* 28(4): 509–529.

Stott, C., Adang, O., Livingstone, A. and Schreiber, M. (2008). Tackling football hooliganism: A quantitative study of public order, policing and crowd psychology. *Psychology, Public Policy, and Law* 14(2): 115.

Stott, C. J., Hoggett, J. and Pearson, G. (2012). "Keeping the peace": Social identity, procedural justice and the policing of football crowds. *British Journal of Criminology* 52: 381–399.

Suchman, M. C. (1995). Managing legitimacy: Strategic and institutional approaches. *The Academy of Management Review* 20: 571–610.

Sundaramurthy, C. and Lewis, M. (2003). Control and collaboration: Paradoxes of governance. *Academy of Management Review* 28(3): 397–415.

Sunshine, J. and Tyler, T. R. (2003a). The role of procedural justice and legitimacy in shaping public support for policing. *Law and Society Review* 37(3): 555–589.

Sunshine, J. and Tyler, T. R. (2003b). Moral solidarity, identification with the community, and the importance of procedural justice: The police as prototypical representatives of a groups moral values. *Social Psychology Quarterly* 66(2): 153–165.

Swanson, J. A. (1992). *The Public and the Private in Aristotle's Political Philosophy*. Ithaca, NY, and London: Cornell University Press.

Tajfel, H. E. (1978). *Differentiation between Social Groups: Studies in the Social Psychology of Intergroup Relations*. Oxford: Academic Press.

Tajfel, H. (1981). *Human Groups and Social Categories: Studies in Social Psychology*. Cambridge: Cambridge University Press.

Tajfel, H. (1982). Social psychology of intergroup relations. *Annual Review of Psychology* 33:1–39.

Tajfel, H. and Turner, J. C. (1986). The Social Identity Theory of Intergroup Relations, in S. Worchel and W. G. Austin (eds), *Psychology of Intergroup Relations*. Chicago, IL: Nelson-Hall: 7–24.

Tankebe, J. (2009). Public cooperation with the police in Ghana: Does procedural fairness matter? *Criminology* 47(4): 1265–1293.

Tankebe, J. (2013). Viewing things differently: The dimensions of public perceptions of police legitimacy. *Criminology* 51(1): 103–135.

Tankebe, J. (2015). Re-thinking police legitimacy. Seminar given at All Souls College, Oxford, 12 March 2015.

Taylor, I. (1999). *Crime in Context*. Cambridge: Polity Press.

The Guardian (2012). Reading the riots: Investigating England's summer of disorder. *The Guardian*, 19 July, www.guardian.co.uk/uk/series/reading-the-riots, last accessed 22 July 2013.

Thomas, G. (2011). A typology for the case study in social science following a review of definition, discourse, and structure. *Qualitative Inquiry* 17(6): 511–521.

Thomas, R. and Linstead, A. (2002). Losing the plot? Middle managers and identity. *Organization* 9(1): 71–93.

Tilly, C. (1995). Contentious Repertoires in Great Britain, 1758–1834, in M. Traugott (ed.), *Repertoires and Cycles of Collective Action*. Durham, NC: Duke University Press, pp. 15–42.

Tilly, C. (2003). *The Politics of Collective Violence*. Cambridge: Cambridge University Press.

Timmins. N. (1995). *The Five Giants: A Biography of the Welfare State*. London: HarperCollins.

Tomasic, R. (2011). The Failure of Corporate Governance and the Limits of Law: British Banks and the Global Financial Crisis, in W. Sun. J. Stewart, and D. Pollard (eds), *Corporate Governance and the Global Financial Crisis: International Perspectives*. Cambridge: Cambridge University Press, pp. 28–49.

Townley, B. (1995). "Know thyself": Self-awareness, self-formation and managing. *Organization* 2(2): 271–289.

Toynbee, P. (2015). If police have to make these cuts, what exactly should they stop doing? *The Guardian*, 17 November, available on https://www.theguardian.com/commentisfree/2015/nov/17/britain-police-cuts-theresa-may?CMP=share_btn_tw.

Traugott, M. (1995). *Repertoires and Cycles of Collective Action*. Durham, NC: Duke University Press.

Travis, A. (2010). Theresa May scraps Labour police beat pledge. *The Guardian*, 29 June, available on https://www.theguardian.com/uk/2010/jun/29/theresa-may-labour-police-beat.

Trinkner, R., Tyler, T. R., and Goff, P. A. (2016). Justice from within: The relations between a procedurally just organizational climate and police organizational efficiency, endorsement of democratic policing, and officer well-being. *Psychology, Public Policy and Law* 22(2): 158–172.

Tullock, G. (1984). A (partial) rehabilitation of the public interest theory. *Public Choice* 42: 89–99.

Turner, V. (1974). *Dramas, Fields, and Metaphors: Symbolic Action in Human Society*. Ithaca, NY: Cornell University Press.

Tyler, T. R. (2006). *Why People Obey the Law*, 2nd edition. New Haven, CT: Yale University Press.

Tyler, T. R. (2011). *Why People Cooperate: The Role of Social Motivations*. Princeton, NJ: Princeton University Press.

Tyler, T. R. (2017). Procedural justice and policing: A rush to judgement? *Annual Review of Law and Social Science* 13: 29–53.

Tyler, T. R. and Blader, S. L. (2000). *Cooperation in Groups: Procedural Justice, Social Identity, and Behavioral Engagement*. Philadelphia, PA: Psychology Press.

Tyler, T. R. and Blader, S. L. (2003). Procedural justice, social identity, and cooperative behavior. *Personality and Social Psychology Review* 7: 349–361.

Tyler, T. R. and Blader, S. L. (2005). Can businesses effectively regulate employee conduct? The antecedents of rule following in work settings. *Academy of Management Journal* 48(6): 1143–1158.

Tyler, T. R., Callahan, P. and Frost, J. (2007). Armed, and dangerous(?): Can self-regulatory approaches shape rule adherence among agents of social control. *Law and Society Review* 41(2): 457–492.

Tyler, T. R. and Fagan, J. (2008). Legitimacy and cooperation: Why do people help the police fight crime in their communities? *Ohio State Journal of Criminal Law* 6: 231–276.

Tyler, T. R. and Huo, Y. (2002). *Trust in the Law: Encouraging Public Cooperation with the Police and Courts*. New York: Russell SAGE Foundation.

Tyler, T. R. and Jackson, J. (2014). Popular legitimacy and the exercise of legal authority: Motivating compliance, cooperation, and engagement. *Psychology, Public Policy, and Law* 20(1): 78.

Tyler, T. R. and Wakslak, C. J. (2004). Profiling and police legitimacy: Procedural justice, attributions of motive, and acceptance of police authority. *Criminology* 42: 253–281.

Tyler, T. R., Jackson, J. and Mentovich, A. (2015). The consequences of being an object of suspicion: Potential pitfalls of proactive police contact. *Journal of Empirical Legal Studies* 12(4): 602–636.

UN General Assembly (UNGA) (1994). *International Assistance for the Rehabilitation and Reconstruction of Nicaragua: Aftermath of the War and Natural Disasters. G. A. Resolution 49/16.* New York: United Nations.

U.S. Treasury (2009). Treasury Secretary Tim Geithner's written testimony for Congressional Oversight Panel, 21 April, available on https://www.treasury.gov/press-center/press-releases/Pages/tg94.aspx.

Van Bueren, E. M., Klijn, E. H. and Koppenjan, J. F. (2003). Dealing with wicked problems in networks: Analyzing an environmental debate from a network perspective. *Journal of Public Administration Research and Theory* 13(2): 193–212.

Van Damme, A. (2017). The impact of police contact on trust and police legitimacy in Belgium. *Policing and Society* 27(2): 205–228.

Van de Ven, A. H. (2007). *Engaged Scholarship: A Guide for Organizational and Social Research.* Oxford: Oxford University Press.

van Hulst, M. (2013). Storytelling at the police station: The canteen culture revisited. *British Journal of Criminology* 53(4): 624–642.

Van Maanen, J. (1975). Police socialization: A longitudinal examination of job attitudes in an urban police department. *Administrative Science Quarterly* 20(2): 207–228.

Van Maanen, J. (1979). The fact of fiction in organizational ethnography. *Administrative Science Quarterly* 24(4): 539–550.

Van Maanen, J. (1984). "Two Cultures of Policing: Street Cops and Management Cops" by Elizabeth Reuss-Ianni (Review). *Contemporary Sociology* 13(4): 448–449.

Van Marrewijk, A. and Yanow, D. (2011). *Organisational Spaces: Rematerializing the Workaday World.* Cheltenham: Edward Elgar.

Vickers, M. H. and Kouzmin, A. (2001). New managerialism and Australian police organizations: A cautionary research note. *International Journal of Public Sector Management* 14(1): 7–26.

Vigoda-Gadot, E. and Meisler, G. (2010). Emotions in management and the management of emotions: The impact of emotional intelligence and organizational politics on public sector employees. *Public Administration Review* 70(1): 72–86.

Villiers, P. (1997). *Better Police Ethics: A Practical Guide.* London: Kogan Page.

Villiers, P. (2009). *Police and Policing: An Introduction.* Hook: Waterside Press.

Vinzant, J. and Crothers, L. (1996). Street-level leadership: Rethinking the role of public servants in contemporary governance. *The American Review of Public Administration* 26(4): 457–476.

Vitellone, N. (2010). Just another night in the shooting gallery?: The syringe, space, and affect. *Environment and Planning D: Society and Space* 28(5): 867–880.

Waddington, D. (2012). The law of moments: Understanding the flashpoint that ignited the riots: David Waddington on how the shooting of Mark Duggan led to the August rioting. *Criminal Justice Matters* 87(1): 6–7.

Waddington, P. A. J. (1999). *Policing Citizens: Authority and Rights.* London: University College Press.

Waddington, P. A. J. (2007). Policing of public order. *Policing* 1(4): 375–377.

Waddington, P. A. J., Williams, K., Wright, M. and Newburn, T. (2015). Dissension in public evaluations of the police. *Policing and Society* 25(2): 212–235.
Wahlström, M. (2010). Producing spaces for representation: Racist marches, counter-demonstrations, and public-order policing. *Environment and Planning D: Society and Space* 28(5): 811–827.
Wain, N., Ariel, B., and Tankebe, J. (2017). The collateral consequences of GPS-LED supervision in hot spots policing. *Police Practice and Research* 18(4): 376–390.
Walker, D. (2012). How far can we trust our public sector professionals? It's a thin and delicate line between trusting professionals and keeping them in check. *Guardian Professional*, 5 July.
Wallington, P. (1985). Policing the miners' strike. *Industrial Law Journal* 14(1): 145–159.
Walsh, D. (1983). *The Use and Abuse of Emergency Legislation in Northern Ireland*. London: The Cobden Trust.
Walsh, D. J. and Conway, V. (2011). Police governance and accountability: Overview of current issues. *Crime, Law and Social Change* 55(2–3): 61–86.
Walsh, J. P., Weber, K. and Margolis, J. D. (2003). Social issues and management: Our lost cause found. *Journal of Management* 29: 859–881.
Wasserman, V. and Frenkel, M. (2011). Organizational aesthetics: Caught between identity regulation and culture jamming. *Organizational Science* 22(2): 503–521.
Weick, K. E. (1995). *Sensemaking in Organizations*. London: SAGE.
Weinfass, I. (2017). Chief Constable in public call for more police resources. *Police Oracle*, 5 June.
Weisburd, D., Groff, E. R. and Yang, S.-M. (2012). *The Criminology of Place*. Oxford: Oxford University Press.
Weitzer, R. (1995). *Policing under Fire: Ethnic Conflict and Police-Community Relations in Northern Ireland*. New York: State University of New York Press.
Westley, F. R. (1990). Middle managers and strategy: Microdynamics of inclusion. *Strategic Management Journal* 11(5): 337–351.
Westmarland, L. (2001). Blowing the whistle on police violence: Gender, ethnography and ethics. *British Journal of Criminology* 41(3): 523–535.
Westmarland, L. (2002). *Gender and Policing*. London: Routledge.
Whitfield, J. (2004). *Unhappy Dialogue: The Metropolitan Police and Black Londoners in Post-War Britain*. Cullompton: Willan.
Whyte, D. (ed.) (2015). *How Corrupt is Britain?* London: Pluto.
Wicks, D. and Carney, D. (2009). Recent judicial decisions. *The Police Journal* 82(4): 349–361.
Wikström, P. O. H. (2006). Individuals, Settings, and Acts of Crime: Situational Mechanisms and the Explanation of Crime, in P. O. Wickström and R. Sampson (eds), *The Explanation of Crime: Context, Mechanism, and Development*. Cambridge: Cambridge University Press, pp. 61–107.
Wikström, P. O. H., Oberwittler, D., Treiber, K. and Hardie, B. (2012). *Breaking Rules: The Social and Situational Dynamics of Young People's Urban Crime*. Oxford: Oxford University Press.
Wolfe, J. (2004). Those that live by the work of their hands: Labour, ethnicity and nation-state formation in Nicaragua, 1850–1900. *Journal of Latin American Studies* 36: 57–83.
Wolfe, S. E. and Piquero, A. R. (2011). Organizational justice and police misconduct. *Criminal Justice and Behaviour* 38(4): 322–353.
Wolfe, S. E. and Nix, J. (2016). The alleged "Ferguson effect" and police willingness to engage in community partnership. *Law and Human Behavior* 40(1): 1–10.

Wolfe, S. E., Nix, J., Kaminski, R. and Rojek, J. (2016). Is the effect of procedural justice on police legitimacy invariant? Testing the generality of procedural justice and competing antecedents of legitimacy. *Journal of Quantitative Criminology* 32(2): 253–282.

Wood, D. A. (2016). The importance of liberal values within policing: Police and crime commissioners, police independence and the spectre of illiberal democracy. *Policing and Society: An International Journal of Research and Policy* 26(2): 148–164.

Wood, D. A. and Williams, E. (2017). The Politics of Establishing Reflexivity as a Core Component of Good Policing, in S. Armstrong, J. Blaustein and A. Henry (eds), *Reflexivity and Criminal Justice*. London: Palgrave Macmillan, pp. 215–236.

Woodward, K., Jones, J. P. and Marston, S. A. (2012). The politics of autonomous space. *Progress in Human Geography* 36(2): 204–224.

Wright Mills, C. (1959). *The Sociological Imagination*. New York: Oxford University Press.

Wright, T. A. and Goodstein, J. (2007). Character is not "dead" in management research: A review of individual character and organizational-level virtue. *Journal of Management* 33(6): 928–958.

Yin, R. K. (2004). *Case Study Research: Design and Methods*. Thousand Oaks, CA:SAGE.

Yong, A. G. and Pearce, S. (2013). A beginner's guide to factor analysis: Focusing on exploratory factor analysis. *Tutorials in Quantitative Methods for Psychology* 9(2): 79–94.

Zhu, J., Tatachari, S. and Chattopadhyay, P. (2017). Newcomer identification: Trends, antecedents, moderators and consequences. *Academy of Management Journal* 60(3): 855–879.

INDEX

Note: Page numbers in *italics* denote references to Figures and page numbers in **bold** denote references to Tables.

accountability infrastructure 56
accreditations **11**
agency, structure and 139–140
agency myth 116–117
Aristotle 17–18, 97, 101, 103–104, 104n1
August riots: background 110–111; client base of rioters 111–113; conflict among stakeholders 113–115; copycatting 112; crowd behaviour 112; stand-and-observe order 112; technology, use of 111; training and 121–122. *See also* mass public disorder, riot policing

Bache, I. 5
Barabashev, A. 22
Barwell, Gavin 114–115
Basic Command Units (BCUs) 74
"being something vs becoming someone" 72, 80, 82
belonging, sense of 49
Berkman, M. B. 32
Bevir, M. 6
Bies, A. L. 22
Bittner, E. 29
BlackBerry riots 116
Blair, Ian 118
Blakelock, Keith 116
body-worn video (BWV) cameras 58
Boyer, R. 7
Bradford, B. 51, 57

British model of policing 54–55, 114
Brixton (London) riot 118
Broadwater Farm riot 116
budget cuts to policing 2–3, **9**, 81–83
business case justification 136
Business Managers 74

Cameron, David 110–111, 118
canteen culture 74
career progression, police officer **10**
Chakraborti, Neil 42
change programmes 60–61
character: developing over time 71; police work and 69–70; recognizing in others 71; role-playing and 70; as source of moral agency 71, 90–91. *See also* virtue ethics
Chin, Nathan 112
civilian-managers 74, **76**, 83, 84, 85
collaborative working **10**
collective consciousness 73, 78
collective social identity 73–74
College of Policing (CoP) 3, 129–130
common good: definition of 14, 22–23; public interest vs 22; stories and 139. *See also* public good
comparative governance studies 27–28
compliance 47
condensation symbol, policing as 48
consensus 144

consequentialism 16
cop-managers 74, **76**, 77–79, 84, 85
copycatting 112, 124
corporate governance 2, 8
corporate scandals 2
crowd behaviour 112–113

Davies, A. 73, 75
decision-making quality 42, 119
deliberative democracy 27
democracy, as necessary for public good 27–28
democratic policing 54–55
deontological policing 16
deterrence 58
dilemmatic policing 74, 87, 98–99, 123, 132–133, 144 *See also* impossible jobs policing
discretion, police 73
disorder, public. *See* mass public disorder
distributive justice 41
domain consensus **10**
Dorries, Nadine 114
Dubber, Markus Dirk 55
Duggan, Mark 110
"duty to obey" 39

Elliott, I. 50
emotional labour 101–102
English Defence League (EDL) 30
eudaimonia 17–18, *20*, 24, 139
evidence-based medicine 133–134
evidence-based policing: achieving credibility 135; antipathy to stories 128–129, 138; commodification techniques 134; definition of 129–130; emphasis on 'what works' 135–137; hierarchical modes in policing **12**; implications of 137–138; promoting 132. *See also* experimentation methods in policing
excessive force in policing 30–31
experimentation methods in policing: focus of 130–131; resistance to 130–131; usefulness of 131
extrinsic motivations for behaviour 57–58

Fahy, Chief Constable 114, 116
fairness 41–43, 50–51
Farrell, W. 111
field experimentation methods. *See* experimentation methods in policing
football hooliganism 115
force, use of 30–31, 54
Frederickson, H. G. 31

gemeinsinn 14
Ghoshal, S. 135–136
Giddens, A. 49
Glidewell, John 105–106
Godwin, Tim 112
good citizen 47–51
good life 87–88
good policing *20*, 24, 26, 85
governance: challenges to 3–5; comparative work on 28; definition of 1, 6; description of 5–6; disciplines of 5; failure in 100; focusing on individual forces 14; hierarchical changes **9–13**; modes of 7–8, **9–13**, *20*; network modes of 80; ownership and control sense of 8; as perpetual process 24; rhetorical flexibility of 6
governance in policing: allowing people to flourish 19; miners' strike 21; as production of order *20*
governance reforms, types of 68
Grandy, C. 22

habituation 98, 101, 102, 104
Hamilton, D. 75
Hargrove, Erwin 105–106
Harrington-Buhay, N. 28
Hart, Ben 140
hate-crime victims 42
Her Majesty's Inspectorate of Constabulary and Fire and Rescue Service (HMIC) 29, 57
hierarchical modes in policing 7, **9–13**, 52
Hillsborough 36
Hinsch, Wilfried 37–38
Hollingsworth, J. R. 7
Holt, R. 72, 80
Hope, Tim 137

identification 45, **63**
identity: change in policing and 59–66; legitimacy and 49; middle managers and 69; organizational identification and 62–64. *See also* social identity
impossible jobs policing: criteria of 106–109; definition of 105–106; impossible tasks vs 120–123; professional authority **108**; public good and **107–108**; stakeholder conflict **107**; street-level bureaucrats and 123–124; unpopular/illegitimate clients **107**; volatile client base 124–126; weak/negative agency myth **108**
impossible tasks 120–123

Independent Police Complaints Commission (IPCC) 29
individual liberty principle 15–16
individual virtues 25, 33, 85, 89–90 *See also* virtue ethics
institutional normativity 39
institutional trust 39
institutional virtues 24–25, 33, 72–73, 85, 87 *See also* legitimacy, virtue ethics
institution-building 79
interaction quality 42
internalization 45
internal value systems 46
intrinsic motivations for behaviour 59

Jackson, J. 57
Johnson, Boris 118
Johnson, J. 111

Kantian ethics 16–17, 87

Lammy, David 110
L.A. riots 111
leadership 91, 119–120
legitimacy: compliance with law and 44–45; concepts vs conceptions of 37; definition of 37–38; empirical concept of 37–38; legality and 43; motivating power of 44–47; normative concept of 37–38, 39; public good in 88; social identity and 44; trust and 39–41, *40*; two component model of 38–39, 43–44; values beyond fairness 43. *See also* police legitimacy
Lewis, P. G. 22
Lipsky, M. 73, 105–106
Loader, Ian 48, 90
London Metropolitan Service Police 35
Louden, R. B. 90–91

MacIntyre, A. 70–71
management-cop label 69
management cops 65–66
Manning, P. K. 54–55
Mark, Robert 118
marketization 7–8, **10**, 68, 85
markets 7
mass public disorder: arrest decisions during 119–120; BlackBerry riots 116; Brixton (London) riot 118; collective will of crowd 122; copycatting 112, 124; crowd dynamics 94; crowd hostility 122; dispersal tools 116; impossible tasks at front line in 121; individual police officers and 93–94; L.A. riots 111;

leadership changes during 119–120; Molotov cocktails and 103; opportunistic looting 111; petrol bombs and 103; protective clothing changing crowd behaviour 113; protective riot clothing 116; riots/rioting 94, 109–110; spontaneous disorder 124–125; training for 102–103, 109–110, 121; unlawful demonstrations 97; virtue perspective on 92–93; water cannon use 116. *See also* August riots, riot policing
May, Teresa 118
McNee, David 118
Meisler, G. 22
middle managers: coping with change 85; definition of 67; identity and 69; professional bureaucracies posing challenges to 68–69
Milliband, Ed 111
moral agency 70, 71, 90–91
moral legitimacy 38–39
moral norms 47
Morrell, K. 28
Moynihan, D. P. 22
Mulcahy, A. 48, 90
Multi-Agency Safeguarding Hubs (MASH) **10**
multiple publics 31–32

National Crime Agency (NCA) 3
network governance 18, 80
networks 7, 85
New Public Management (NPM) 68, 75
Nicholson-Crotty, S. 126
normative judgements 39, 40, 42, 43, 62
Nozick, R. 15
Nussbaum, M. C. 104

O'Brien, Thomas W. 23
ontological security 49–50
opportunistic looting 111
Orde, Hugh 118
order: benefits of 1; disadvantages to 1; in social systems 1
organizational identification 62–64, **63**
organizational justice 65
O'Toole, L. J. 126
over-socialized accounts 70

Pandey, S. K. 22
Parlett, M. 75
partnership working **10**
Peelian principle 6, 21, 26, 35

PEEL reviews **13**, 36
performance management **13**, 33
Pickhardt, M. 14
Plutzer, E. 32
police and community support officers (PCSOs) **9**
Police and Crime Commissioner (PCC) model 2–3, **9**
Police and Criminal Evidence Act 1984 (PACE) 57
Police Authority 74
police authority 118–119, 120 See also professional authority
police culture 64–65, 74
Police Effectiveness, Efficiency and Legitimacy programme (PEEL reviews) **13**
Police Executive Research Forum 120
police legitimacy 35–37, 53–54 See also legitimacy
police malfeasance 90
police organizations: change within 60; feelings of membership 64
police/police officers: career paths of **10**; character development 97–98; cohorts **10**; competing obligations of 92–93; controlling 54–55; defending from missiles in rots 123; democratic oversight of 56; developing character 25, 73–74; direct entry recruits **10**; effects of reform on 77–79; effects on public order 92–93; emotional labour 101–102; extrinsic motivations for behaviour 57–58; fast track schemes **10**; individual responsibility and 99–100; intrinsic motivations for behaviour 59; as mediator of relations in power 6; professionalization agenda **11**; public's relationship with 48; racial impartiality of 116; recording critical decisions 98–99; relational identification with 49; representing social identities 44; responding to 2011 disorder 30–31; role of 29; self-worth of 64; storying events 98–99, 138–139; task of 55–56; unwilling to implement change programmes 61; wielding power 36; working personality of 71. See also identity, public servants
police power 55–56, 57
Police Professional (Hart) 140
police reform: case study 74–77; civilianization and 83–85; cost cutting 81–83; description of 72–74; differential effects of 84; reactions to change 77–79; structure 79–81

police surveillance 55
police training: habits associated with 87; for riots 121–122; virtue and 86–87. See also public order training
police work: character and 69–71; characterizing 68; as dilemmatic 99; management and 67–68; middle managers and 68–69; in producing order 67; reform initiatives 68
Policing and the Condition of England (Loader) 48
policing reform 2–3
poverty 28–29
power: justification of 37; moral performance of 44; police power 55–56; of the state 137; from virtue perspective 91. See also legitimacy
private police schemes **12**
privatization 7–8, **12**
procedural fairness See procedural justice
procedural justice 41–42, 48–51, 56, 61–62, 136
procedure, definition of 43
professional authority 106, **108**, 117–120, 122, 124
professional bureaucracies 68–69
professionalization agenda **11**
progressive focusing 75
public confidence in police authority 118–119
public good: accounting for alternatives 30–31, 33; assessment of 14–15; avoiding bad outcomes 29–30, 33; citizenship behaviors of the policed 48; in comparative governance 28–32; contributing to 15, 50; corrosion of 22; democracy and 27–28; feminist scholars on 23; individual liberty principle 15–16; individual virtues 25; institutional virtues 24; lowest common denominator of values 31, 33; measuring 26–32; narrative/story approach and 138; performance indicators and 15; police reform and 82; policing and 23, *33*; public services enhancing 27; pursuing and understanding of 89; recognizing multiple publics 31–32, 33; shock absorber role of 28–29, 33; utopia problem of 24; virtue ethics perspective on 16
public interest: common good vs 22; definition of 22–23; use of 27
public order longitudinal project: account of actions 97–99; background 94–97; character development and 97–98; data

sources relating to **96**; role of emotion in 101–102
public order training 92–97, 102–103, 109–110 See also disorder, public
public servants 6, **11**, 14, 25, 69, 117 See also police/police officers, street-level bureaucracies, *individual public servants*
public services: enhancing public good 27; policing in tension with 28–29

Radose, Lynn 119
randomized controlled trial (RCT) 130, 135
rational choice theories 47
Rawls, J. 14
reductionism 90–91
reflexivity 98
reform. See policing reform
Reicher, S. 92
Reiner, R. 6
relational identification with police 49
research process 132–133
resilience, failures as lack of 91
responsibility, definition of 71
responsibilization 91
Reuss-Ianni, E. 69
rewards 58
Rhodes, R. A. W. 5–6
riot policing 109, 113–114, 120, 123–124 See also August riots, mass public disorder
riots/rioting. See August riots, mass public disorder
risk assessment 140, **141**, **142**
risk management 23, 76
role-playing, in relation to moral agency 70–71
Rowe, Sharon 116
rule of law 93

Sackett, D. L. 133–134
Schubert, G. 26
security guards **12**See also privatization
self, the 71–72
self-actualization 59, 62
self-awareness 71–72
self-formation 71–72
self-preservation of the state 55
self-worth 50, 62
Sennett, R. 120–121
sentencing guidelines 15
Sherman, L. 129–130
Simo, G. 22
Sims, Chris 115
situated judgments 139
Situational Action Theory (SAT) 46–47

Skolnick, J. H. 71, 74
social identification **63**
social identity 44, 49, 62–64, **63**, 73–74 See also identity
social order, memberships of 4
social scripts 140
spontaneous disorder 124–125
stakeholders **76**, 81, **107**, 113–115, 126
stand-and-observe order 112
state power 137
Stephen Lawrence enquiry 36, 57
Stephenson, Paul 117–118
stop and search 57–58
storytelling/storying of events 98, 138–144, **141–143**
Stott, C. 92
Straussman, J. D. 22
street-level bureaucracies 25, 73, 105–106, 109, 123–124 See also public servants
street-level policing tasks 120–121
Suchman, M. C. 38–39, 43

teleological ethics 18 See also virtue ethics
Thomas, R. 73, 75
Threats to Life (TTL), value of stories in understanding 140, **141–143**
Tottenham 110
Townley, B. 71
training. See police training
trust, legitimacy and 39–41, *40*
Tullock, G. 22

UAF (Unite against Fascism) 30, 113
under-socialized accounts 70
Unite against Fascism (UAF) 30, 113
unlawful demonstrations 97
utilitarianism 16–17, 87
utopia problem 24, 33

Van Maanen, J. 73
Vaz, Keith 118
Vigoda-Gadot, E. 22
virtue ethics: Aristotle and 17–18; case studies 18–19; compatible with Kantianism 17; compatible with utilitarianism 17; contextual complexities 88–89; police power and 56; social complexities of 88; solving utopia problem 24, 33; storytelling/storying of events 138–144; temporal complexities 88; training and 86–87; working with 87.

See also institutional virtues, *individual virtues*
volatility in client base 124–126

Waddington, P. A. J. 48
Walker, N. 49
Weller, P. 6

"what works" policing 135–137
Wikström, P. O. H. 46
working personality 71
Wright Mills, C. 138

Yates, John 117–118